The Confederate State of Richmond

The Confederate State of

RICHMOND

A BIOGRAPHY OF THE CAPITAL

by Emory M. Thomas

Louisiana State University Press
Baton Rouge

Louisiana Paperback Edition, 1998
07 06 05 04 03 02 01 00 99 98   5 4 3 2 1

Library of Congress Cataloging-in-Publication Data

Thomas, Emory M., 1939–
    The Confederate State of Richmond : a biography of the capital /
by Emory M. Thomas.—Louisiana pbk. ed.
        p.   cm
    Originally published: Austin : University of Texas Press, 1971.
    Includes bibliographical references and index.
    ISBN 0-8071-2319-6 (paper)
    1. Richmond (Va.)—History—Civil War, 1861–1865.   2. Richmond
(Va.)— Social life and customs.   I. Title.
    F234.R557T47   1998
    975.5'23—dc21   98-27396
                                                                        CIP

The paper in this book meets the guidelines for permanence and durability
of the Committee on Production Guidelines for Book Longevity of the
Council on Library Resources. ∞

FOR MY WIFE

Frances Taliaferro Thomas

INTRODUCTION TO THE 1998 EDITION

This is an old book. It began life in 1964(!) as an idea for a Ph.D. dissertation. Actually it began as a capitulation to Frank E. Vandiver, who had let me discover that I really did not want to write a biography of Jubal Early and that I would not live long enough to do the research for a study of the image of Jefferson Davis in the American mind. Then he politely refused to direct a study of Bourbonism in late-nineteenth-century Virginia. So, more out of desperation than anything else, I capitulated. I agreed to undertake an investigation of the city of Richmond as the capital of the Confederate States of America. Following Vandiver's lead, I sought to find and define the impact of the Confederacy and its war upon the city in which I had been born and raised.

Irony abounded. A native of Richmond, educated in its public schools, holding an undergraduate degree from the state university all of sixty miles away, had traveled 1,500 miles, had endured the rigors of graduate school at Rice University, and had come to love Houston—just so he could write a dissertation about Richmond.

Yet the apparent absurdity made sense. For me, as a boy in Richmond, the American Civil War in general and the Confederacy in particular were lots of sad stories told principally by people in flowered dresses, floppy straw hats, and white gloves. I knew that I would never learn all those stories, and the main reason I would not was that I did not want to hear them, much less learn them. I well remember that class with Vandiver, from which I emerged with the startling revelation that the Civil War and the Confederate experience possessed genuine intellectual viability. Questions, issues, ideas, and thoughts about this period reached to the core of the human condition and evoked excitement, nay passion,

among respectable intellectuals. My 1,500-mile sojourn had convinced me
that the impact of the Confederate experience upon southern urban history was important. So I set out to do the research on Richmond in Richmond, and found that I was fascinated with the story I subsequently told.
At some point during the arduous process of producing a dissertation, I
became committed to doing history. I began with an academic hoop
through which I had to jump and emerged with a profession. This sounds
melodramatic, but it is true—and it is consistent with my tendency to do
the right things for the wrong reasons.

Then some other things happened, and my dissertation became a book.
Of course, it was not that simple. Huge amounts of blood, sweat, toil, and
tears intervened. Written initially in Houston, the manuscript underwent
revision over a period of four years in places pretty disparate—El Paso,
Texas; Christ Church, Virginia; Blanchester, Ohio; and Athens, Georgia,
for examples.

Recently I reread this book and discovered that I like it. I still agree
with the thesis—that Richmond underwent major transformations as a result of the Confederacy and its war, and the city became a great capital.

My greatest surprise has been that no scholar has undertaken to redo
my study. Mike Chesson has written *Richmond after the War, 1865–1890,* in
which he argues that Richmond betrayed the country of which she was
the capital. I disagree, but applaud Chesson's meticulous research and attention to the urban South in the nineteenth century. Very good, very different general histories of Richmond written since my study are Virginius
Dabney's *Richmond: The Story of a City* and Marie Tyler-McGraw's *At the
Falls: Richmond, Virginia, and Its People.* And Louis Manarin's edited volume *Richmond at War: The Minutes of the City Council* appeared after (!) I
read it on microfilm. But no consequential work has emerged to challenge
or supplement mine. Nor have historians flocked to other Confederate
cities to assess the war's impact and tell the stories of the upheaval in those
settings.

As I reread this book, my most consistent response was the wish to
know more about all manner of topics I introduced here. What about hospitals, law enforcement, prostitution, skilled and unskilled labor, courts,
and more? Material is in these pages on these subjects, yet I can now
think of sources for and methods of expanding an understanding of these

matters. Michael Chesson's article "Harlots or Heroines?: Another Look at the Richmond Bread Riot" (*Virginia Magazine of History and Biography* 92 [April 1984], 131–75) certainly illustrates the importance of using court records to add flesh to the story. However, Chesson's work is all too lonely, and even he did not answer the question in his title. The urban history of the Confederacy remains a fertile field for the most part unplowed, even less planted and harvested. And Richmond, too, is "ripe."

History can become too old. If this reissue accomplishes nothing else, I hope that it will inspire some bright graduate student casting about for a dissertation topic to settle upon this one. That bright student can then join me in thanking Sylvia Frank, acquisitions editor at Louisiana State University Press, for bringing *The Confederate State of Richmond: A Biography of the Capital* once more into print.

EMORY M. THOMAS

Athens, Georgia

PREFACE

Ideally, written history should offer interpretations of the past that enable us to live meaningfully in the present. And written history should offer narratives of the past that enable us to share a greater portion of the human drama.

The Civil War in American historical memory survives primarily on its battlefields. To these fields generations of Americans have followed generations of historians to interpret the war period and to reenact the national drama. A thin but firm rank of historians have always insisted that the most significant events of the period happened quietly behind the battle lines, away from the sounds of trumpet and drum. Yet, too few serious scholars have given attention to the history of cities during wartime, and almost none have dealt with Confederate urban history.

Hopefully this book will offer interpretations of life in Richmond during the Confederate period that have significance to and beyond 1861–1865 and that have importance greater than analyses of battles and campaigns. Hopefully, too, this book will do justice to the narrative drama of home front war, which in Richmond's case at least rivaled the dramatic events of the battlefields.

During my period of writing and researching, many people have earned my sincere gratitude. Professor Frank E. Vandiver of Rice University provided inspiration and guidance. My thanks go to Mrs. Douglas Southall Freeman, Mrs. Mary Wells Ashworth, and Mr. Ambler Johnston for their interest and understanding. Mr. John Dudley and Mr. Robert Bricker of the Virginia State Library were most generous with their time and knowledge. The staff of the Virginia Historical Society and especially Miss Eleanor Brockenbrough at the Confederate Museum, Richmond, extended help and sympathy during my search for manuscript materials. The staffs at the National Archives, the Fondren Library at Rice University, the Alderman Library at the University of Virginia, and the University of Georgia Library have given patient assistance. And Miss Vivian Ward rendered invaluable service in typing the final drafts. Especial thanks are given to the publishers for permission to reproduce the map of Richmond from *Richmond at War*, edited by Louis H. Manarin.

I should like to express my appreciation to my parents for their aid and to my father-in-law, Harry Tinsley Taliaferro, Jr., for his keen interest and suggestions. Finally, I thank my wife, Fran, for her talent, energy, and understanding as editor, typist and counselor.

EMORY M. THOMAS

Athens, Georgia

CONTENTS

ILLUSTRATIONS

PART I   SEAT OF GOVERNMENT

Secession

RICHMOND SEEMED TO ATTRACT REVOLUTIONS. Even before there was a Richmond, Nathaniel Bacon settled on land that would become Richmond, and in 1676 he began the rebellion that bears his name. Patrick Henry preached revolution at Richmond in 1775 when he asked for "liberty or death" at St. John's Church. In 1779 the rebel colony of Virginia made Richmond its capital, and soon thereafter the rebel Benedict Arnold raided the town on behalf of the British. The slave Gabriel in 1800 unsuccessfully attempted a general black insurrection in Richmond. The presumed rebel Aaron Burr stood trial for his western machinations in Richmond in 1807. And it could be said that Nat Turner's slave rebellion in 1831 concluded in Richmond when the aroused state convention of 1831–1832 debated gradual abolition of slavery, but finally settled on tightening the bonds of the slave system. The irony was that, though men seemed periodically to begin or end revolutions in Richmond, the city itself was a quiet place, and Richmonders were for the most part conservative folk.[1]

[1] General histories of Richmond include W. Ashbury Christian, *Richmond, Her Past and Present*; Samuel Mordecai, *Richmond in By-Gone Days*; *Richmond, Capital of Virginia: Approaches to Its History by Various Hands*; John P.

Nevertheless revolution came again to Richmond on April 13, 1861. This pleasant spring Saturday dawned on clamorous confusion as houses emptied and citizens swarmed into the street! On nearly every corner strangers congregated to seek one another's reactions to news dispatches about the Confederate bombardment of Fort Sumter.[2]

Throughout the hard winter of 1860–1861 Richmond had watched the formation of the Southern Confederacy and had agonized over the dissolution of the Union. A diverse, urban area, the city had little in common, save tradition, with the agrarian radicals of the Cotton South. Richmond and the Commonwealth had waited and temporized and warned. On April 12 Richmond was a Union town. But the action at Sumter transformed her. Lincoln's reinforcement represented coercion, an overt, decisive challenge to the city. Southern traditions plus Yankee aggression would justify secession. Richmond and Virginia would wait no longer.[3]

The agony of indecision behind her, Richmond sought release. The excited knots on the street corners coalesced into a mob during the early afternoon, and three thousand citizens marched on the Tredegar Iron Works near the James River. Accompanied by cannon fire and the "Marseillaise" the eager secessionists raised the Stars and Bars over the Works. When the shouting subsided, the speeches began. Joseph R. Anderson, master of Tredegar, Virginia Attorney General John Randolph Tucker, and others told the crowd what they wanted to hear. Virginia would secede. The Yankee tyranny was over. Those Richmonders unable to hear the speeches at Tredegar could hear the theme repeated in the hundred-gun salute of the Fayette Artillery climaxed by the roar of massed cannons.

Little, *History of Richmond*; Julia Cuthbert Pollard, *Richmond's Story*; and Mary Newton Stanard, *Richmond, Its People and Its Story*.

2 The firing at Sumter began at 4:30 A.M. on April 12, and J. B. Jones (*A Rebel War Clerk's Diary at the Confederate States Capital*, ed. Howard Swiggett, I, 16) states that "extras" announced the news of the engagement on the twelfth. News of Sumter's fall and the full reaction to the event came on Saturday, the thirteenth.

3 Jones, *Rebel War Clerk's Diary*, I, 17.

Having exhausted the potential for Southern fervor at Tredegar, the jubilant demonstration moved on. With a cannon from the state arsenal in tow, 2,500 citizens started for Capitol Square to confront Governor John Letcher.[4] Until this day the middle-aged and middle-class governor had been a personal embodiment of Richmond's sentiments in the secession crisis. Obsessed with law, order, and Union, he had answered a query on his state's probable course of action by stating, ". . . whatever Virginia does she is not going to be dragged out of the Union at the tail of a Southern Confederacy."[5] However, the events of the day and the aroused populace had overridden Virginia's conservative leadership. Union men had been noticeable for their absence from the streets on this day. John Letcher sat in the Governor's Mansion and wondered whether the approaching crowd would want his guidance or his head.[6]

While the governor collected himself, two boys from the crowd raced for the flag pole atop the Capitol. They sought to haul down the Stars and Stripes and replace it with a Confederate ensign. The swifter of the two youths reached the roof and had begun to climb the lightning rod, when suddenly the clamps holding the rod began to let go. A breathless, impotent crowd stood hypnotized below. Surely the young lad would meet death in his fall from the Capitol roof to the ground far below. But as the boy rolled down the slope, his companion, who had lodged himself in the gutter, was able to break the momentum of the fall. To the relief of the spectators, both lads were unharmed.[7] Near tragedy did not prevent the sub-

[4] Good accounts of the reaction in Richmond to Sumter's fall are found in the *Richmond Daily Dispatch*, April 15, 1861; the *Daily Richmond Enquirer*, April 15, 1861; Sallie Brock Putnam, *Richmond during the War: Four Years of Personal Observation*, p. 18; and Christian, *Richmond, Her Past and Present*, p. 215.

[5] John Herbert Claiborne, *Seventy-five Years in Old Virginia, With Some Account of the Life of the Author and Some History of the People amongst Whom His Lot Was Cast,—Their Character, Their Condition, and Their Conduct before the War, during the War, and after the War*, p. 173; Tucker Randolph, Journal.

[6] F. N. Boney, *John Letcher of Virginia: The Story of Virginia's Civil War Governor*, p. 111.

[7] Mrs. Fannie A. Beers, *Memories: A Record of Personal Experience and Adventure during Four Years of War*, pp. 29–30.

stitution of flags, however. The Stars and Bars soon waved over the Capitol, and the strains of "Dixie" mingled with the calls for Letcher.

Finally the governor appeared. The harassed executive was probably relieved at the good humor of the crowd, but he did not fully appreciate his serenade. Stiffly he thanked the assemblage for their consideration and pledged that he would do his constitutional duty. His only concession to the spirit of the hour was his assurance that he would defend Virginia's honor. Perhaps with some irritation at the sight of an unlawful flag on the Capitol, he reminded the crowd that Virginia had not yet seceded. Letcher then bowed, bade the people good evening, and retired.[8] Undaunted by this mild rebuff the crowd listened to a number of fiery speeches and shouted approval of a proposed resolution: "That we rejoice with high, exultant, heartfelt joy at the triumph of the Southern Confederacy over the accursed government at Washington in the capture of Fort Sumter."[9]

Darkness heightened the enthusiasm. An estimated ten thousand persons, nearly one-third of the city's population, thronged Main Street. Bonfires crackled on major street corners. Across Shockoe Valley more fires lighted Church and Union hills. Torches and illuminated buildings increased the spectacle. Amid pealing bells and exploding fireworks there were speeches at the Spotswood Hotel, at the Exchange Hotel, and in front of the *Dispatch* and the *Enquirer* offices.[10] A band was still playing at 11:30 P.M.,[11] and the *Dispatch* termed the demonstration "one of the wildest, most enthusiastic and irrepressible expressions of heartfelt and exuberant joy on the part of the people generally, that we have ever known to be the case before in Richmond."[12] Next morning the more rabid secessionists were no doubt disturbed to learn that Governor Letch-

[8] Boney, *Letcher*, pp. 111–112; *Dispatch*, April 15, 1861; *Enquirer*, April 16, 1861.

[9] *Enquirer*, April 16, 1861.

[10] *Ibid.*; *Dispatch*, April 15, 1861; Putnam, *Richmond during the War*, p. 18; Christian, *Richmond, Her Past and Present*, p. 215.

[11] Randolph, Journal.

[12] *Dispatch*, April 15, 1861.

er had called out the Public Guard to secure the property and buildings belonging to the United States.[13] During the night the governor had removed the Confederate flag from the Capitol. But he had replaced it with a Virginia flag instead of the Stars and Stripes.[14] In general, Richmonders shared their governor's concern for order and legality. Having made the decision for secession and vented their feelings the night before, the populace, on Sunday, April 14, was content to eye the bulletin boards at the *Dispatch* office for late news and to await the next session of the Virginia Secession Convention.[15]

For two months the state Secession Convention had sat in the city and voted in compliance with the unionist views of Governor Letcher and probably three-fifths of the state's population.[16] At its outset the convention contained approximately thirty secessionists, seventy moderates, and fifty unionists.[17] By April 4 a test vote revealed that the conservative margin had dwindled considerably. A motion to submit an ordinance of secession to the people in the regular May election failed by only three votes.[18] Now that war had begun, it seemed that the convention would have to pass an ordinance of secession or adjourn.[19]

On February 4 Richmond had elected three delegates to the Secession Convention. Characteristically, the conservative-minded city had selected one secessionist, George Wythe Randolph, and two unionists, William H. MacFarland and Marmaduke Johnson. Although the voters had expressed unionist convictions in the selection of delegates, they had rejected the extreme views of John

---

[13] Boney, *Letcher*, pp. 111–112.

[14] *Enquirer*, April 16, 1861; Jones, *Rebel War Clerk's Diary*, I, 21.

[15] *Dispatch*, April 15, 1861.

[16] Claiborne, *Seventy-five Years in Old Virginia*, p. 145; Henry T. Shanks, *The Secession Movement in Virginia, 1847–1861*, pp. 142–143; Jones, *Rebel War Clerk's Diary*, I, 17.

[17] Shanks, *Secession Movement in Virginia*, pp. 159–160.

[18] *Ibid.*, p. 190.

[19] As the tide of popular enthusiasm ran more and more toward disunion, the convention's moderates kept the body in session to await action from Washington and Montgomery, and also to prevent the call of another convention whose delegates would doubtless be more radical.

Minor Botts, a strong nationalist candidate.[20] Randolph, lawyer
and grandson of Thomas Jefferson, had declared himself for disunion, though he was not a leader in the convention's "southern
rights" faction.[21] MacFarland, lawyer and president of the Farmers
Bank,[22] and Johnson were moderates, although both had stated
that, if the Union offered no protection for slavery, they would favor separation.[23] On March 19 the *Richmond Examiner* characterized Johnson as "the dark sleek fat Pony from Richmond, supposed
to be much affected with Botts" who "neighed submission." Johnson, according to the *Examiner*, was a "curly-headed poodle . . .
nearly overcome with dignity and fat" and was unwilling to exert
himself against the status quo. As late as April 13 Johnson's views
had so clashed with John Moncure Daniel, secessionist editor of the
Examiner, that the delegate was forced by the Mayor's Court to
post three thousand dollars as surety that he would keep peace with
Daniel.[24] To make sure that the Richmond delegates and the convention generally were aware of the city's current sentiments,
leading secessionists planned another demonstration for the night
of Monday, April 15, and all that day enthusiastic crowds packed
the galleries in the Capitol.[25]

Despite the popular enthusiasm, many secessionists despaired of
John Letcher and his "terrapin convention." Former Governor
Henry A. Wise, leader of the extreme southern rights wing of the
Democratic Party, feared that it would be autumn before Virginia
finally seceded.[26] Ever an opportunist, Wise had formulated plans
for a "Spontaneous Southern Rights Convention" to organize "a
resistance party for the spring elections. Once organized we will be
ready to concert action for any emergency, mild, middle, or ex-

20 Christian, *Richmond, Her Past and Present*, p. 214.
21 Lyon G. Tyler, ed., *Encyclopedia of Virginia Biography*, III, 32.
22 *Ibid.*, p. 42.
23 Shanks, *Secession Movement in Virginia*, p. 156.
24 *Dispatch*, April 15, 1861; Frederick S. Daniel, ed., *The Richmond Examiner during the War; or, the Writings of John M. Daniel with a Memoir of His
Life*, p. 10; Randolph, Journal.
25 *Dispatch*, April 15, 16, 1861.
26 Jones, *Rebel War Clerk's Diary*, I, 17. Wise told Jones that, in the event
that Virginia remained in the Union, he would offer his services to the Confederacy and fight against his state.

treme."[27] This radical assembly was scheduled to meet on Tuesday, April 16, in Metropolitan Hall on Franklin Street, just a block-and-a-half from the Capitol. Portrayed by the secessionist press as a "Peoples" convention in defiance of the regular convention called by the legislature, the "Spontaneous" body would not likely countenance moderation. The secessionist leaders postponed the parade and demonstration scheduled on Monday night, but this did not lessen the fervor of growing revolution. An observer recorded on Monday: "Business is generally suspended, and men run together in great crowds to listen to news from the North, where it is said many outrages are committed on Southern men and those who sympathize with them. . . . These crowds are addressed by the most inflamed members of the Convention, and never did I hear more hearty responses from the people."[28]

In desperation the Secession Convention had sent commissioners to Washington to seek guarantees from Lincoln. The President had none to offer.[29] Were this not enough to disturb Governor Letcher's sleep, on Monday he received Secretary of War Simon Cameron's requisition for Virginia troops to aid in suppressing the Southern "combinations in rebellion."[30] On Tuesday the rival conventions would meet in the city: the regularly constituted body and a "spontaneous" assembly in violent opposition to it. Wise's fears were ill-founded. Virginia would act before autumn.

A guard with drawn sword protected the entrance of Metropolitan Hall, while the four hundred delegates to the Spontaneous Convention, observed by ticket-holding spectators, assembled in "secret" session. In the first major address of the day, P. H. Aylett, grandson of Patrick Henry, urged moderation. In defiance of his fiery heritage and the spirit of the hour, Aylett counseled delay in

[27] Shanks, *Secession Movement in Virginia*, p. 202.

[28] Jones, *Rebel War Clerk's Diary*, I, 20.

[29] Christian, *Richmond, Her Past and Present*, p. 216. Lincoln told the commissioners, William Ballard Preston, George Wythe Randolph, and Alexander H. H. Stuart, that his inaugural address expressed his views. He had nothing to add to it.

[30] On February 25 Lincoln gave Letcher's informal representative, James D. Davidson, the impression that there would be no coercion of the Southern states (Boney, *Letcher*, pp. 108–109).

the hope that the other convention would do its duty promptly. A torrent of oratory answered. Captain O. Jennings Wise, son of the former governor, and editor of the *Richmond Enquirer*, "thrilled every breast" in denunciation of Yankee tyranny and Virginian hesitation. Richmonders James A. Seddon, James Lyons, and George W. Randolph joined in the radical tirade. Finally the delegates agreed to give the Secession Convention one more day. What they would do if it delayed further was unclear. Yet the very absence of plan was ominous enough. Just after adjournment an excited messenger rushed into the hall, and announced that the governor had blocked the channel of the James River at Norfolk to trap Federal ships then in the river. Letcher had finally moved. The same day he refused to honor Cameron's requisition of troops. Secessionists in the city were exultant.[31]

Next day, Wednesday, April 17, the Virginia Secession Convention passed an ordinance of secession, eighty-eight to fifty-five. All three of Richmond's delegates voted with the majority. Fearing a border incident with the United States before the state was prepared, the convention acted in secret session.[32] In essence the legal façade of secession merely endorsed a *fait accompli* in the popular mind. The only concession to the moderates was a provision to submit the ordinance to the voters for ratification. The tenor of popular opinion throughout most of Virginia reduced this provision to the level of a technicality. Since the arrival of the news from Sumter, Richmond's sentiments had shifted away from the legal-minded pronouncements of the Secession Convention toward the fire-eating secessionist speeches of delegates to the Spontaneous Convention.

Lieutenant Governor Montague announced the adoption of the secret ordinance to the Spontaneous Convention within an hour of its passage. Bedlam broke loose in Metropolitan Hall. Hats filled the air. The cheering finally subsided to permit an address by John

---

[31] Jones, *Rebel War Clerk's Diary*, I, 20–21; Mrs. Roger A. Pryor, *Reminiscences of Peace and War*, p. 122; *Dispatch*, April 18, 1861; *Enquirer*, April 18, 1861; Christian, *Richmond, Her Past and Present*, p. 216.

[32] J. N. Brenaman, *A History of Virginia Conventions*, pp. 53–58.

Tyler. The impassioned words of the aged ex-President had a "supernatural effect" on the throng. Henry A. Wise was next on the platform. An admirer termed his speech a "burst of eloquence, perhaps never surpassed by mortal orator." Toward the end of the speaking Letcher entered the hall. The happy secessionists applauded their "tortoise Governor" and his resolve to fulfill his duty to the newly independent state.[33] Finally the delegates shouted hoarse assent to resolutions tendering cordial thanks to the Secession Convention for the "noble act of patriotic duty which they have just performed" and pledged themselves, "their fortunes and sacred honors in defense of their native soil."[34]

Because of the "secrecy" of both conventions' proceedings, the glad tidings of Virginia's secession were reduced to widespread whispers on the streets of Richmond.[35] Then on the night of April 19 the city abandoned all pretense of secrecy. Ten thousand people assembled at City Hall and followed Smith's Armory Band on a torchlit parade about the city. Sympathetic spectators lined the route. Illuminated buildings and Confederate flags expressed the unanimity of feeling in the city. A transparency depicting Abraham Lincoln in full flight from Washington was one of several hundred seen in Richmond during the night.[36] The *Dispatch* when referring to the procession stated that "nothing that ever transpired here has served to infuse so much enthusiasm in the people of all classes, conditions and colors."[37] The wild parade ended at the Governor's Mansion in Capitol Square. Unlike the last time a secessionist demonstration had filled his front yard, Governor Letcher was now in complete accord with the throng. In anticipation of the crowd's desires, the Stars and Bars of the Confederate States floated unmolested above the Capitol.[38]

[33] Jones, *Rebel War Clerk's Diary*, I, 22–23.
[34] *Enquirer*, April 20, 1861.
[35] Jones, *Rebel War Clerk's Diary*, I, 24.
[36] Putnam, *Richmond during the War*, pp. 20–21; Christian, *Richmond, Her Past and Present*, p. 216; Jones, *Rebel War Clerk's Diary*, I, 25; *Enquirer*, April 20, 1861; *Dispatch*, April 20, 1861.
[37] *Dispatch*, April 20, 1861.
[38] Jones, *Rebel War Clerk's Diary*, I, 25.

The spectacle of the flag atop the Capitol filled many Richmond-ers with pride. With the *Enquirer* they would beam, "The spirit of patriotism which animated our forefathers in the days of '76 still burns in the hearts of their sons! God bless the old Common-wealth!"[39] The presence of the rebel banner, however, was odious to some of the western members of the Secession Convention. They met in the Powhatan Hotel on April 19 and while the city was wildly celebrating secession from the United States in the streets outside, these men took the first steps toward secession from Vir-ginia and the creation of West Virginia.[40]

Also a bit disconcerted with the presence of the Confederate flag over Richmond were the Confederates themselves. According to secessionist logic, Virginia had asserted her sovereignty and dis-solved the bonds of union with the United States. But she had not yet joined the Confederate States. Although it was a foregone con-clusion that Virginia would eventually enter the Southern fold, the question was when. If she waited until her people ratified the ordinance of secession on May 18, Virginia might well be overrun with Federal armies and reduced to a purely nominal ally of the Confederacy.[41] Fearful of gaining the sympathies of the Common-wealth only to lose her desperately needed men and material, Presi-dent Jefferson Davis dispatched his Vice-President, Alexander H. Stephens, to Richmond to hasten a firm alliance between Virginia and the Confederacy.[42] In order to underscore his concern for the success of Stephens's mission, Davis sent thirteen regiments of troops to Richmond three days later.[43]

Stephens was an excellent choice as a commissioner to the Vir-ginia Convention. The wizened Georgian was a thorough-going Whig. He had made up his mind on secession just in time to win

[39] *Enquirer*, April 23, 1861.

[40] Boney, *Letcher*, p. 116.

[41] J. B. Jones emphasized the fear that Jefferson Davis would respect the tech-nicality of Virginia's position and not send troops for fear such action be con-strued as an invasion of Virginia by the Confederacy (*Rebel War Clerk's Diary*, I, 26–27).

[42] Jefferson Davis to John Letcher, April 19, 1861, *Jefferson Davis, Constitu-tionalist; His Letters, Papers, and Speeches*, ed., Dunbar Rowland, V, 64–65.

[43] Davis to Letcher, telegram, April 22, 1861, *ibid.*, p. 65.

the Confederacy's second highest office. Talent he had. But the stigma of his late decision and the doctrinaire bent of his brilliant mind were to plague his Confederate career and render him more a liability than an asset to the Davis government.[44] When Stephens arrived in Richmond on April 22, however, he was at the height of his influence and powers in the young government. He addressed the Virginia Secession Convention the day after his arrival. After pointing out that he, like the convention, had exhausted every avenue of reconciliation with the old Union before deciding on secession, Stephens made a strong appeal for immediate action. He recounted the advantages of the Confederate constitution and flattered the Virginians by his very eagerness for them to treat with him. He proposed a temporary arrangement with his government; an arrangement which would become permanent when the voters ratified the ordinance of secession. He closed his plea with a mild warning, a bit more flattery, and a very interesting proposition:

The enemy is now on your border—almost at your door—he must be met. This can best be done by having your military operations under the common head at Montgomery—or it may be at Richmond. For, while I have no authority to speak on that subject, I feel at perfect liberty to say, that it is quite within the range of probability that, if such an alliance is made, the seat of our government will, within a few weeks, be moved to this place. There is no permanent location at Montgomery—and should Virginia become, as it probably will, the theatre of the war, the whole may be transfered here. . . . We want the voice of Virginia in our Confederate Councils.[45]

Stephens's logic of a temporary alliance satisfied the convention's legal minds. The volunteers assembling across the Potomac and the Vice-President's eager suit speeded Virginia's union with the Confederacy. Stephens and six Virginia commissioners drew up an agreement on April 24. and the Secession Convention ratified it and

[44] Stephens's role in the Confederate government is well discussed in James Z. Rabun's "Alexander H. Stephens and Jefferson Davis," *American Historical Review*, 58 (January, 1953): 290–321.

[45] Henry Cleveland, *Alexander H. Stephens, in Public and Private: with Letters and Speeches, before, during, and since the War*, pp. 729–744.

the Confederate constitution the next day.[46] On April 27, the convention resolved: "That the President of the Confederate States
and the constituted authorities of the Confederacy be, and they are
hereby cordially and respectfully invited, whenever in their opinion the public interest or convenience may require it, to make the
city of Richmond, or some other place in the State, the seat of the
Government of the Confederacy."[47] If Stephens's speech on the
twenty-third had proposed a bargain, the convention had upheld its
part. And if the Confederacy accepted the convention's invitation,
Richmond would once again be at the center of a revolution.

[46] *Ibid.*, pp. 743–744; Virginia Convention, *Ordinances Adopted by the Con-*
vention of Virginia, in Secret and Adjourned Sessions in April, May, June and
July 1861, pp. 3–5.
[47] *Enquirer*, May 3, 1861.

Old Town, Young City
Richmond in 1861

THE NIGHT BEFORE HIS APPEAL on the floor of the convention for Virginia's prompt alliance with the Confederacy, Vice-President Stephens received a serenade from the citizens of Richmond. Perhaps it was as the First Regiment Band played and those assembled raised three cheers for him and for Jefferson Davis, that Stephens began to think of the removal of the Confederate government to Richmond.[1] His broad hint the next day would be no idle promise. Montgomery was small and seemed far from the probable scene of the conflict that would decide the fate of the young nation. Richmond and Richmond's advantages over Montgomery and other possible capitals would indeed be worthy of further contemplation.

Stephens had entered Richmond from the south. This approach allowed the city to display her best side. Another traveler to Richmond in the spring of 1861 described the city from this direction: "Passing out of the cut through the high bluff, just across the 'Jeems' river bridge, Richmond burst beautifully into view; spread-

---

[1] *Richmond Daily Dispatch*, April 23, 1861.

ing panorama-like over her swelling hills, with the evening sun
gilding simple houses and towering spires alike into a glory. The
city follows the curve of the river, seated on amphitheatric hills,
retreating from its banks; fringes of dense woods shading their
slopes, or making blue background against the sky. No city of the
South has grander or more picturesque approach; . . ."[2]

On the left of Richmond's panoramic site along the James,
Gambles Hill rose above the flats of the river. Here, in 1607, Captain Christopher Newport of the Jamestown expedition had planted
a cross to mark the end of his exploration up the James. A string
of islands interspersed with rocks and swirling rapids had halted
his voyage and marked the beginning of the falls of the river. By
1861, the view from Gambles Hill to the James River included the
Kanawha Canal which by-passed the falls and allowed packet and
barge traffic up river to Lynchburg. Still another of man's accommodations with nature lay under the hill in the flat land next to
the river. Glowing and smoking, the Tredegar Iron Works had
become a Richmond landmark and one of the city's important
industrial and military assets.

Viewed from Gambles Hill, Richmond spread to the right by the
James. Warehouses, tobacco factories, and flour mills crowded the
river bank. Behind them, on the long slope ending in Council
Chamber Hill, was the commercial and residential center of the
city. Paralleling the river, Main Street and Franklin Street were
avenues of trade and promenade respectively. Dominating the center of the scene, atop Council Chamber Hill, sat the classically col-
umned Capitol, designed in 1785 by Thomas Jefferson. Within a
block of the Capitol were most of the city's public buildings: the City
Hall, the former United States Customs House, and the Governor's
Mansion among others. From the crest of Council Chamber Hill
the land fell away into the valley of Shockoe Creek. Beyond the
creek the middle-class residential areas on Church and Union hills
were visible. And on the right of the scene were the wharves of
Rocketts, a suburb of the city. The houses of the poorer class of

2 T. C. DeLeon, *Four Years in Rebel Capitals: An Inside View of Life in the
Southern Confederacy from Birth to Death*, p. 85.

Richmonders seemed to follow Shockoe Creek to its mouth and overflow onto the flats at Rocketts. From a distance Richmond in 1861 gave the Confederate Vice-President and other visitors the impression of an emerging, urban metropolis whose mills and market places had not yet overshadowed the taste and natural beauty of their provincial setting.[3]

Beyond the city's physical attractiveness, Alexander H. Stephens, Whig politician, was no doubt pleased with Richmond's political record. Democrats in Richmond were so few in number that they were known as the Spartan Band. The city was "the abode of that class who proclaimed that they were Whigs, and that 'Whigs knew each other by the instincts of gentlemen.' "[4] The conservative nature of the city's Whiggery was demonstrated in the two-to-one majority Richmond's voters gave to the Constitutional Unionist ticket in the election of 1860.[5] Like Stephens, Richmonders had decided on secession after exhausting the possibilities of reconciliation. Until February, 1859, a chapter of the American Colonization Society in Richmond was still attempting to solve the problem of Negro emancipation by supporting voluntary emigration to Liberia.[6] Stephens probably felt his political kinship with the city most strongly when he visited Richmond's newest statue, that of Henry Clay, which had been unveiled in the spring of 1860.[7]

Closely associated with Richmond's political posture were the city's four daily newspapers. The secession crisis in the state and nation had fanned the fires of journalistic partisanship to white heat. Like Stephens, the *Richmond Daily Whig* and its editor, Robert Ridgeway, had supported the Constitutional Union ticket of

[3] For descriptions of Richmond see especially Agnes M. Bondurant, *Poe's Richmond*; and Samuel Mordecai, *Richmond in By-Gone Days*.

[4] John S. Wise, *The End of an Era*, pp. 58–59.

[5] B. G. Garner, Jr., "Political History of Richmond," in Sketches of Societies and Institutions, Together with Descriptions of Phases of Social, Political and Economic Development in Richmond, Virginia, comp. Virginia Capital Bicentennial Commission, pt. 31, p. 14.

[6] Virginia Branch American Colonization Society, Minutes, November 4, 1823–February 5, 1859. In 1854 the chapter raised $16,000 and sent 273 emigrants, and in 1858 the group called on ministers of Richmond's churches to make special collections to finance the work.

[7] W. Ashbury Christian, *Richmond, Her Past and Present*, pp. 207–208.

Bell and Everett in 1860,[8] and for a time had counseled against secession. Ridgeway told his readers that disunion was not only illegal,[9] but also impractical. He argued that the seceded states had taken the cowardly way out by withdrawing from the Union rather than remaining and defending Southern rights within the Union.[10] In 1861 secessionist feeling in the city and state forced Ridgeway to resign his editorship.[11] The *Whig*, by the time Stephens arrived in Richmond, was steering the popular course regarding disunion. And, like Stephens, the *Whig* would become one of the Davis government's sternest critics.[12]

Richmond's other three dailies had a background of Democratic editorial policy. Edited by O. Jennings Wise, the *Daily Richmond Enquirer* was known as the "Democratic Bible."[13] During the war the *Enquirer* would carry on its ancient rivalry with the *Whig* by generally defending the Davis government against the assaults of the *Whig* and the *Richmond Daily Examiner*.[14] The *Examiner* had stood for secession and Southern rights under the editorship of Robert Old during the critical winter of 1860–1861. In the spring John Moncure Daniel returned to Richmond from a diplomatic post in Sardinia and resumed control of the paper. Daniel intensified the *Examiner*'s secessionist policy,[15] and during the war he and his associate, Edward A. Pollard, would voice almost irrational opposition to the Davis administration.[16] Richmond's largest daily paper in terms of circulation was the *Daily Dispatch*, which

8 Marvin Davis Evans, "The Richmond Press on the Eve of the Civil War," *The John P. Branch Historical Papers of Randolph-Macon College*, New Series, 1 (January, 1951): 42–43.

9 *Richmond Daily Whig*, November 9, 1860, cited in Evans, "Richmond Press on the Eve," p. 45.

10 *Whig*, December 22, 1869, cited in Evans, "Richmond Press on the Eve," p. 45.

11 *Ibid.*, p. 21.

12 Harrison A. Trexler, "The Davis Administration and the Richmond Press, 1861–1865," *Journal of Southern History* 16 (May, 1950): 185–191.

13 Evans, "Richmond Press on the Eve," pp. 16–20.

14 Trexler, "Davis and the Richmond Press," pp. 178–181.

15 Evans, "Richmond Press on the Eve," pp. 37–39; Frederick S. Daniel, ed., *The Richmond Examiner during the War; or, the Writings of John M. Daniel with a Memoir of His Life*, pp. 230–231.

16 Trexler, "Davis and the Richmond Press," pp. 181–185.

boasted eighteen thousand readers.[17] Editors James A. Cowardin and John D. Hammersley pursued a moderately Democratic policy, and had advocated Virginia's secession only after a tortuous editorial monologue from the summer of 1860 until January, 1861.[18] The *Dispatch* sustained its large circulation by the accuracy of its reporting and the moderation of its editorial policy in contrast to its polemical competitors. The Richmond press was an active institution. In the spring of 1861 its unanimity for secession and its enthusiasm for the Confederacy gave weight to Richmond's claim to be a suitable location for the seat of government. As far as the Confederate Vice-President could then discern, it seemed that his government would receive sympathetic support from the city's press.

In keeping with the soundness of Richmond's national and state political record was a city government ably run by urban aristocrats. Joseph Mayo, elected mayor of the city each year since 1853, had originally come to Richmond to study law under Abel Upshur, later Whig President John Tyler's Secretary of State.[19] Despite his seventy-six years, Mayo administered the city well and daily dispensed justice in minor criminal offenses at the Mayor's Court. Fifteen aldermen, five from each of the city's three wards, also sat in the Mayor's Court. An elected judge heard civil cases and all felonies, except those punishable by death, at monthly sessions of the city's Hustings Court.[20] A state circuit court and the Virginia Supreme Court of Appeals also sat in the city.

Richmond's legislative power was vested in a fifteen-member city council. The city charter, as amended by the Virginia General Assembly in March, 1861, granted the city council authority to make and enforce rules and ordinances "which they shall deem necessary for the peace, comfort, convenience, good order, good

[17] Evans, "Richmond Press on the Eve," pp. 25–35.
[18] *Ibid.*, pp. 27–35.
[19] Mrs. Madge Goodrich, "The Mayors of Richmond," in Sketches, comp. Virginia Capital Bicentennial Commission, pt. 24, pp. 24–25.
[20] Virginia General Assembly, *Acts of the General Assembly of the State of Virginia, Passed in 1861 in the Eighty-fifth Year of the Commonwealth*, chap. 88.

morals, health and safety of said city." The council through standing committees oversaw the work of the various administrative officials and departments within the city.[21]

During the war years, eighteen men served on the Richmond City Council. Only one member acquired national prominence— George Wythe Randolph, grandson of Thomas Jefferson, Confederate general officer, and Secretary of War. Several councilmen achieved local distinction by serving in the Virginia House of Delegates or by excelling in their chosen professions. As a group, the members of the city council were solid citizens and successful men—no more, no less. The oldest councilman in 1861 was sixty, the youngest twenty-eight. The average age at the beginning of the war was fifty-three. Most of the city fathers were natives. Twelve councilmen came from Richmond and the adjacent counties; all but two were born and raised in the state of Virginia. With few exceptions Richmond's councilmen were substantial members of the city's industrial or mercantile economy. Among the eighteen councilmen, ten made their living from commerce as merchants, bankers, managers, or investors; four were manufacturers; two were practicing lawyers. Only three members of the council worked at trades. In sum the Richmond City Council was a stable body of practical urbanites.[22] Led by such men as Peachy R. Gratton, David I. Burr, Thomas H. Wynne, and its president, David J. Saunders, Richmond's council gave promise of rising to the challenges that war and being the Confederate capital would bring.

Perhaps Richmond's strongest appeal as a seat of government was her economic potential. Vice-President Stephens and the Confederate leaders could find other cities in the South with picturesque settings, stable municipal governments, and active secessionist presses. Richmond, however, offered a balanced commercial economy, easy transportation by rail or water to at least the eastern

21 *Ibid.*, pp. 159–170.

22 Louis H. Manarin, ed., *Richmond at War: The Minutes of the City Council, 1861–1865*, pp. 627–636. In many respects the observations of George Cary Eggleston (*A Rebel's Recollections*, p. 27) describe the atmosphere of Richmond's traditional, political and social life.

Confederacy, and virtually the only heavy industrial facilities in the young nation.

Like most Southern cities, Richmond rested her economy on an agrarian base. She had come into being and grown as a center of trade with the countryside. Situated between the great plantations of Tidewater and the farms of Virginia's Piedmont, Richmond received tobacco, cotton, and grain in exchange for the products of her domestic manufacturing and for articles imported from Europe or the North. During the 1850's, cargoes at Richmond's port averaged 100,000 tons per year.[23] The five railroads serving the city entered from all directions of the compass and prospered with the aid of sound management, ample traffic, and good relations with the State Board of Public Works.[24] Great planters and prosperous yeomen made Richmond the commercial and social center of central and eastern Virginia. They came to the city at regular intervals to sell their staple crops and purchase large quantities of goods for their farms, chattels, and families.[25]

By the spring of 1861 Richmond was no mere way-station in the exchange of staples for manufactures; she was coming of age. Her transportation facilities and trade with the interior spawned further economic opportunities. Although (according to the United States census of 1860) she stood twenty-fifth in population among the nation's cities, she ranked thirteenth in order of manufactures.[26] Much of this manufacturing activity utilized the local agrarian staples—tobacco and grain. Twelve flour and meal mills ground a product worth over three million dollars. Also refining the area's

[23] G. M. Bowers, "Richmond as a Port, Its History and Development," in Sketches, comp. Virginia Capital Bicentennial Commission, pt. 32, p. 3.

[24] Railroads serving Richmond were the Richmond, Fredericksburg and Potomac; Richmond and Petersburg; Virginia Central; Richmond and Danville; and Richmond and York River (Angus J. Johnston, II, "Virginia Railroads in April, 1861," *Journal of Southern History* 22 [August, 1957]: 309, 329).

[25] For direct mention of the influence of trade with the planters see Wise, *End of an Era*, p. 63; and Mrs. David J. Greenberg, *Through the Years: A Study of the Richmond Jewish Community*, p. 12.

[26] U.S., Bureau of the Census, Eighth Census, 1860, *Statistics of the United States, (including mortality, property, etc.) in 1860; Compiled from the Original Returns and Being the Final Exhibit of the Eighth Census, under the Direction of the Secretary of the Interior*, XVIII.

grains were Richmond's three bakeries, a distillery, and a brewery;
not to mention Elijah Baker's company making a patent medicine,
"Baker's Bitters." In 1860 there were in Richmond and surrounding Henrico County fifty-two tobacco manufacturers whose annual
gross product was valued at nearly five million dollars. Seven
major warehouses, an exchange, six tobacco-box factories, and two
cigar makers also served the industry.[27] In November, 1860, a
British traveler summed up the influence of tobacco on the city:
"The atmosphere of Richmond is redolent of tobacco; the tints of
the pavements are those of tobacco. One seems to breathe tobacco,
to see tobacco, and smell tobacco at every turn. The town is filthy
with it."[28]

Besides the great mills and tobacco factories there were many
smaller manufacturing enterprises. Cobblers, saddlers, coopers, carriage makers, blacksmiths, brick makers, and bookbinders supplied
the needs of planter and worker in the city.[29] Also profiting from
Richmond's basic trade patterns with the countryside and the expanding market within the city, were 964 merchants who reported
over twelve million dollars in gross sales during 1860.[30] Planters,
merchants, and other visitors supported several first class hotels.
The Exchange Hotel, Ballard House, Spotswood Hotel, and the
American Hotel were most popular with the city's guests. The ur-
bane Tucker DeLeon claimed that Richmond hotels had been "always mediocre,"[31] but the somewhat naive Kentuckian, Lieutenant
W. M. Clark, termed the Exchange Hotel the "finest building I

[27] U.S. Bureau of the Census, Eighth Census, 1860, *Manufactures of the
United States in 1860; Compiled from the Original Returns under the Directions
of the Secretary of the Interior*, pp. 216–217; B. G. Garner, Jr., "History of
Business and Industry: Tobacco," in Sketches, comp. Virginia Capital Bicentennial Commission, pt. 14, p. 26.

[28] Catherine Cooper Hopley, *Life in the South: From the Commencement of
the War by a Blockaded British Subject. Being a Social History of Those Who
Took Part in the Battles, from a Personal Acquaintance with Them in Their
Homes. From the Spring of 1860 to August, 1862*, I, 135.

[29] Eighth Census, *Manufactures of the United States in 1860*, pp. 216–217.

[30] Virginia General Assembly, *Documents of the Session of 1861*, Document
II, "Financial Statement and Suggestions Relative to Defects in the Revenue
Laws by the Auditor of Public Accounts," pp. 76–77.

[31] DeLeon, *Four Years in Rebel Capitals*, p. 87.

was ever in."[32] An accurate appraisal no doubt lay somewhere in between the two opinions.

Alexander H. Stephens, as he mentally surveyed Richmond's economy, no doubt appreciated its sound agrarian base. The Vice-President and other Confederate leaders, however, coveted most the newer trends in the city's economic development—finance and iron manufacture. In 1861 each of the four major Richmond banks boasted more than a million dollars in capital, and the combined capital of the four totaled over ten million. The growth of insurance companies brought further financial prestige to Richmond's economy. Should the city become the Confederate capital, her financiers and economic resources could become assets contributing to the stability of the young nation's currency and economy.[33]

Iron was the key to Richmond's greatest economic advantage to the Confederacy. The city was the center of the industry south of the Potomac. In 1860 she claimed four rolling mills, fourteen foundries and machine shops, a nail works, six works for manufacturing iron railing, two circular-saw works, and fifty iron and metal works.[34] The industry employed 1,550 workers, 20 per cent of Richmond's 7,589 engaged in manufacturing. Iron manufacture in the city produced nearly $2 million in sales annually and claimed $837,700 invested capital.[35] Joseph R. Anderson's Tredegar Works was the city's largest and most diversified plant, employing 900 men by the spring of 1861.[36] However, Tredegar was far from being alone in Richmond's iron industry. Talbott and Brother, Old Dominion Iron and Nail Works, Richmond Foundry, Burr and Ettenger, and Richmond Stove Company were some of Anderson's

[32] Sam L. Clark, ed., "A Confederate Officer Visits Richmond," *Tennessee Historical Quarterly* 11 (March, 1952): 88.

[33] According to the statements published in the *Daily Richmond Enquirer*, April 2, 1861, the leading banks in the city in order of capital were Farmers Bank of Virginia, $3,150,900; Exchange Bank of Virginia, $3,137,100; Bank of Virginia, $2,651,250; Bank of the Commonwealth, $1,074,300. One example of financial aid was a Trader's Bank $50,000 loan to the state (*Enquirer*, April 20, 1861).

[34] Kathleen Bruce, *Virginia Iron Manufacture in the Slave Era*, p. 323.

[35] Eighth Census, *Manufactures of the United States in 1860*, pp. 216–217.

[36] Bruce, *Virginia Iron Manufacture*, p. 342.

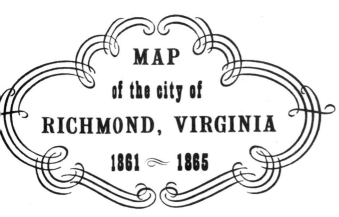

MAP
of the city of
RICHMOND, VIRGINIA
1861 ~ 1865

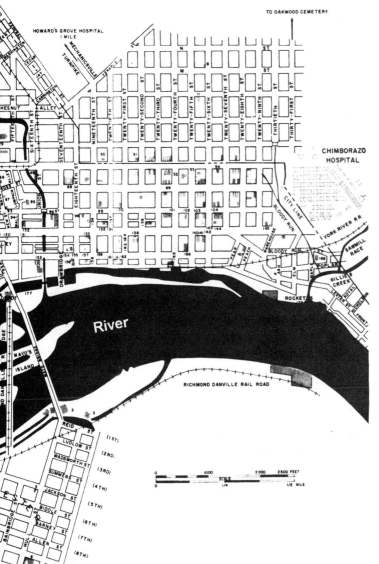

1. General Hospital No. 1—Alms House
2. Hebrew Cemetery
3. Powder Magazine—burned April 1865
4. City Hospital and Poor House
5. Tan Yard
6. St. Francis de Sale Hospital—formerly Goddin's Tavern
7. St. John's Evangelical Church—Lutheran
8. General Hospital No. 26—Springfield Hall

LEIGH STREET

9. Residence of Mrs. R. E. Lee, fall of 1863 (210 East Leigh)
10. Richmond Female Orphan Asylum
11. Leigh Street Baptist Church

CLAY STREET

12. Clay Street Free School—Methodist Chapel
13. Wickham House, residence of C. G. Memminger ca. 1863–1864—now part of Valentine Museum
14. James Caskie House, residence of Mrs. R. E. Lee, winter of 1862–1863
15. R. H. Maury House—submarine electrical torpedo invented here by M. F. Maury
16. Bruce House, residence of Senator Semmes and Col. Ives—A. H. Stephens lived here 1861–1862
17. White House of the Confederate States—now Confederate Museum

MARSHALL STREET

18. Residence of John H. Reagan 1863
19. St. Mary's German Catholic Church
20. St. Joseph's Orphanage—Catholic
21. St. James's Episcopal Church
22. Second Market and Watch House
23. John Marshall House—now A.P.V.A. headquarters
24. General Hospital No. 4, for officers—formerly Richmond Female Institute
25. Sycamore Church—Disciples of Christ
26. Beth Ahaba Synagogue
27. College Hospital—Medical College Infirmary
28. Medical College of Virginia
29. Lancasterian School—free school
30. City Jail

BROAD STREET

31. Breeden & Fox Store used as hospital 1862
32. Richmond Lyceum or Broad Street Theatre—formerly Monticello Hall
33. Richmond Theatre—burned 1862, rebuilt same year
34. Richmond, Fredericksburg & Potomac Rail Road Depot
35. Broad Street Hotel used as hospital—formerly Swan Tavern
36. Hoyer & Ludwig, Lithographers (printed C.S. currency), second floor; commutation office, first floor
37. Valentine Store (residence faced Capitol St.), office of Transportation Bureau
38. Confederate Government Stables, for over 100 horses exclusive of ambulance horses
39. Winder Building—offices of Provost Marshal, Medical Director, Dept. of Henrico, Passport etc.
40. First Presbyterian Church
41. Broad Street Methodist Church
42. City Hall
43. Powhatan House
44. First Baptist Church
45. Carlton House
46. Monumental Church of Richmond

47. First African Baptist Church
48. Temporary tracks to connect R.F.&P. with Virginia Central Railroad in case of necessity
49. Virginia Central Railroad Depot
50. Trinity Methodist Church
51. Bellevue Hospital
52. St. John's Episcopal Church
53. St. Patrick's Catholic Church
54. Crenshaw House where J. E. Johnston was nursed after Battle of Seven Pines

GRACE STREET

55. Brewer House where J. E. B. Stuart was brought mortally wounded
56. Residence of Samuel Preston Moore 1861–1865
57. Grace Street Baptist Church
58. Residence of Samuel Cooper 1863
59. Centenary Methodist Church
60. Residence of Mrs. Robert Craig Stanard until 1862
61. St. Peter's Cathedral—Catholic
62. Central (Monumental) Hotel—office of second auditor
63. St. Paul's Episcopal Church
64. Capitol Square—
   A. Washington Monument where Davis was inaugurated Feb. 22, 1862
   B. Bell Tower
   C. Capitol Building where C.S. Congress met
   D. State Court House
   E. Governor's Mansion
   F. Governor's Kitchen
   G. Governor's Stables
65. Richmond House—War Tax Bureau in annex
66. Universalist Church
67. Beth Shalome Synagogue
68. General Hospital No. 9—Seabrook's prison hospital
69. Residence of Elizabeth Van Lew, Union spy

FRANKLIN STREET

70. Residence of Dr. Robert Archer, President Armory Iron Works
71. Residence of Joseph R. Anderson, President Tredegar Iron Works
72. Clopton Hospital
73. Residence of C. G. Memminger 1861
74. Residence of George W. Randolph 1861—probable site
75. Stewart House—residence of Mrs. R. E. Lee 1864–1865
76. Baskerville House—residence of Alexander H. Stephens 1863–1865
77. United Presbyterian Church
78. C.S. War Department (& Navy)—formerly Virginia Mechanics Institute
79. Block of C.S. offices—Signal Corps, Nitre & Mining Bureau, Blues Hall, containing Q.M. Dept. 1861, Paymaster etc.
80. C.S. Treasury Building—formerly U.S. Custom House
81. General Post Office—Goddin's Hall
82. *Southern Literary Messenger* Building
83. Belvin's Block—C.S. offices
84. *Whig* Building
85. *Examiner* Building
86. Naval or Marine Hospital
87. *Sentinel* Building
88. Metropolitan Hall
89. Clifton House

90. Ballard House
91. Exchange Hotel
92. Richmond Varieties Theatre
93. Odd Fellows Hall
94. Henningsen Hospital
95. Lumpkin's Jail, probably "Castle Godwin" in 1861–1862
96. Scott's Drug Store
97. First Market, Watch House and Public Hall
98. Masonic Hall
99. General Hospital No. 12—Banner or Wm. H. Grant's Factory
100. Third Alabama Hospital—Robinson's Factory
101. Third Georgia Hospital—General Hospital No. 19
102. Second Alabama Hospital—Yarbrough-Turpin Factory, now Pohlig's
103. General Hospital No. 20—Royster's Factory
104. Residence of John L. Ligon

MAIN STREET

105. Penitentiary Spring
106. Residence of J. P. Benjamin 1861–1865
107. Robertson Hospital
108. Residence of S. R. Mallory 1862
109. A. Second Presbyterian Church
    B. Residence of Rev. Dr. Moses D. Hoge
110. Second Baptist Church
111. Arlington House—Comptroller's Office
112. Spotswood Hotel—Post Office in basement
113. Bosher's Hall—Q.M. Dept. 1863—Archer & Daly, steel engravers
114. St. Lawrence House—offices
115. Corinthian Hall
116. Crawford's Saloon Hospital—Ezell's Hospital
117. Farmers Bank
118. Bank of Virginia
119. American Hotel
120. Bank of the Commonwealth
121. Exchange Bank of Virginia
122. Telegraph Office
123. *Southern Punch* Office
124. General Hospital No. 5—Kent, Paine & Co.
125. *Enquirer* Office
126. *Dispatch* Office
127. General Hospital No. 6—Keen, Baldwin & Co.
128. Mitchell & Tyler
129. Richardson's Hospital
130. Traders Bank
131. Bread Riots of April 1863 started here
132. General Hospital No. 8—St. Charles Hotel
133. General Hospital No. 10—Union Hotel
134. General Hospital No. 11—Globe Hospital—probable site
135. Old Stone House—now Poe Foundation
136. General Hospital No. 13—Christian & Lea —probable site
137. General Hospital No. 14—Second Georgia
138. Henrico Court House
139. General Hospital No. 18—Creanor's Factory
140. General Hospital No. 23—Ligon's Factory
141. General Hospital No. 22—Howard's Factory
142. General Hospital No. 24—Moore Hospital or Harwood's Factory
143. Ross Factory Hospital
144. Atkinson Factory Hospital
145. Residence of Luther Libby

CARY STREET

146. General Hospital No. 2—Baily's Factory
147. Packet Office—canal packet boats docked here
148. Bowers Foundry
149. C.S. Custom House
150. General Hospital No. 7—Bacon & Baskerville's
151. Navy Ordnance Store
152. Columbian Hotel
153. Talbott's Foundry
154. Factory for making Confederate coffee—burned Feb. 1864
155. Military Prison for U.S. officers
156. City gas storage tanks
157. Castle Thunder—prison
158. Castle Lightning—prison
159. Engineer Bureau Hospital—Friends' Meeting House—probable site
160. Dibrell's Warehouse—hospital
161. Libby Prison, showing tunnel to east dug by prisoners
162. Kerr's tobacco stemmery
163. General Hospital No. 15—Crew & Pemberton's Factory
164. General Hospitals Nos. 16 and 17—First and Fourth Georgia
165. York River Railroad Depot
166. General Hospital No. 21—Gwathmey's Factory
167. General Hospital No. 23—Randolph's Factory for Texas and Arkansas soldiers
168. City Gas Works

CANAL STREET

169. C.S. Artillery Work Shops
170. Gallego Mills
171. Shockoe Warehouses

BYRD STREET

172. Second African Baptist Church
173. Samson & Pae's Foundry
174. Richmond & Petersburg Railroad Depot
175. General Hospital No. 3—Byrd Island or Gilliam's Factory
176. Richmond & Danville Railroad Depot
177. Mayo's Warehouse—hospital
178. Rocketts Landing—boats for Drewry's Bluff docked here and occasionally the schoolship *Patrick Henry*

ARCH STREET

179. Pratt's Castle
180. Asa Snyder Stove Works—probable site
181. Arsenal & Ordnance shops covered this area
182. Franklin Paper Mill
183. Haxall and Crenshaw Flour Mills
184. C.S. Armory and Shops—formerly Virginia State Armory
185. Richmond Iron and Steel Works
186. Gauge House and Boat Yard
187. Tredegar Iron Works
188. Crenshaw Woolen Mills (near Tredegar)
189. C.S. Laboratory

MANCHESTER

1. Manchester Cotton Factories
2. Taliaferro Mills—later Dunlop Mills
3. James River Cotton Factories
4. Danville Railroad Workshops—General Hospital No. 28
5. Temperance Hotel—hospital
6. Methodist Church

prosperous competitors.[37] By 1861 the iron manufacturers in Richmond had a well-established trade with the South,[38] and had sought to improve their products and profits by establishing a Mechanics Institute with a night school for apprentices.[39] Without Richmond and her iron industry, the Confederates' war-waging capacity would suffer a staggering blow. And what better way to emphasize the importance of the city's security than to make her the Confederate capital?[40]

Evidences of Richmond's economic well-being were everywhere in the city. Most of the 37,910 persons who lived within the limits of the city were financially secure.[41] During 1860 the city supported only 426 paupers, and the same year the council had built a new Alms House to accommodate any increase.[42] Richmond taxpayers owned real property worth over $19 million in 1861.[43] Manufacturing, trade, and the professions had made some Richmonders affluent by 1861, and with flour selling for eight cents per pound in the markets, a day laborer could manage well on $1.25 a day.[44]

Family and professional standing joined financial status as dictators of class in nineteenth-century Richmond. As one student of the city's social mores expressed it:

... family first, with the concomitant of polish, education and "manner," were the sole "open sesame" to which the doors of the good old city would swing wide.

The learned professions were about the sole exceptions. "Law,

[37] *Ibid.*, pp. 290–305.
[38] *Ibid.*, pp. 277–280.
[39] *Ibid.*, pp. 315–318.
[40] *Ibid.*, pp. 345–347; cf., pp. 381–383.
[41] Eighth Census, *Statistics of the United States . . . in 1860*, XVIII. Taxable personal property totaled $4,065,365 (City of Richmond, Personal Property Tax Books, 1860).
[42] Bureau of the Census, Eighth Census, Social Statistics, MS; Christian, *Richmond, Her Past and Present*, p. 207.
[43] City of Richmond, Real Estate Tax Books, 1861, MSS in Virginia State Library.
[44] *Dispatch*, April 5, 1861; *Enquirer*, April 2, 1861; Eighth Census, Social Statistics MS.

physic, the church," . . . were permitted to condone the "new families."

Trade, progressive spirit and self-made personality were excluded from the plane of the elect, as though germiniferous. The "sacred soil" and the sacred social circle were paralleled in the minds of their possessors.[45]

The lines of class hardened in the urban South in a way unknown outside the cities. The same observer noted, "In the country districts habit and condescension often overrode class barriers, but in the city, where class sometimes jostled privilege, the line of demarcation was so strongly drawn that its overstepping was dangerous."[46] In general the upper classes, possessed of wealth, name, profession, or some combination of the three, resided on the high ground near the center of the city. Marshall, Cary, Franklin, and Grace streets were most popular.[47]

The middle strata of society occupied a unique position in antebellum Richmond. The successful tradesmen, shopkeepers, manufacturers, commercial people, and the like, who composed Richmond's middle class were numerous and important in the city's political and economic life. Yet in the larger context of state and section, the urban middle class, albeit sometimes reluctantly, accepted the social values and political leadership of the planters. It was ironic, and ultimately tragic, that these forgotten men of the ante-bellum South should give themselves so completely to the planter-inspired Confederacy, and should share so fully in the Confederacy's destruction.

Richmond's lower-class whites generally inhabited the lower ground near the James River and Shockoe Creek. For the most part they worked as skilled and semi-skilled laborers in the city's industries. A significant percentage of working class Richmonders were foreign born, mostly German and Irish.[48] The existence of

---

45 T. C. DeLeon, *Belles, Beaux, and Brains of the 60's*, p. 59.
46 *Ibid.*
47 Mary Wingfield Scott (*Old Richmond Neighborhoods*) gives a thorough description of the city's residential areas and their inhabitants.
48 Samuel Mordecai, *Richmond in By-Gone Days*, pp. 292–295; Eighth Census, Social Statistics MS.

this incipient proletariat was rare in the South, and rarer still was the degree of class awareness this unsouthern element would display as Confederates.

In 1861 relations among classes, and among foreign and native born, were usually harmonious in Richmond. Newspapers in covering the activities of municipal courts did employ the stereotyped image of Irishmen as drunkards and brawlers.[49] And the economic pressures of wartime would bring out a latent anti-Semitism among some Richmonders. On the whole, however, in the spring of 1861 white Richmonders lived together in general amity.

Prime among reasons for this good will was the existence of black Richmonders. The census of 1860 recorded 11,739 slaves in the city.[50] Some of these bondsmen were household servants, cooks, maids, and the like. Many toiled in tobacco factories, iron works, and flour and cotton mills. Richmond was first among American cities in her adaptation of slave labor to factories.[51] The city itself owned hands to maintain streets, man the gas works, and do other such menial duties. In short, Richmond depended upon slaves for a wide variety of tasks. Not only did bondsmen do the city's unskilled, dirty work, but also slaves served as skilled operators in Richmond's growing industries.

Although many Richmonders owned the slaves they employed, many others rented servants. The hiring out system permitted a master to rent his excess chattels to anyone who needed them. Normally, owner and user agreed upon term, price, duties, and some standard of treatment. In some rare cases, the slave himself was free to strike the best bargain he could, pay his owner a fixed fee, and keep the balance. Usually, however, the arrangement originated with owner and user or with the aid of a middleman broker. Economically, hiring out effected a fluid distribution of slave labor in that bondsmen were always available when and where needed, without the exchange of the large amounts of capital

[49] *Richmond Daily Examiner*, September 3, 1861.
[50] Eighth Census, *Statistics of the United States . . . in 1860*.
[51] Richard C. Wade, *Slavery in the Cities: The South 1820–1860*, pp. 33–36.

necessary to buy them. Socially, hiring out tended to liberalize significantly the institution of slavery. The hired slave worked for someone who was not his master and therefore could take unusual liberties. Often the renter allowed his hireling to work overtime and earn money.[52] Most important, the hired-out slave lived out also.

The traditional Southern urban pattern of slave quarters within a compound behind the master's house existed in Richmond. But when the slave was an iron puddler and his master was the Tredegar Iron Works, this pattern would not fit. Although the law required the slave's owner to provide quarters, in practice an increasing number of urban chattels were free to find their own housing under the nominal supervision of their owners. Live out quarters were often shanties, but they were sufficiently beyond the master's dominance to allow the slave at least some measure of individuality and to afford Richmond's black community some degree of sub rosa society.[53]

Richmond officialdom countered this liberalizing effect with stringent laws governing slave conduct and "place." The Ordinance Concerning Negroes of 1857 provided for a rigid pass system restricting the rights of slaves to be abroad at night. The same ordinance restricted Negro presence in carriages, public grounds, graveyards, and in any assembly of five or more "whether free or not." More than this, Negroes were prohibited from smoking in public, swearing, carrying canes, and from purchasing weapons or "ardent spirits." The penalties for violations of the municipal

[52] *Ibid.*, pp. 38–43.

[53] *Ibid.*, p. 64. Parallel to the genuine black society, which existed beyond the cognizance of most whites, was the "Colored Aristocracy" of domestic servants who aped the manners, dress, and attitudes of their masters. Mordecai (*Richmond in By-Gone Days*, pp. 359–360) recorded: "Like their betters, the negroes of the present day [1860] have their mock-gentility, and like them, they sustain it chiefly in dress and pretension. . . . These gentry leave their visiting cards at each other's kitchens, and on occasion of a wedding, Miss Dinah Drippings and Mr. Cuffie Coleman have their cards connected by a silken tie, emblematic of that which is to connect themselves, and a third card announces, 'At home from ten to one,' where those who call will find cake, fruits, and other refreshments." C.f., H. J. Eckenrode, "Negroes in Richmond in 1864," *Virginia Magazine of History and Biography* 46 (July, 1938): 193–200; City of Richmond Ordinances, December 22, 1857, cited in Wade, *Slavery in the Cities*, pp. 106–109.

discipline were "stripes well laid on" for bondsmen, often together with fines for the negligent master.[54]

Motivation for these regulations went beyond concern for good order and discipline among Richmond's chattel population. At the heart of the matter was the lingering fear of a slave insurrection. Gabriel's plot in 1800 and Nat Turner's blind fury in Southhampton County in 1831 impressed all white Virginians with the volatile nature of their servile institution. Their fears were well founded. In May, 1861, a slave, Maria Scott, attempted to murder a white child entrusted to her care. Although the *Examiner* stated that this was the first instance of such a crime in Richmond, at least one other bondswoman would do away with her master and his family and Richmond's captive population would become manifestly restive[55] during the Confederate period.

Despite the fears and repressive laws of Richmond's master class, slaves lived better in the city than in the rural areas. Because of the practices of hiring out and living out, the distinctions between free Negro and slave in Richmond were becoming narrower in 1861. At the same time the gulf between black and white in the city was broadening. The victims of this squeeze were Richmond's 2,576 free blacks.[56] Free persons of color did not enjoy the economic security of their enslaved brethren. They competed for employment with slave labor and whites. They were often unemployed.[57] They shared many of the legal restrictions imposed upon bondsmen. Neither could assemble freely or speak "uppity." The law required free blacks to have papers proving their freedom and to register with the Hustings Court when they established residence in Richmond.[58]

Black and white lived in close contact in Richmond, but in spite of this proximity, perhaps because of it, law and customs kept the black in his prescribed place. In May, 1861, the Mayor's Court

[54] Wade, *Slavery in the Cities*, pp. 106–109.

[55] *Examiner*, May 25, 1861, September 10, 1863.

[56] Eighth Census, *Statistics of the United States . . . in 1860.*

[57] *Examiner*, September 5, 1861.

[58] City of Richmond Ordinances, December 22, 1857, cited in Wade, *Slavery in the Cities*, pp. 106–109.

sentenced Christopher Mitchell to jail for "conduct unbecoming a white man and a Christian" and for being "too intimate" with Sarah Mosly, a free Negro.[59] On June 3, 1861, the mayor ordered Susan Moxley, a free Negro, whipped for "not going home and staying there" when told to do so.[60] A court case in 1863 reveals the full extent to which race was significant in Richmond. Edward S. Gentry struck a white boy. If Gentry were a Negro, this action was a crime; if Gentry were white, the incident became a mere scuffle —disorder, but no crime. Before the Mayor's Court, Gentry pled that he was of less than one-quarter Negro blood, therefore not a mulatto, therefore white. Mayor Mayo agreed that Gentry was not a mulatto and that, according to law, he did not have to register himself as a Free Person of Color, but the mayor insisted that Negro blood constituted a black man, and that Gentry did not have the privileges of whites.[61] In the context of the nineteenth century, race per se was not an issue in Richmond. White Richmonders in the main believed unquestioningly in their racial superiority. Most black Richmonders, too, accepted the racial status quo. The Confederate experience would give Richmonders second thoughts about the wisdom and justice of slavery, but no serious thoughts about equality.

To round out his impression of Richmond's social institutions, Vice-President Stephens might have investigated the state of education, religion, and culture in the city. Richmonders had long been committed to the ideal of public education. A series of mass meetings and conventions had petitioned the state of Virginia to establish a system of public instruction. In spite of this fervor, by 1861 scarcely more than 200 pupils in Richmond received secondary instruction at public expense. The Lancasterian School, established in 1816 at Fifteenth and Marshall streets, served 150 children whose parents could not afford to pay the tuition of a private school. The city's strongest educational asset was the Medical College of Virginia, a rarity below the Potomac. Equally rare was a

[59] *Examiner*, May 24, 1861.
[60] *Ibid.*, June 5, 1861.
[61] *Ibid.*, January 26, 1863.

college for women, the Richmond Female Institute. Richmond College, founded by Virginia Baptists, also gave indication of the city's commitment to higher education. Richmond supported six public schools and twenty-three private primaries and academies in 1860.[62]

The city's thirty-three churches were led by such excellent men as Charles M. Minnegerode, Moses D. Hoge, Seth Doggett, and Bishop McGill. A white pastor, Jeremiah Jeter, served a Negro congregation in excess of three thousand in one of Richmond's four African Baptist Churches. Richmond's congregations were primarily comprised of members of the major evangelical Protestant denominations. However, the existence of three Roman Catholic churches, three Jewish synagogues, one Quaker meeting house, and a Universalist church demonstrated the variety of religious faiths in the city.[63]

Richmond's newspapers and periodicals had a circulation of nearly 84,000 in 1860.[64] Editor George W. Bagby from his office across from Capitol Square produced one of the finest literary journals in the nation, the *Southern Literary Messenger*.[65] Special engagements by such popular entertainers as Blind Tom, the young black pianist, supplemented the prestigious regular offerings at the Richmond Theater.[66] In sum, Richmond offered the Confederacy educational, religious, and cultural institutions equal to any city in the South.

In the spring of 1861 the city contained a happy blend of rural provincialism and urban potential. Richmond was an old town and a young city combined. The land, its fruits and its possessors, still greatly influenced the town. Planter dominance was visible in both

[62] Eighth Census, Social Statistics MS; F. W. Boatwright, "Education," in *Richmond, Approaches to Its History by Various Hands*, pp. 208–213.

[63] Dover Baptist Association, *Minutes of the Dover Baptist Association*, Richmond, 1860; Eighth Census, Social Statistics MS. In 1860 Richmond's thirty-three congregations were divided as follows: Baptist, eight; Methodist, six; Episcopal, five; Presbyterian, four; Roman Catholic, three; Jewish, three; Lutheran, two; Quaker, one; Universalist, one.

[64] Eighth Census, Social Statistics MS.

[65] Lyon G. Tyler, ed., *Encyclopedia of Virginia Biography*, III, 160.

[66] Christian, *Richmond, Her Past and Present*, p. 211.

society and economy. Bankers, merchants, and industrialists, however, had begun to challenge the supremacy of the planter, and in 1861 they had equaled him in the market place, if not in the drawing room. Richmond's zest for local government and atmosphere of gentle noblesse were distinctly Southern traits. Yet the city's Whiggish policies, diverse economy, and heterogeneous population gave her a youthful, cosmopolitan air exceptional in the ante-bellum South.

The young city offered much to the Confederacy, but the Confederacy had more to offer Richmond. The Confederate experience would strain every phase of Richmond's life, but war would bring maturity to the city's social, economic, and political institutions. The Cause would inspire her finest years, and in the end, when she had made her last sacrifice, the city would feel herself the very embodiment of the Confederacy.[67]

[67] For some further discussion of what the Confederate experience meant to Richmond see Frank E. Vandiver, *Jubal's Raid: General Early's Famous Attack on Washington in 1864*, pp. 15–18; Douglas S. Freeman, "The Confederate Tradition of Richmond," an essay written for the *Richmond Magazine* and reprinted in William J. Kimball, ed., *Richmond in Time of War*, pp. 158–162; and, Freeman, *The Last Parade*.

Permanent Capital

WITH THE COMPLETION of Virginia's temporary alliance with the Confederacy, Stephens's official mission to the state ended. Doubtless he returned to Montgomery with some convictions about the advantages of the removal of the Confederate capital to Richmond. On April 29 the Secession Convention appointed five men to represent Virginia in the provisional Congress at Montgomery.[1] Among these R. M. T. Hunter, former United States senator, was especially anxious to effect a change of capitals.[2] In late March a knowledgeable diarist recorded, "There are people who already say that the detestable hotels at Montgomery will drive Congress elsewhere."[3] A bill seeking removal of the government had been on the calendar since May 1. Hunter presented the Virginia convention's invitation to a secret session of Congress on May

---

[1] *Daily Richmond Enquirer*, April 30, 1861. The five included R. M. T. Hunter, William C. Rives, Gideon D. Camden, Waller R. Staples, and J. W. Brockenbrough.

[2] J. B. Jones, *A Rebel War Clerk's Diary at the Confederate States Capital*, ed. Howard Swiggett, I, 41.

[3] Mary Boykin Chesnut, *A Diary from Dixie*, ed. Ben Ames Williams, p. 30.

10. That same day Congress resolved to adjourn on May 23 and to meet again in Richmond on July 20, unless an emergency intervened. However, on May 17 President Davis vetoed the resolution on the grounds that the legislative branch of the government should not meet at a point several days' travel from the executive departments. Thus on May 20, Congress resolved that the entire government should move to Richmond before July 20. (Alabama could muster only Mississippi and South Carolina in her defense and lost the capital, six votes to three.) The following day Davis signed the resolution, and Congress appropriated forty thousand dollars to defray the expenses of moving the governmental departments.[4]

In the final analysis, the reason for the move combined appreciation of Richmond's status as a city with understanding of immediate military requirements. Many historians have criticized the decision to move the capital so close to Federal territory.[5] Yet the security of Richmond's industrial potential was essential to the young nation during the first months of war. And a glance at the map convinced the Confederate leadership that the five-day march between Washington and Richmond could be made extremely costly to an invader. If shore batteries or a Confederate navy could keep Union gunboats out of Virginia's large rivers, the distance and terrain between the rival capitals favored a determined defense. Dense forests, river obstacles, and swampy areas would impede an advance on Richmond from the north. A resourceful Southern commander could choose his battlefield and strike the enemy anywhere in the hundred-mile corridor between the Blue Ridge Mountains and the Chesapeake Bay. As long as the opposing armies bore any relation to each other in size, "on to Richmond" would

[4] U.S., Congress, Senate, *Journal of the Congresses of the Confederate States of America, 1861–1865*, vol. I, *Journal of the Provisional Congress of the Confederate States of America*, pp. 173–174, 206–211, 225, 254–264; James D. Richardson, ed., *A Compilation of the Messages and Papers of the Confederacy including the Diplomatic Correspondence, 1861–1865*, pp. 100, 112; James M. Matthews, ed., *Statutes at Large of the Provisional Congress of the Confederate States of America*, pp. 161–162, 165.

[5] See, for example, Clement Eaton, *A History of the Southern Confederacy*, p. 61.

be a siren's song luring Union troops onto a killing ground. Beyond these defensive capabilities, an army in northern Virginia would always threaten Federal territory and the Federal capital.[6]

On the same day that Vice-President Stephens reached Richmond to cement relations between Virginia and his government, Colonel Robert E. Lee, late of the U.S. Army, arrived in the city to assume command of Virginia's troops.[7] Lee's military reputation was well known to Richmonders. As a young engineer officer he had won praise and recognition in Scott's Mexican War. He had commanded at Harpers Ferry during the John Brown hysteria. The dignity of his aristocratic lineage and the gentle charm of his manner may have obscured for the moment the essence of this middle-aged Virginian—duty and genius. But a humble noblesse was also his characteristic. Presented to the Virginia Convention on April 23, he spoke but few words.[8] On the night of April 22, after the crowd of citizens had serenaded and cheered Alexander H. Stephens, they marched to the Spotswood House in search of Lee. Mayor Mayo appeared and informed the well-wishers that Lee was at work.[9] Others might have the time to make speeches. Lee had much else to do.

Events of the preceding day had demonstrated the chaotic unpreparedness of Richmond's defenses. April 21 had begun routinely, a quiet Sunday in the city. But as Richmond families were leaving the city's churches and anticipating their Sunday dinners, the alarm bell on Capitol Square began suddenly to toll. Rumor passed in whispers, then shouts, through the streets. "The *Pawnee* is coming!" "A Yankee gunboat is steaming up the James to shell the city!" Military companies collected hastily. A Howitzer Corps and the Fayette Artillery scrambled to Rocketts with their weapons; women and civilians joined the march. Cavalry companies scoured

6 See Frank E. Vandiver, "Jefferson Davis and Confederate Strategy," in *The American Tragedy: The Civil War in Retrospect*, ed. Bernard Mayo.

7 *Enquirer*, April 23, 1861; W. Ashbury Christian, *Richmond, Her Past and Present*, p. 218.

8 Christian, *Richmond, Her Past and Present*, p. 218.

9 *Richmond Daily Dispatch*, April 23, 1861.

the countryside south of the city. The Young Guard and the Virginia Life Guard formed on the wharf, perhaps intending to repel a landing party. The swearing of teamsters mingled with cries of small boys, as Richmond in her Sunday best went en masse to war.

Then as swiftly as the fright had begun, the alarm passed. Even if the *Pawnee* had been coming up the river (and she was not), her heavy draught would not have permitted passage to the city. Richmond laughed at its folly. Relieved citizens, a bit amused at their gullibility, left the heights above Rocketts' landing and resumed their Sunday routine. Some of the spectators remained to watch the assembled artillery companies engage in some impromptu, badly needed practice with their pieces. One idle rumor had panicked virtually the entire city. The local militia force was eager, but it was small and inexperienced. "*Pawnee* Sunday" had been a good joke on the city, but it had also revealed a very uncomical state of unreadiness.[10]

Throughout May, Lee worked to increase the efficiency of his rapidly expanding command of Virginia volunteers. The activating of a long dormant state militia provided confusion and excitement enough in Richmond. In addition, however, troops from all parts of the nation joined their government in the migration to the new capital.

Anxiety over Virginia's security and the selection of Richmond as a mustering place transformed the peaceful town into an armed camp. The streets were full of "soldiers singly, soldiers in pairs, in squads, in files. Drums and fifes and crowds of soldiers, and nothing more."[11] Richmond's fairgrounds became a Camp of Instruc-

---

[10] Almost everyone in the city recorded a good description of "*Pawnee* Sunday." See for example, *Dispatch*, April 22, 1861; *Enquirer*, April 23, 1861; Sallie Brock Putnam, *Richmond during the War: Four Years of Personal Observation*, pp. 24–26; Jones, *Rebel War Clerk's Diary*, p. 28; T. C. DeLeon, *Four Years in Rebel Capitals: An Inside View of Life in the Southern Confederacy from Birth to Death*, pp. 103–104; John H. Worsham, *One of Jackson's Foot Cavalry, His Experience and What He Was during the War 1861–1865, including a History of "F Company," Richmond, Va., 21st Regiment Virginia Infantry, Second Brigade, Jackson's Division, Second Corps, A. N. Va.*, pp. 14–16.

[11] Catherine Cooper Hopley, *Life in the South*, I, 368.

tion, and cadets from the Virginia Military Institute came down from Lexington to serve as drill masters.[12] As early as April 27 the *Enquirer* reported nearly two thousand troops in the city and almost a thousand more at the Camp of Instruction.[13] Richmond militia units drilled nightly, and many businesses suspended operation early in the day to allow their employees time to fulfill their military obligations.[14] By November the *Whig* would estimate that 2800 of Richmond's 4000 voting population had entered the army.[15] One participant in the transformation of this armed mob into an army remembered: "The drilling, of which there was literally no end, was simply funny. Maneuvers of the most utterly impossible sort were carefully taught to the men. Every amateur officer had his own pet system of tactics, and the effect of the incongruous teachings, when brought out in battalion drill, closely resembled that of the music at Mr. Bob Sawyer's party, where each guest sang the chorus to the tune he knew best."[16] The horseless adjutant of a cavalry regiment summarized a common predicament in the young army in a letter to his mother: "I have no uniform and no sabre yet. I conduct Dress Parade in my grey pants and blue coat and borrow a sabre from some one on the sick list. If we should receive marching orders I can probably obtain a horse and sabre in this way and march with the regiment."[17]

Throughout May and June of 1861 the troops poured into the city. Volunteers came armed with shotguns, bowie knives, muskets, or squirrel guns. As soon as practicable the companies were mustered into the Confederate service.[18] Then the men drilled,

[12] John C. Shields, "Old Camp Lee," reprinted from Richmond *Dispatch*, May 22, 1898, in *Southern Historical Society Papers* 26 (1898): 241–246.

[13] *Enquirer*, April 27, 1861.

[14] *Ibid.*, April 23, 1861; *Dispatch*, April 30, 1861.

[15] *Richmond Daily Whig*, November 6, 1861.

[16] George Cary Eggleston, *A Rebel's Recollection*, p. 64.

[17] "T" to Mother, May 15, 1861, Kate Mason Rowland Papers.

[18] Virginia troops were turned over to the national government in accord with the convention which allied the state with the government on June 8, soon after the voters ratified the ordinance of secession. Although there was some dispute over ordnance supplies and works, Governor Letcher eventually honored the state's commitment. For a discussion of the friction between Virginia Chief of Ordnance Charles Dimmock and his Confederate counterpart, Josiah Gorgas,

loafed, and awaited orders dispatching them to a probable front.

Elite corps such as the Washington Artillery from New Orleans joined the local "Grays" and "Blues" (Richmond Light Infantry Blues). The young Louisianians with Edward, their French chef from Victor's Restaurant, were popular guests at a round of teas and dances in the city.[19] In the many companies composed of the wealthy and prominent, "whenever a detail was made for cleaning the campground, the men detailed regarded themselves as responsible for the proper performance of their task by their servants, and uncomplainingly took upon themselves the duty of sitting on the fence and superintending the work."[20] Women and girls made regular visits to the camps bearing cakes and other delicacies. Reviews and parades in camp, parties and the theater in the city, added to the gaiety of the season. The horseless cavalry officer reassured his mother about the rigors of army life: "We have had two horse-races this week gotten up by way of amusement. The soldiers using their own horses. You know we are quartered at the Ashland Race-Course. On Friday the officers give a military ball to which $500 have already been subscribed by the different companies. You ask how we live. We occupy a very nice house that belongs to the racing club and have a mess of eighteen or twenty and a caterer who was one of the proprietors of a hotel in Richmond before he joined the army, we of course live well."[21] Enlisted men did not fare so well. For the most part, they lived in tents and subsisted on a diet of bacon, bread, and coffee.[22] Nevertheless, uniforms concealed the marks of social class, and "regardless of social distinction, or castes of society, the barriers which hedge familiar intercourse were broken down, and the man was almost forgotten in the soldier."[23]

---

see Frank E. Vandiver, *Ploughshares into Swords: Josiah Gorgas and Confederate Ordnance*, pp. 67–72; and Virginia Executive Council Minutes, June 1, June 7, 1861.

[19] William Miller Owen, *In Camp and Battle with the Washington Artillery of New Orleans: A Narrative of Events during the Late Civil War from Bull Run to Appomatox and Spanish Fort*, p. 21.

[20] Eggleston, *Rebel's Recollections*, p. 73.

[21] "T" to Mother, June 18, 1861, Kate Mason Rowland Papers.

[22] Tucker Randolph, Journal.

[23] Putnam, *Richmond during the War*, p. 32.

These were the gala days when the excitement of war was enjoyable in Richmond. One diarist, Mary Boykin Chesnut, wife of a South Carolina provisional congressman, recorded: "Noise of drums, tramp of marching regiments all day long, rattling artillery wagons, bands of music, friends from every quarter coming in. We ought to be miserable and anxious, and yet these are pleasant days. Perhaps we are unnaturally exhilarated and excited."[24]

On June 7 the New Orleans Zouaves reached Richmond. On June 10 one of the company married a Richmond girl. Resplendent in blue jackets, red baggy trousers, red caps, black leather leggings, and white gaiters, these gay warriors were reputed to have been recruited from the New Orleans jails. From the time of their arrival the chicken population in Richmond declined.[25] At least one of the Zouaves brought a *vivandière* with him. She dressed like the men, and from the description of Mrs. Chesnut who saw her, "she frisked about in her hat and feathers, did not uncover her head as a man would have done, played the piano, sang war songs. She had no drum but she gave us a rataplan! She was followed at every step by a mob of admiring soldiers and boys."[26] Mrs. Chesnut missed very few of the gay scenes in the young capital. On July 4 she noted: "A young Carolinian with queer ideas of a joke rode his horse through the barroom of this hotel [Spotswood House]. How he scattered people and things right and left! Captain Ingraham was incensed at the bad conduct of his young countryman. 'He was intoxicated, of course,' said Captain Ingraham. 'But he was a splendid rider.' "[27]

Not all of Richmond's property-owners thought the onslaught of soldiers was so exhilarating. Owners of restaurants where Zouaves ate sumptuously and charged the fare to the government resented the newcomers. So did almost anyone who had a henhouse near one of the encampments. And when young Carolinians, drunk or

---

24 Chesnut, *Diary from Dixie*, p. 75.
25 *Dispatch*, June 8, June 15, 1861; Putnam, *Richmond during the War*, p. 36.
26 Chesnut, *Diary from Dixie*, p. 82; Sam L. Clark, ed., "A Confederate Officer Visits Richmond," *Tennessee Historical Quarterly* 11 (March, 1952): 89.
27 Chesnut, *Diary from Dixie*, p. 75.

sober, spoke of "coming to fight Virginia's battle for her," retorts were swift and bitter.[28] Not all Richmond girls limited their services to the soldiers to bearing them baskets of cakes and goodies. The world's oldest profession had had its prosperous practitioners in ante-bellum Richmond. With the coming of armies to the city, however, prostitution boomed.[29] The record of one house of ill fame, that run by Mary Wilson and Mary Walker at the head of Adams Valley near Shockoe Creek, illustrates the general trend of increased activity. On June 6 the night-watch police first closed down Mary Wilson's business activity.[30] Less than a week later Mary Walker charged three soldiers with "violating her person."[31] It would seem that she had over-advertised. At any rate she recovered rapidly, for on July 20, the night watch found the Wilson-Walker establishment in full operation. This time Mayor Mayo fined the two Marys two hundred dollars and sent them to jail.[32] In less than two months, then, one or both of the partners had been before the Mayor's Court three times. And it would be safe to speculate that the women resumed their trade as soon as they had served their time in jail. Despite the best efforts of the military and civil authorities, prostitution flourished in Richmond throughout the Confederate period.

Drunken rowdiness, too, increased with the influx of Richmond's defenders. Fights, knifings, and shootings alarmed the once quiet city.[33] The *Whig* concluded a paragraph lamenting the scarcity and high price of whiskey by observing that even at fifteen cents per drink "judging by the number of drunken Sons of Mars" liquor was cheap and plentiful.[34]

Some Richmonders began to have second thoughts about becoming the Confederate capital. The city council enacted ordinances

[28] Putnam, *Richmond during the War*, p. 30.
[29] Bell I. Wiley, *The Life of Johnny Reb: The Common Soldier of the Confederacy*, pp. 54–56.
[30] *Richmond Daily Examiner*, June 8, 1861.
[31] *Ibid.*, June 15, 1861.
[32] *Whig*, July 22, 1861.
[33] For examples see *Examiner*, May–June, 1861.
[34] *Whig*, July 22, 1861.

closing barrooms at 10:00 P.M. and later shut them down completely on Sundays. The council also requested Mayor Mayo to impress upon the military commanders the necessity of making troops leave their side arms in camp when they visited the city.[35] Ladies generally remained off the streets until most of the troops had departed for field positions.[36] Some irritation was no doubt inevitable. Richmond, however, adjusted to the presence and occasional high spirits of her defenders and, once the initial shock had passed, made every effort to aid the new army and its cause.

The national army that gathered about the capital found the city alive with preparations for war. Immediately after the news of fighting at Fort Sumter reached Richmond, the city council appropriated $50,000 for arming and equipping volunteers. To finance this appropriation and other expenses of the emergency, the council on its own initiative began issuing $300,000 worth of notes in denominations less than two dollars. Throughout the spring and summer, Richmond's military units received clothing, tents, and other supplies from city funds.[37] To enforce the unanimity of secessionist feeling in the city, on April 22 the council enacted an ordinance controlling suspicious persons. Citizens were to report persons holding seditious opinions to the mayor who would treat them as vagrants or persons of ill-fame.[38] Further action of the council to prepare the city included appointing a committee to wait on the governor and seek his advice in preventing "monopolies of provisions."[39] In response to a petition from Richmond's physicians, the council authorized druggists to charge medicines needed by the families of volunteers to the city.[40] And volunteers' families re-

[35] Richmond City Council, Minutes, April 22, 1861, and July 8, 1861. Proceedings of the council are available in Louis Manarin, ed., *Richmond at War: The Minutes of the City Council, 1861–1865*. Meeting dates are given in the margins.

[36] *Dispatch*, July 13, 1861.

[37] City Council, Minutes, April 13, 22, 1861.

[38] *Ibid.*, April 22, 1861; see *Enquirer*, April 25, 1861, for text of the ordinance. One example of action taken under the ordinance is the case of John Frost reported in the *Dispatch*, May 7, 8, 10, 1861.

[39] City Council, Minutes, April 22, 1861.

[40] *Dispatch*, May 4, 1861; City Council, Minutes, May 13, 25, 1861.

ceived city water free, if they should be unable to afford the service.[41] As significant as these actions of the council were, the individual citizens of Richmond more than matched the patriotic zeal of their municipal authorities.

As soon as the Secession Convention called for volunteers from the state, Richmond began contributing to the cost of equipping soldiers and of assisting their families. Meetings, subscription blanks, and benefit entertainments raised thousands of dollars.[42] The county court of surrounding Henrico County floated a ten-thousand-dollar bond issue to raise and equip volunteers.[43] Fifty prominent citizens, most past military age, formed the Richmond Ambulance Corps to assist the wounded.[44] And the ladies of Richmond sewed. Almost every church in the city converted its lecture hall or Sunday school room into a clothing factory. Women made uniforms, knitted socks, rolled bandages, and carded lint.[45] The government soon assumed most of the responsibility for clothing and supporting its troops, but contributions from Richmond's private citizens never ceased to aid the cause.

Into the midst of Richmond's preparations for war came Jefferson Davis and the government of the Confederate States. On May 25 the Richmond City Council resolved that the government's advent gave the "liveliest satisfaction" and that "no proper efforts will be omitted to manifest the public sense of the high distinction." Specifically, the council resolved to "tender to His Excellency Jefferson Davis, on his arrival, the hospitalities of the city, and assure him of the high consideration in which he is held, for his official and personal virtues and services."[46] Enthusiasm for the

41 City Council, Minutes, June 5, 1861.

42 For examples see *Enquirer*, April 23, 25, and May 10, 1861.

43 James H. Bailey, *Henrico Home Front, 1861–1865: A Picture of Life in Henrico County, Virginia: Based on Selections from the Minute Books of the Henrico County Court*, pp. 2–4.

44 "The Richmond Ambulance Corps," reprinted from the Richmond *Dispatch*, December 12, 1897, in *Southern Historical Society Papers* 25 (1897): 113–115.

45 *Enquirer*, April 23, 25, and May 10, 1861; *Dispatch*, April 23, 25, 1861; Putnam, *Richmond during the War*, p. 39.

46 City Council, Minutes, May 25, 1861.

President did not confine itself to the pronouncements of Richmond officialdom. The *Dispatch* called Davis "an instrument of Providence for accomplishing its own beneficent designs," and added, "It is impossible that the South should not feel secure with such a man as this at the helm; and thrice welcome is he in Richmond, where all respect, admire, and confide in him."[47] The *Enquirer* termed Davis "one of the few men of the age who combine the Caesarian faculty of writing with the pen, speaking with the tongue, and fighting with the sword."[48]

Richmond expressed her admiration with lusty cheers when the President's train reached the city in the early morning of May 29. Cannon roared as Davis and his party, behind four splendid bays, left the depot and proceeded to the Spotswood Hotel. From the window of his flag-draped suite, the President thanked the crowd for their attentions and pledged his concern for the defense of Virginia. By five o'clock in the afternoon Davis was in the saddle reviewing troops.[49]

Next day the President and his lady received Richmonders at the Governor's Mansion for two-and-a-half hours.[50] When they had the opportunity to see the President at close range and shake his hand, the citizens were pleased. Davis was tall, and the ramrod posture of a lean frame accentuated his practiced dignity. A carefully cultivated charm and pleasant smile brightened his otherwise stern features. He possessed reputation, administrative skill, and the same indomitable will that later characterized his capital. Davis should have been Richmond's first citizen; for a time he was.[51]

The President had been quietly tending the roses on his Mississippi plantation when the telegram arrived announcing his election as provisional President. Mrs. Davis remembered, "he looked so

---

47 *Dispatch*, May 30, 1861.
48 *Enquirer*, April 27, 1861.
49 *Dispatch*, May 30, 1861; *Enquirer*, May 31, 1861.
50 *Dispatch*, May 30, 1861.
51 For a good physical description of Davis see Jones, *Rebel War Clerk's Diary*, I, 36–37.

grieved that I feared some evil had befallen our family. . . . he told me, as a man might speak of a sentence of death."[52]

Later he wrote his wife from Montgomery, "We are without machinery, without means, and threatened by a powerful opposition; but I do not despond, and will not shrink from the task imposed upon me."[53] Davis would fulfill his responsibilities and do his duty, but he probably would not enjoy it.

The President's policies, as his contemporaries and later historians saw them, were at the same time too revolutionary and too prosaic. He ran his administration as though the Confederacy had existed a thousand years earlier. His armies fought a defensive revolution, while red tape, proper channels, and official formalities multiplied.[54] At the same time, the Davis government would virtually overturn the Southern way of life in defense of Southern independence. His administration would suspend the writ of habeas corpus, conscript troops, impress goods, and finally arm Negroes in desperate attempts to win its war.[55] While critics attacked his efforts as being those of a pedant or a despot, Davis stubbornly did his duty as he saw it. He drove himself so hard that his health faltered and his temper sometimes flared. Never possessed of great personal magnetism and often exhausted from his labors, the President, in time, withdrew into his round of official tasks. He lived four years in the capital, but Richmond never really knew him.

But at the time of his arrival in Richmond, Davis was the man of the hour. On June 1 three thousand citizens and the Armory Band serenaded the President.[56] He was cheered every afternoon when he rode out to see the troops. He was doing the work of Presi-

[52] Varina Howell Davis, *Jefferson Davis, Ex-President of the Confederate States of America: A Memior by His Wife*, II, 18.

[53] Dunbar Rowland, ed., *Jefferson Davis, Constitutionalist; His Letters, Papers and Speeches*, V, 53–54.

[54] Best exponents of this view of Davis were Edward A. Pollard, *The First Year of the War*, pp. 265–268; and later Clifford Dowdey, *The Land They Fought For: The Story of the South as the Confederacy, 1832–1865.*

[55] See especially Frank E. Vandiver, *Jefferson Davis and the Confederate State*, for the best recent statement of these events.

[56] *Dispatch*, June 3, 1861.

dent and five cabinet-level departments, and Richmonders were delighted.[57]

Davis's arrival signaled an acceleration in the already furious activities of governmental machinery in the new capital. Executive offices were provided in the old United States Customs House for the President, Cabinet, and the Departments of War, Justice, Navy, and the Treasury. The clerks of the War Office had barely occupied these quarters and sorted out the boxes of papers brought from Montgomery, when permanent facilities were leased at Mechanics Hall.[58] Workmen fashioned offices and committee rooms day and night, and hammers punctuated the swearing of departmental secretaries.[59]

Richmond's carpenters could not hope to keep pace with the political construction going on at the Spotswood Hotel. Richmond's council purchased the $35,000 home of L. D. Crenshaw on Cary Street for the President, but while the mansion was being furnished, the President, cabinet officials, and would-be officials lived at the Spotswood.[60]

Although the Congress assumed the cost of purchasing and furnishing the executive mansion,[61] the Richmond City Council paid for the presidential family's residence at the Spotswood at over fifty dollars per day.[62] Presiding over social arrangements here for her harassed husband was Varina Howell Davis. A handsome, if not pretty, woman, Mrs. Davis would never be beloved by Richmond. She was forced to become First Lady of an established society that was easily piqued by this direct, "western person" with her circle of "foreign" (non-Virginian) ladies. Varina Davis ultimately made some strong friends among Richmond natives and melted the early coolness of the Richmond ladies; but twice when Richmond was in peril, this professed First Lady would abandon

[57] DeLeon, *Four Years in Rebel Capitals*, pp. 102–103.
[58] Jones, *Rebel War Clerk's Diary*, p. 46.
[59] DeLeon, *Four Years in Rebel Capitals*, p. 87.
[60] City Council, Minutes, June 8, 10, 1861.
[61] *Dispatch*, July 9, 1861.
[62] Council paid $3,288 for the President's board from May 29 to August 1 (City Council, Minutes, August 14, 1861).

the city for a safer locale.[63] Nevertheless, for this hour she found herself matriarch of the mad, microcosm Confederacy within the Spotswood. Mrs. Chesnut wrote:

This Spotswood is a miniature world. The war topic is not so much avoided. Everybody has some personal dignity to take care of, and everybody else is indifferent to it. A Richmond lady told me under her breath that Mrs. Davis had sent a baby's dress to her friend, Mrs. Montgomery Blair (wife of Lincoln's Postmaster General), and Mrs. Blair had responded: "Even if the men kill one another, we will abide friends to the bitter end, the grave." I said nothing, because I will be taken aside and told by somebody else: "That Blair story is all false, made up by these malicious, gossipy women." In this wild confusion, everything likely and unlikely is told you, and then everything is flatly contradicted.[64]

The "official family" was a huge one. General P. G. T. Beauregard arrived on May 30, and the Hero of Sumter graciously received the praise due him before hurrying off to another field.[65] Congressman Chesnut of South Carolina assisted the President, while his wife joined the circle of Mrs. Davis and "worked like a beaver, or rather a mole, for her friends."[66] Leroy Pope Walker, Secretary of War, lived at the Spotswood until the confusion there and the press of his duties sent the Alabamian to the country for a rest.[67] Louis T. Wigfall, congressman and later influential senator from Texas, came to town with the President and was soon making four speeches a day to admirers.[68] Secretary of the Treasury Christopher G. Memminger, Commissary General Lucius B. Northrop, and Secretary of the Navy Stephen D. Mallory made the Spotswood their home during these hectic months.[69]

---

[63] See Douglas S. Freeman, *The South to Posterity: An Introduction to the Writings of Confederate History*, pp. 128–134; T. C. DeLeon, *Belles, Beaux, and Brains of the 60's*, pp. 66–68; and Varina Howell Davis, *Memoir*, II, 202–210.

[64] Chesnut, *Diary from Dixie*, p. 68.

[65] *Dispatch*, June 1, 1861.

[66] Chesnut, *Diary from Dixie*, p. 68.

[67] Jones, *Rebel War Clerk's Diary*, I, 62–64.

[68] Letter of Mrs. Wigfall to daughter, May 30, 1861, quoted in Mrs. D. Giraud Wright, *A Southern Girl in '61: The War-Time Memories of a Confederate Senator's Daughter*, p. 55.

[69] *Dispatch*, May 30, June 4, 1861; *Enquirer*, June 4, 1861.

Attorney General Judah P. Benjamin of Louisiana, capable and smiling, scurried about seeking good restaurants and stimulating conversation.[70] An admirer said of him, "Hebrew in blood, English in tenacity of grasp and purpose, Mr. Benjamin was French in taste," and went on to point out, "There was no circle, official or otherwise, that missed his soft, purring presence, or had not regretted so doing."[71] In contrast to the well-oiled Benjamin, fiery Secretary of State Robert Toombs soon sickened of wartime politics, resigned his post, and in July followed Virginia's ex-governors John B. Floyd and Henry A. Wise to field commands.[72] Toombs's successor in the State Department was Robert Mercer Taliaferro Hunter, one of the nation's ablest public men and a member of the old Virginia aristocracy. He would spend most of the Confederate period as President pro tem of the Senate, but for the moment, the dark, Indian-looking Virginian held his portfolio because the cabinet needed a Virginian for political purposes.[73]

Politics was the business of Davis's official circle, and they plied their trade day and night at the Spotswood. The Richmond government wielded even more power perhaps than its counterpart in Washington. The Confederacy was new, and avenues of power were opening everywhere. For example, about one thousand civil servants came with the government from Montgomery. The Confederacy eventually employed over seventy thousand civilians.[74] Add to this the number of military positions available, and it is obvious that the privilege of dispensing the "loaves and fishes" of official patronage presented decided political opportunities.

As civil servants, politicians, and hangers-on joined the military in Richmond, the new capital became horribly overcrowded. In the

[70] The standard biography of Benjamin is Robert D. Meade, *Judah P. Benjamin: Confederate Statesman.*

[71] DeLeon, *Belles, Beaux, and Brains*, pp. 91–92.

[72] Jones, *Rebel War Clerk's Diary*, p. 60.

[73] A good sketch of Hunter appeared in an article in the *New York Leader*, and is quoted in Charles G. Haysine to R. M. T. Hunter, April 14, 1861, in Charles Henry Ambler, ed., *Correspondence of Robert M. T. Hunter, 1826–1876*, *American Historical Association Annual Report, 1916*, II, 351.

[74] Paul P. Van Riper and Harry N. Schreiber, "The Confederate Civil Service," *Journal of Southern History* 25 (November, 1959): 450–451.

hotels men made their beds in parlors, halls, and on billiard tables. Vacant seats in the dining rooms produced scrambles among hungry guests. One newcomer stated, "Such a thing as a clean room, a hot steak, or an answered bell were not to be bought by flagrant bribery."[75] Another sojourner complained, "Boarding is rising rapidly, and so are the blood-thirsty insects at the Carleton House."[76] Boardinghouses and rented dwellings eased the crush at the hotels, but Richmond would never be underpopulated. Despite some discomfort, however, those connected with the government remarked the vast difference of its reception by the Richmond and Montgomery people. As one official expressed it: "Richmond, having given the invitation, made the best of it when accepted. The people united in a sincere effort to show a whole-souled hospitality to all strangers deserving of it. Gentlemen in the government were received with frank and freehanded kindness; and even a wretch, who had wintered in the shade of Washington upas, was allowed to flutter about and not be gunned for by the double-barreled spectacles of every respectable dowager."[77] The new capital had little time to scrutinize the government's hordes, for before she could prepare herself, war began.

Throughout the spring the Richmond City Council had made efforts to defend the city. Besides general aid to military organizations, the body appropriated $5,000 for the city's immediate defenses.[78] Colonel Andrew Talcott of the State Engineer Corps put three topographical parties in the field and selected four or five positions for redoubts.[79] By May 21 Talcott reported to Lee that work on two outworks would begin in a few days, and estimated that six hundred men would be sufficient to garrison the works.[80] On June 8 Governor Letcher turned over Virginia's military organization to

[75] DeLeon, *Four Years in Rebel Capitals*, pp. 86–87.
[76] Jones, *Rebel War Clerk's Diary*, I, 47.
[77] DeLeon, *Four Years in Rebel Capitals*, p. 103.
[78] City Council, Minutes, June 3, 1861.
[79] Andrew Talcott to R. E. Lee, May 15, 1861, U.S. Congress, House, *War of the Rebellion: A Compilation of the Official Records of the Union and Confederate Armies* ser. I, vol. 2, p. 851.
[80] Talcott to Lee, May 21, 1861, *ibid.*, p. 864.

the Confederate government. Nevertheless, local work on Richmond's fortifications continued, as the city street cleaners abandoned their usual duties.[81] However, on June 14, Lee, in his new capacity as military advisor to the President, wrote Governor Letcher expressing alarm at the slow progress of Richmond's defense preparations. Lee suggested that more laborers be found for the work on the fortifications, and that a home defense organization be formed and armed for any emergency.[82]

Accordingly the police and local military units swept down upon black neighborhoods and commandeered unemployed free Negroes to serve the Cause. Ultimately the free blacks received eleven dollars per month, the pay of an army private, for their services. Though work on the fortifications relieved a chronic unemployment among the city's free Negroes, a private's pay proved inadequate compensation for the degradation attached. The council also appropriated eleven thousand dollars to arm and equip the Richmond Home Artillery, a unit commanded by Thomas H. Ellis and consisting of three eighty-man companies.[83] Such were the city's preparations on the eve of the first battle for her life.

Richmond's first war news was glorious. On June 10 a small contingent under Colonel John Magruder repulsed a Union force twice its size in a "very animated" battle of two-and-a-half hours. The fight took place at Big Bethel Church on the peninsula between the James and York rivers. The Confederates suffered eight casualties to the Federals' seventy-six.[84] Although the action involved little more than a frontal assault against artillery, the news of a victory stirred imaginations in Richmond. This confidence collapsed, however, when a Union victory at Rich Mountain on July 11 canceled the success at Big Bethel.[85] But Richmonders knew that

[81] *Dispatch*, June 7, 1861.

[82] Clifford Dowdey, ed., Louis H. Manarin, assoc., ed., *The Wartime Papers of R. E. Lee*, p. 50.

[83] City Council, Minutes, July 8, 1861; *Examiner*, September 4, 1861.

[84] Report of Col. J. B. Magruder, *War of the Rebellion: Compilation of Official Records*, ser. I, vol. 2, pp. 91–92; Report of Benjamin F. Butler, *ibid.*, pp. 80–82.

[85] DeLeon, *Four Years in Rebel Capitals*, pp. 111–112, 114–115.

these engagements were petty. The great battle was still to come, and on it depended the fate of the young nation.

As the summer moved along the tension increased. "A hushed, feverish suspense—like the sultry stillness before the burst of the storm—brooded over the land, shared alike by the people and the government."[86] Then suddenly most of the troops were gone from Richmond. They had joined Beauregard near Manassas, or Magruder on the peninsula. The citizens were alone in the city.

Richmond slept poorly, if at all, on the night of July 21. There had been fighting at Manassas. "Each splashed and weary-looking man was stopped and surrounded by crowds . . ."[87] Reports were unclear. President Davis had gone to the front. In Mechanics Hall, at Franklin and Ninth streets, a cluster of officials of the provisional government fidgeted and paced. The telegraph brought fragmentary dispatches as Secretary of War Walker cursed his office and longed to be in the field. The entire Cabinet was present. Howell Cobb, president of the Provisional Congress, pronounced the battle a draw and an argument ensued. Then Judah Benjamin burst into the office and gave out the news. Benjamin had memorized the text of the President's telegram to Mrs. Davis, "Night has closed on a hard fought field. . . . Our forces have won a glorious victory." Secretary of State Hunter's face relaxed; Postmaster General Reagan's eyes resumed normal size; and Attorney General Benjamin fairly glowed. The new nation would indeed have a *permanent* government, and Richmond would be its capital.[88]

[86] *Ibid.*, p. 120.
[87] *Ibid.*, p. 124.
[88] Jones, *Rebel War Clerk's Diary*, I, 65–66; for text of Davis's telegram see *Enquirer*, July 26, 1861.

PART II   "SHELL AND BE DAMNED"

4

Adolescent Capital

JEFFERSON DAVIS RETURNED to his capital on the night of July 23. Standing before an immense assembly outside the Spotswood Hotel, Davis delivered a glowing account of the glorious battle of Manassas. The President praised his generals, Johnston and Beauregard, and the Old War Horse described the maneuvers which had brought victory. Although declining any direct credit for the triumph, Davis recalled how wounded soldiers had cheered him as their leader, and how his presence had rallied the broken ranks to the final victorious charge. The President delighted his audience by describing the immense quantities of supplies left on the field by the fleeing Federals. He closed by lauding the gallantry of Southern arms, but warned the throng of citizens that a hard fight still remained.[1] However, on this night, no one in Richmond doubted there would be an eventual Southern victory.

Some in the mob that heard and cheered the President that night were disappointed that Davis had not taken literally his constitu-

[1] *Richmond Daily Dispatch*, July 24, 1861; Mary Boykin Chesnut, *A Diary from Dixie*, ed. Ben Ames Williams, p. 89.

tional role as commander-in-chief and personally led his army.[2]
Perhaps Davis himself shared this disappointment. Still others, in
the days that followed, would lament the failure of the Confederates to pursue their foes into Washington to seize the rival capital.[3]
But for now the single triumph sufficed. "Men were beside themselves with joy and pride,—drunk with glory."[4] The *Dispatch* in
reporting the arrival of Davis stated, "The excitement in the city
yesterday reached a height such as we never before witnessed."[5]
The *Whig* termed the action at Manassas the "greatest battle since
Waterloo,"[6] and the *Enquirer* abandoned all restraint: "Then let
the songs of rejoicing swell through all our beautiful land, for God
hath given us the victory! Let our whole people join in the loud
and joyful acclaim. . . . This day our freedom and independence
stand secure!"[7] In this hour following a glorious victory and the
President's triumphal return, Richmond was an exultant capital.
During the weeks to come, she would learn the cost of her exulta-
tion and of being the capital of a nation at war.

Casualties of the great battle arrived in three waves. On the first
wave the walking wounded came stumbling into the city. Next
came special trains carrying the coffins. The body of Georgia's Colonel Bartow lay in state at the Capitol, while many of his comrades
filled new graves at Hollywood, Oakwood, and Shockoe cemeteries.
Finally came stretchers bearing the seriously wounded.[8] As each
train arrived: "The whole city was there—the rich merchant—the
rough laborer—the heavy features of the sturdy serving-woman—
the dusky, but loving face of the negro—the delicate profile of the

[2] J. B. Jones, *A Rebel War Clerk's Diary at the Confederate States Capital*,
ed. Howard Swiggett, I, 65–66.

[3] For a discussion of this issue and pertinent letters of Davis, Johnston, and
Beauregard, see Varina Howell Davis, *Jefferson Davis, Ex-President of the Confederate States of America: A Memoir by His Wife*, II, 120–137.

[4] Mrs. Fannie A. Beers, *Memories: A Record of Personal Experience and Adventure during Four Years of War*, p. 25.

[5] *Dispatch*, July 24, 1861.

[6] *Richmond Daily Whig*, July 22, 1861.

[7] *Daily Richmond Enquirer*, July 26, 1861.

[8] T. C. DeLeon, *Four Years in Rebel Capitals: An Inside View of Life in the
Southern Confederacy from Birth to Death*, pp. 125–126; Jones, *Rebel War
Clerk's Diary*, I, 66.

petted belle—all strained forward in the same intent gaze, as car after car was emptied of its ghastly freight."[9] After a time the *Dispatch* implored its readers to stay away from the depot, as the crush there was impeding the removal of the wounded.[10]

The day after the battle many Richmond people answered Mayor Mayo's call for a mass meeting in Capitol Square to make arrangements for care of the wounded. The citizens appointed one committee to go to Manassas and aid in bringing the soldiers to Richmond and another to secure facilities for the care of the military men in the city.[11] Hospital accommodations in Richmond were painfully limited, and until more could be provided, "almost every house in the city was a private hospital, and almost every woman a nurse."[12] Richmond's citizen committee solicited rooms, nurses, and supplies for the wounded, while a subcommittee called on those in the surrounding countryside to donate fresh farm produce to the effort.[13] R. H. Dickinson offered free of charge his St. Charles Hotel at the corner of Main and Wall streets as a hospital, and the day after President Davis's return, Charles Bates was collecting volunteer cooks and nurses for a new hospital at the Second Market, on Sixth Street between Marshall and Broad. Within a month Richmonders had contributed nearly eight thousand dollars to care for 1,336 patients.[14] The city council resolved to pay the cost of medicine for soldiers lodged with private families or cared for by voluntary associations. The council also provided a lot in Oakwood Cemetery for the interment of soldiers who died in the city.[15] Although Richmond was almost totally unprepared for the large numbers of casualties, her citizens met the crisis individually with a generous spirit that won the praise and admiration of many a wounded man. These soldiers would remember Richmond as the

[9] DeLeon, *Four Years in Rebel Capitals*, p. 126.
[10] *Dispatch*, July 25, 1861.
[11] *Dispatch*, July 22, 1861; *Enquirer*, July 26, 1861.
[12] Sallie Brock Putnam, *Richmond during the War: Four Years of Personal Observation*, p. 65.
[13] *Dispatch*, July 27, 1861.
[14] *Whig*, July 24, August 29, 1861.
[15] Richmond City Council, Minutes, August 12, 1861.

residence, not of government officials, but of brave and kindly ladies. Senator Wigfall's daughter recalled:

. . . droll story of one of these ministering angels in the hospital when she approached the bedside of an ill soldier. He looked wan and weary and infinite pity filled her heart. "Can I not do something for you?" she asked. "Would you like me to bathe your face?" He raised his eyes and looked at her, replying in dead earnest, with real gratitude for her good intentions, and not the slightest appreciation of the humor of the situation:

"I have had it washed seventeen times to-day, Miss, but you can do it again if you want to!"[16]

To channel the city's patriotic energies, benevolent associations were formed by many leading citizens and sojourners. Richmond's Young Men's Christian Association established a depot on Main Street to collect and distribute articles for the sick and wounded.[17] The ladies of St. James Episcopal Church secured the home of Judge John Robertson and converted it into a hospital.[18] Several other ladies opened "Soldiers Rest" in a school building on Clay Street.[19] Throughout the fall and winter, local amateurs and touring professionals presented benefit concerts in behalf of wounded soldiers and families of volunteers.

Men and women from other Confederate states who were residing in Richmond organized and operated hospitals for their state's wounded soldiers. Mrs. A. F. Hopkins established an Alabama hospital on August 1 and eventually managed four hospitals in the city.[20] One of her nurses remembered: "She neglected no detail of business or other thing that could afford aid or comfort to the sick or wounded. She kept up a voluminous correspondence, made in person every purchase for her charges, received and accounted for hundreds of boxes from Alabama containing clothing and delicacies for the sick, and visited the wards of the hospitals every day."[21]

[16] Mrs. D. Giraud Wright, *A Southern Girl in '61: The War-Time Memories of a Confederate Senator's Daughter*, p. 151.
[17] *Dispatch*, August 1, 1861.
[18] *Whig*, August 6, 1861.
[19] Beers, *Memories*, pp. 40–42.
[20] *Whig*, August 31, 1861.
[21] Beers, *Memories*, p. 34.

Howell Cobb, president of the Provisional Congress, presided over a meeting of the city's Georgians on August 24 when that group selected an executive committee to found a hospital in Richmond and solicit funds from Georgia.[22] By December there were three Georgia hospitals in the capital.[23] In September, South Carolina natives set up a hospital in Manchester, south of the James near Mayo Bridge.[24] During the coming years, citizens of North Carolina, Louisiana, and Texas would also establish hospital facilities in Richmond for their states' troops.[25] Although these state hospitals primarily served the wounded from the respective states, in the aftermath of battle the soldier's birthplace made no difference. When Mrs. Chesnut asked if there were Carolinians in one hospital, a matron expressed the prevailing spirit, "I never ask where the sick and wounded come from."[26]

Although the flood of wounded after great battles would always necessitate individual volunteer efforts in Richmond, the Confederate government operated the largest hospital facilities in the city. As the casualties poured in from Manassas, Confederate Surgeon General S. P. Moore dispatched many of them to Richmond's new Alms House. The municipal building became General Hospital Number One, and its former inmates were gainfully employed as a maintenance staff.[27] After a tour of the city's hospitals in mid-August, a *Whig* reporter pronounced the General Hospital best managed.[28] The surgeon general was a brusque man who offended fellow officers and private citizens with equal facility. However, one of his most critical subordinates conceded that "he was an able executive officer, and I believe an efficient and impartial one."[29] Impeded by shortages of drugs, trained personnel, and equipment,

[22] *Enquirer*, August 27, 1861.
[23] William A. Carrington to E. S. Gaillard, December 8, 1862, War Department Collection of Confederate Records, Letters sent file of the Medical Director at Richmond.
[24] Carrington to Gaillard, December 6, 1862, *ibid.*
[25] Robert W. Waitt, Jr., *Confederate Military Hospitals in Richmond*, pp. 8–10.
[26] Chesnut, *Diary from Dixie*, p. 26.
[27] City Council, Minutes, February 23, 1863.
[28] *Whig*, August 17, 1861; cf., Chesnut, *Diary from Dixie*, p. 116.
[29] John Herbert Claiborne, *Seventy-five Years in Old Virginia*, p. 200.

Moore's bureau would establish and operate twenty-eight general hospitals.[30]

Richmond's greatest medical asset was an entrepreneur, Dr. William Brown McCaw. In the fall of 1861, this thirty-eight–year–old Richmonder received authority from Surgeon General Moore to convert some recently constructed barracks on Chimborazo Hill into a military hospital. McCaw secured for his hospital the status of an independent army post, and, aided by the resultant freedom of action, he built the largest military hospital in the world.[31] Chimborazo Hospital treated 76,000 patients during the war and maintained a mortality rate of less than 10 per cent. The complex covered the slopes of Chimborazo Hill with 150 buildings accommodating 40 to 60 patients each, and 100 tents providing space for 8 to 10 convalescents each. McCaw supported his enterprise by commuting patients' rations into money. With the money drawn from the commissary department in lieu of food, McCaw not only supplied his charges with food, but also financed the remainder of his hospital's work. The commandant and his energetic staff baked up to ten thousand loaves of bread a day in Chimborazo's bakery, made soup in boilers from the Grant and Mayo tobacco factories, and stored as many as four hundred kegs of home-brewed beer in caves under the eastern end of the hill. Several hundred cows and goats belonging to the hospital grazed Tree Hill Farm loaned to the hospital by its patriotic owner. The hospital's canal boat, the *Chimborazo*, made regular trips to Lynchburg to secure provisions. Even in times of great scarcity, McCaw's operation was so successful that, in addition to its outstanding medical service, Chimborazo showed a profit. At the war's close, the Confederate treasury owed the hospital $300,000 in repayment of a loan.[32]

[30] Waitt, *Hospitals in Richmond*.

[31] Major Edgar Erskine Hume, "The Days Gone By: Chimborazo Hospital Confederate States Army—America's Largest Military Hospital," *The Military Surgeon: Journal of the Association of Military Surgeons of the United States* 75 (September, 1934): 161. Chimborazo was surpassed only during World War I in total number of patients treated.

[32] *Ibid.*, pp. 158–161; Chimborazo Hospital, Hospital Fund Statement, October 11, 1861–January 1, 1862, Claiborne Family Papers.

By September 17 the *Enquirer* reported fifteen hospitals in Richmond.[33] A report on hospitals presented to the Provisional Congress by William H. MacFarland stressed the need for more attention to cleanliness, but found conditions generally favorable. Because of the strain of converting housewives to nurses and of caring for hordes of wounded troops, however, some of Richmond's makeshift hospitals were not much improvement on battlefield aid stations. An *Enquirer* reporter noted that in one hospital a dead body had remained in the cellar for four days. And in other places amputated arms and legs lay rotting in back yards.[34] Perhaps the most indicative statement on the work being done in Richmond's hospitals during the latter half of 1861 came in response to the request of a doctor's wife for some new finery from the capital. Dr. Jacob Harrison brusquely wrote his wife, "I have not time to do any business at all."[35]

However much the large influx of wounded warriors after Manassas burdened Richmond's resources and energies, the sick and wounded were welcome guests in the city. The approximately one thousand Federal prisoners brought into Richmond following the battle were an entirely different matter. In August:

Mrs. [George Wythe] Randolph presided in all her beautiful majesty at an aid association. The ladies were old ones, and all wanted their own way. They were crossgrained and contradictory, and the blood would mount rebelliously in Mrs. Randolph's clear-cut cheek, but she held her own with dignity and grace. One of the causes of disturbance was that Mrs. Randolph proposed to divide everything sent in equally with the Yankee wounded and sick prisoners. Some were enthusiastic from a Christian point of view; some shouted in wrath at the bare idea of putting our noble soldiers on a par with Yankees, living, dying or dead. Shrill and long and loud it was.[36]

Richmond was immensely proud of her captured abolitionists. For a time curiosity-seekers gathered at the depot and lined the

[33] *Enquirer*, September 17, 1861.

[34] *Whig*, September 4, 1861; *Enquirer*, July 11, 1861.

[35] Dr. Jacob Prosser Harrison to Mrs. Harrison, October 19, 1861, Harrison Family Papers.

[36] Chesnut, *Diary from Dixie*, p. 115.

streets in front of improvised prisons to catch a glimpse of "Lincoln's hirelings." Among the Manassas prisoners was the Honorable Alfred Ely, congressman from New York, who had driven down to watch the engagement. The spectacle of a captured congressman became such an attraction that several fellow prisoners suggested Ely be caged and a fee charged for seeing him.[37] The city mocked its captives by reminding them that their "on to Richmond" desires had been fulfilled, but Richmonders seldom, if ever, jeered or reviled the Federals as they passed through the streets to prison.[38]

For all their pride in possessing prisoners, the Confederates at Richmond had little idea what to do with them. A Richmond minister remembered:

They had not been expected in such numbers, and due preparation had not been made for their reception. There was not a Confederate official in the land who had any experience in taking care of prisoners of war. They were therefore necessarily subjected to many inconveniences and privations, which a suddenly improvised commissariat and superintending staff could not at once remedy. They slept upon the floor on their blankets, if they had been thoughtful enough to bring any, and ate their rations from their fingers, or spread them out on boxes or barrel-heads.[39]

The Confederates confined the Manassas prisoners in converted warehouses or factories near the James River. The warehouse and ship chandlery belonging to the estate of Luther Libby became Libby Prison, best known among Richmond's prisons. As the numbers of prisoners increased, only the Union officers remained in buildings. A maze of tents on Belle Isle in the James River housed the enlisted men. During the three months following Manassas the Confederates brought 2,685 prisoners to Richmond.[40] Brigadier

[37] Alfred Ely, *Journal of Alfred Ely: A Prisoner of War in Richmond*, ed. Charles Lanman, p. 35.

[38] Captain Justus Scheibert, *Seven Months in the Rebel States during the North American War, 1863*, trans. Joseph C. Hayes, ed. William Stanley Hoole, p. 101.

[39] J. L. Burrows, "Recollections of Libby Prison," *Southern Historical Society Papers* 11 (February, March, 1883): 83–84.

[40] *Dispatch*, November 4, 1861.

General John H. Winder, commander of the Department of Henrico and commandant of the Richmond prisons, wisely envisioned Richmond as only a receiving station from which the government would dispatch the captives to locations farther from the war zone.[41] Although the authorities did send many prisoners south, Richmond retained from fourteen to eighteen hundred throughout the fall of 1861.[42] The presence of these unwelcome guests presented a constant threat to the city in the event of a wholesale jail delivery, and in addition the prisoners consumed a portion of Richmond's limited supplies of food and fuel. To the misfortune of both the city and the prisoners, the numbers of men crowded into warehouse prisons would increase, and the tent city on Belle Isle would grow.

The Federals' reactions to their makeshift quarters and improvised treatment varied. One of the best, and perhaps the most complimentary, descriptions of General Winder came from his prisoner Alfred Ely. Writing in his journal about the stern, sixty-five–year–old commandant with the striking and commanding appearance, Congressman Ely commented that ". . . has treated me with the utmost kindness and respect, and his demeanor and general courtesy of manner, when he visits the officers, indicate a strict disciplinarian, it is true; but a person at the same time of humane feelings, and not disposed to exercise his power beyond its proper limits."[43] Although one prisoner stated that only one of ten wounded prisoners survived brutal amputations in Richmond,[44] another wounded captive carved a magnificent pipe from mahogany and beef bones to present to his doctor.[45] The prisoners' food consisted

[41] *Enquirer*, November 19, 1861.

[42] *Dispatch*, November 4, 30, 1861.

[43] Ely, *Journal*, pp. 24, 96; cf., James A. Seddon to W. S. Winder, December 29, 1875, quoted in *Southern Historical Society Papers* 1 (March, 1876): 205–206: "His manner and mode of speech were perhaps naturally somewhat abrupt and sharp, and his military bearing may have added more of sternness and imperiousness; but these were mere superficial traits, perhaps, as I sometimes thought, assumed in a manner to disguise the real gentleness and kindness in his nature."

[44] William Howard Merrell, *Five Months in Rebeldom; or, Notes from the Diary of a Bull Run Prisoner, at Richmond*, p. 19.

[45] *Dispatch*, December 6, 1861.

primarily of bread, water, and beef; but in the early months captives were allowed to purchase coffee, tea, butter, and the like, at an average cost of $2.50 a week.[46] As a general rule, the guards enforced prison regulations sternly. They killed one prisoner for violating a rule against leaning from a window.[47] However, Confederate Lieutenant Todd, Mrs. Lincoln's half-brother, prohibited servants from purchasing items for the prisoners only after one prisoner became obstreperously drunk from his purchases.[48] Alfred Ely became president of the Richmond Prison Association, an inmate organization which met for speeches, toasts, and songs.[49] The association later helped to orient new prisoners and to supply them with the eating utensils and bedding of exchanged prisoners.[50] In the confusion of the first weeks of war, however, such luxuries were scarce. On August 17 a sentry brought Ely two blankets, and said that they were the gift of Jefferson Davis. Thus for the first time in four weeks the congressman slept "separate and apart" from his trousers.[51]

These first prisoners gave the Confederate government its opportunity to obtain from the United States recognition of its rights as a belligerent entity. In November the Rebels chose prisoner Michael Corcoran at random and threatened to execute him if authorities in Philadelphia carried out a death sentence passed on a Confederate naval officer for treason. Thirteen Libby inmates spent almost two months in a seventeen-by-eleven-foot cell as hostages for an equal number of Confederates held in New York as pirates.[52] In December the Richmond government exchanged

46 William C. Harris, *Prison-Life in the Tobacco Warehouse at Richmond by a Ball's Bluff Prisoner*, pp. 22–23.

47 William H. Jeffery, *Richmond Prisons, 1861–1862: Compiled from the Original Records Kept by the Confederate Government, Kept by Union Prisoners of War, Together with the Name, Rank, Company, Regiment and State of the Four Thousand Who Were Confined There*, pp. 21–22.

48 Ely, *Journal*, pp. 44–45.

49 *Ibid.*, p. 32.

50 Harris, *Prison-Life in the Tobacco Warehouse*, p. 24.

51 Ely, *Journal*, pp. 63–64.

52 Merrell, *Five Months in Rebeldom*, p. 58.

Congressman Ely for Charles James Faulkner, a Virginian taken prisoner when he returned from a United States mission to France.[53] These actions reinforced the belligerent rights of the Confederacy that Britain and France had recognized the previous spring. Under prevailing international law, their state of belligerency, a halfway status between rebeldom and nationhood, guaranteed equal rights to Southern ships and soldiers. Holding prisoners of war as hostages and bargaining exchanges of prominent civilians were crude methods, but during the opening months of war, such means seemed necessary to a people fighting to become a recognized nation.

Maimed Confederates and Yankee prisoners were vivid reminders of war's stern realities. Richmond adjusted to these less glorious features of war, but would never again view the conflict as the happy picnic it had been the previous spring. Even if the *Enquirer* suggested that mourners not wear black because of the added expense to the bereaved and its depressing effect on the rest of the city,[54] Richmonders were spared very little of war's expense or horror.

Almost every aspect of the city's life felt the war's impact. In the months following Manassas, Richmond was the most governed city in the land. The Confederate seat of government was also the capital of Virginia and the home of active local governing machinery. For a time during the fall of 1861, the Confederate Congress, the Virginia General Assembly, the Virginia Constitutional Convention,[55] and the Richmond City Council all met in Richmond. Astoundingly enough, relations among these bodies were generally amicable.

Richmond's council waited until mid-October to begin charging the Confederate government for gas to light their offices. Besides paying the President's expenses at the Spotswood Hotel and offer-

[53] Ely, *Journal*, pp. 261–263.
[54] *Enquirer*, July 26, 1861.
[55] This convention was the adjourned session of the Secession Convention. During the fall it drew up a state constitution conforming to the Confederate constitution, but otherwise not unlike Virginia's constitution of 1852.

ing to furnish him with a permanent residence,[56] the council loaned the Confederate treasury $50,000.[57] By early November, the city fathers had appropriated $10,000 for equipping Richmond volunteers, $5,000 for support of volunteers' families, and $15,000, of an estimated $100,000 eventually necessary, for erecting fortifications about the city.[58] Further manifestation of the council's contribution to the national war effort was its sale to the Confederate authority of horses originally purchased for local defense.[59] In nearly all of these actions the council had performed locally a function of the national government.

Relations between the city and state were also generally good during this period. Richmond's council had financed emergency wartime expenditures by issuing notes on the city's credit. When this issue was found to violate state law, the signers of the notes, David J. Saunders, council president, and Peachy Gratton, finance committee chairman, were threatened with prosecution.[60] Richmond's delegates in the General Assembly, however, were able to legalize the issuance of notes with less value than one dollar.[61] The crisis passed.

Compromise settled another minor crisis between state and city. In July the council had authorized and financed a battery of Home Artillery commanded by Colonel Thomas Ellis.[62] Three militia companies had organized and stood ready in case war came close to the city. Virginia's military authorities, however, seized the unit's guns for use in the field, and then proposed to muster the men into the regular army. Ellis's troops, who had enlisted for purely local action, felt the state's actions were a breach of faith, and only twenty-five appeared for the mustering-in ceremony.

[56] City Council, Minutes, October 14, 1861.
[57] Ibid., August 12, 1861.
[58] Ibid., November 4, 1861.
[59] Ibid., August 26, 1861.
[60] Ibid., November 4, 1861.
[61] Virginia General Assembly, Acts of the General Assembly of the State of Virginia, Passed in 1861–2, in the Eighty-sixth Year of the Commonwealth, chap. 67.
[62] City Council, Minutes, July 8, 1861.

After an exchange of published letters between Colonel Ellis and Governor Letcher, and after another mustering fiasco, Letcher disbanded the unit and thus removed the problem for the disputants.[63]

Friction among Richmonders and their governments was perhaps inevitable. If the city and state found ways to compromise differences over notes and home defense units, Confederate congressmen never stopped complaining of crowded conditions and high prices in Richmond's hotels and boardinghouses.[64] In September the Irish mechanics at the Tredegar Works struck for higher wages and threatened to go over to the Confederate armory if their demands went unheeded.[65] Such chronic problems as the scarcity of skilled mechanics would always threaten the unity of the war effort. However, considering the state rights political philosophy which underlay the Confederacy's origin, the accord among local, state, and national governments in Richmond was little short of amazing.[66]

Despite the abundance of lawmakers and governments in the city, Richmond suffered in these first months of the war from a decided lack of domestic tranquility. Along with the generals and great public men came the hangers-on and barroom generals. A Confederate officer in the city on business related: "It is quite amusing to stand about the Bar rooms of the Hotels and hear the plots and plans laid for Mr. Lincoln's Army by our Hotel politicians and there are a great number of them. . . . They talk as if the direction of the Army should be with them. Certainly if they act as they talk, some big guns will go off for they use such great swelling words about Beauregard, Davis and Johnston that one would think they were mere pigmies in the hands of these intel-

---

[63] *Whig*, August 31, November 1, 4, 7, 8, 9, 1861.
[64] See Bell I. Wiley, ed., *The Letters of Warren Akin, Confederate Congressman*, pp. 4–6, for a discussion of a Congressman's salary and expenses in the capital.
[65] Kathleen Bruce, *Virginia Iron Manufacture in the Slave Era*, p. 359.
[66] Other Confederate state governments and their officials were notoriously uncooperative, particularly Georgia's governor, Joseph Brown, and North Carolina's Zebulon Vance. This internal conflict, which allegedly doomed the Confederacy from its birth, is the theme of Frank L. Owsley's *State Rights in the Confederacy*.

lectual giants."[67] One wartime resident noted that "all the loose population along the railroad . . . seemed to have clung to and been rolled into Richmond with it."[68] Most of the excitement-seekers and placemongers were harmless enough, but with the merely curious came less worthy elements.

Stringent laws and constant raiding by the night watch never drove the gamblers from the capital. A police officer recalled "that the sporting fraternity had friends from the slums to the pulpit."[69] They usually occupied the upper floors of the stores on Main Street, and specialized in faro. The "Hells," as they were called, segregated their guests into two rooms according to wealth and social status. Prominent men and heavy gamblers refreshed themselves with elegant food and drink from the house buffet, and the humble players too ate and drank at house expense. "So in Richmond high and low gambled—some dashingly and brilliantly—a few sullenly and doggedly going in for gain. Few got badly hurt, getting more in the equivalent of wines, cigars, and jolly dinners than they gave."[70]

During the fall of 1861 the Richmond police made seven raids on gambling operations. One proprietor, John A. Worsham, attempted unsuccessfully to prosecute one of the ax-wielding officers for trespass. On December 27, as a climax to the fall raids, tables, cards, and other impounded gambling devices made a very large bonfire on Broad Street.[71] Tucker DeLeon recalled the "Hells" nostalgically: "They looked upon the hell as a club—and as such used it freely, spending what they had and whistling over their losses. When they had money to spare they played; when they had no money to spare—or otherwise—they smoked their cigars, drank their toddies and met their friends in chaff and gossip, with no idea that there was a moral or social wrong."[72] Regardless of their own

[67] Sam L. Clark, ed., "A Confederate Officer Visits Richmond," *Tennessee Historical Quarterly* 11 (March, 1952): 91.

[68] DeLeon, *Four Years in Rebel Capitals*, p. 86.

[69] *Richmond Police and Fire Department Directory*, p. 19.

[70] DeLeon, *Four Years in Rebel Capitals*, p. 239.

[71] *Whig*, November 11, 25, December 23, 28, 1861; City Council, Minutes, December 16, 1861.

[72] DeLeon, *Four Years in Rebel Capitals*, p. 239.

morality, the gambling houses did not always bring a wholesome element into Richmond's population. And activities were not always conducted genially. At eight o'clock on the morning of December 7, James McCullogh shot and killed Washington J. Wortham in a duel that grew out of slanders made on McCullogh's honesty. McCullogh, though wounded, left town two days later, and by December 11 the witnesses were so scattered that a coroner's inquest concluded that Wortham's death came "from a pistol fired by someone unknown to the jury."[73]

Unfortunately few of Richmond's lawbreakers adhered to the *code duello.* An indignant citizen remembered that "thieving, garroting, and murdering were the nightly employments of the villains who prowled around the city."[74] Richmond police made 214 arrests during July,[75] and later the numbers grew. Most of the offenses were petty, but vexing nevertheless. A man named Ramm went to jail as a nuisance and a pest because he declared himself in favor of Lincoln. Gentlemen declined to "give way" to ladies on the streets. White men promenaded with black women on Brooke Avenue. A hack driver charged nineteen dollars for carrying a wounded soldier six miles. Drunken soldiers and quarreling women crowded the mayor's courtroom daily.[76] The *Whig* diplomatically stated, "In the aggregate, no army in the world is composed of more quiet and orderly soldiers, but the exceptions are numerous enough to justify more rigid discipline at the camp."[77] On August 5 Mayor Mayo warned soldiers not to slash watermelons with their bowie knives or throw the melons into the air and catch them on their bayonets.[78] The third tier at the Richmond Theatre became a "refuge for rowdyism,"[79] and the *Whig* reported that "people huddled together at Metropolitan Hall in most indecent manner."[80]

[73] *Whig*, December 9, 11, 1861.
[74] Putnam, *Richmond during the War*, p. 76.
[75] *Dispatch*, July 31, 1861.
[76] *Whig*, August 2, 1861, October 18, 1861, November 8, 1861; *Dispatch*, August 29, 1861.
[77] *Dispatch*, August 29, 1861.
[78] *Ibid.*, August 6, 1861.
[79] *Dispatch*, September 14, 1861.
[80] *Whig*, December 11, 1861, February 10, 1862.

Not all the huddling was confined to public places. One historian of soldier life in the Confederacy has termed Richmond "the true mecca of prostitutes."[81] Their number had increased since the previous spring, and the "ladies of the town" had become so brazen that they threatened to take over the town.[82] "Ecclesiastes," a correspondent of the *Religious Herald* (Baptist), wrote: "Formerly harlots went afoot, and did not aspire to any location higher than Cary Street. But under the new arrangement, they ride in carriages (not hacks), and wear modest apparel, so that respectable people are continually found stamping their feet in vexation at being told by friends to be careful, or their politeness to *that* female may be misconstrued by the community."[83] Mayor Mayo, as commander of Richmond's police, despaired of closing down all the houses of ill fame and fell back to keeping prostitutes away from respectable places. When Mayo found "Cary Street Women" in theatre boxes and on Capitol Square "promenading up and down the shady walks jostling respectable ladies into the gutter," he issued from the bench of the Mayor's Court stern, if ineffectual, warnings.[84] Perhaps the ultimate defiance of order came when a madam opened for business across the street from the YMCA Soldier's Hospital. The madam's associates "advertised" from their windows and even enticed a few convalescent troopers from one bed to another.[85]

Vice produced the usual results in Richmond. Venereal diseases ran rampant, particularly among the city's soldier population.[86] The *Examiner* observed in December, 1862: "If the Mayor of Richmond lacks any incentive to stimulate . . . breaking up the resorts of ill-fame in the city, let him visit military hospitals, where sick and disabled soldiers are received for treatment, and look upon the human forms lying there, wrecked upon the treacherous shoals of

[81] Bell I. Wiley, *The Life of Johnny Reb: The Common Soldier of the Confederacy*, p. 53.

[82] George W. Bagby to *New Orleans Crescent*, November 16, 1861, Bagby Papers.

[83] *Religious Herald*, July 31, 1862.

[84] *Richmond Daily Examiner*, April 27, 1863; *Enquirer*, August 22, 1864.

[85] *Dispatch*, May 6, 1862.

[86] For partial statistics see Wiley, *Life of Johnny Reb*, pp. 55–56.

vice and passion which encounters the soldier at the corner of every street, lane, and alley of the city."[87]

During the fall of 1861, the "Shoals of Vice" first became visible to the majority of staid Richmonders. The *Examiner* called the city a "bloated metropolis of vice."[88] The *Dispatch* summed up the situation by beginning an article, "Our readers have by this time become prepared for hearing of almost any sort of diabolism," going on to report another bold robbery.[89] The lawlessness in the young capital shocked and horrified the hitherto quiet, provincial city.

The Richmond City Council helped combat the rising crime rate by raising the walls around the jail courtyard[90] and by increasing the day police force from eight to eleven officers. By Christmas of 1861, seventy-two night watchmen patroled the city.[91] In February Mayor Mayo reactivated the city's chain gang to ease the pressure on Richmond's bulging jail.[92] Justice in the Mayor's Court usually required the miscreant to post a surety to guarantee his future good behavior. Failure to meet the surety resulted in jail sentences or chain gang labor.

The President himself joined the municipal authorities' efforts to curb disorder in the capital. Small boys in Richmond since time immemorial had banded into neighborhood gangs called "cats" for fierce rock battles, and the coming of war incited their martial ardor all the more. One Sunday the "Hill cats" from Shockoe Hill engaged the "Butcher cats" from "Butcher-town," and Davis's young Negro serving boy returned home with a bloody scalp wound. The President then strode to the battleground and attempted mediation. After his address to the warring parties, one "Butcher cat" explained, "President, we like you, we didn't want to hurt any of your boys, but we ain't *never* goin' to be friends with them Hill cats." Davis was perhaps consoled in his failure as a

---

[87] *Examiner*, December 5, 1862.
[88] *Examiner*, January 25, 1862.
[89] *Dispatch*, September 16, 1861.
[90] City Council, Minutes, October 14, 1861.
[91] *Ibid.*, December 23, 1861.
[92] *Enquirer*, February 7, 1861.

juvenile diplomat by the fact that the mayor's fines and switchings also had little effect on the belligerent "cats."[93]

Undoubtedly the surgeon-in-charge of the third Georgia Hospital devised the most ingenious deterrent to lawbreaking in Richmond. Having no guard house, this resourceful officer locked offending patients and staff in the hospital *Dead House*. Thereafter, he told an inspecting officer, he "never heard anything more from them."[94]

The influx of wounded soldiers, prisoners, governments, and lawbreakers bewildered and often disturbed Richmonders. But the war's effect on the capital's economy distressed them even more. Business patterns became chaotic, as proprietors joined the army and as new merchants and alien customers filled the city. On the surface all seemed well. The French consul, Alfred Paul, reported that the Federal blockade had affected prices in a "crushing manner," but that all the people seemed to care about was arms for the troops.[95] Newcomer Tucker DeLeon recounted, "Every branch of industry seemed to receive fresh impetus; and houses that had for years plodded on in moldy obscurity shot . . . up to first class businesses."[96]

One interesting index gives some hint as to what was really happening in the city's market places. During 1860 Richmonders owned pleasure carriages and coaches at the rate of one for every 9.0 taxpaying males. In 1861 the ratio increased to one per 7.6 taxpayers. Although the population increased in the same period, the aggregate value of personal property rose only $200,000. The average citizen's wealth rose slightly, but a few Richmonders became affluent enough to purchase their own carriages.[97] Ap-

---

[93] Varina Howell Davis, *Memoir*, II, 198–199; *Whig*, September 10, 18, 1861; John S. Wise, *The End of an Era*, pp. 58–59.

[94] William A. Carrington to E. S. Gaillard, December 6, 1862, War Department Collection of Confederate Records, Letters sent file of the Medical Director.

[95] Remark cited in Gordon Wright, "Economic Conditions in the Confederacy as Seen by the French Consuls," *Journal of Southern History* 7 (May, 1941): 198.

[96] DeLeon, *Four Years in Rebel Capitals*, p. 147.

[97] City of Richmond, Personal Property Tax Books. In 1860 Richmond's white males numbered 4,102. They owned 455 carriages and personal property worth $4,065,365. In 1861 4,245 taxpayers owned 560 carriages and property worth $4,272,874.

parently, economic adjustment to war proved difficult for many, but profitable for a few.

A January, 1862, report of the Richmond City Council Finance Committee defined the dominant commercial trends during the first year of the war. The first portion of the report dealt with Davis, Dupree and Company's petition requesting a refund of their license tax, because they had dissolved their auction business. In this case, however, the committee found that Davis, Dupree and Company had merely ceased to attract customers. "If this should be considered sufficient reason for remitting a tax, the council may expect to be flooded with petitions for the remission of taxes; as it has, unhappily, been the case during the past year that many persons in the city have found their business unprofitable and have stopped it; and to remit the taxes in all such cases will materially and injuriously affect the finances of the city."[98] The second half of the committee's report recommended extending the time allowed for new businessmen to apply for licenses. The extension would accommodate the large numbers of new enterprises.[99] Richmond experienced intense business activity in 1861, yet war brought a great turnover in her commercial economy, and many of the city's business houses passed into new hands or out of the picture.

Naturally the most dramatic changes in Richmond's commercial economy came in response to the demands of war. As the capital's population swelled, the numbers of hotels, boardinghouses, restaurants, bars, and bawdy houses expanded. The blockade and the severance of normal economic relations with the Union severely altered the prewar patterns of trade.[100] Those businessmen enterprising enough, or shrewd enough, to find new sources of supply survived the transition. Sometimes this meant running in goods from the North past the two contending armies. Sometimes it meant running in shipments from Europe past the Federal navy.[101]

[98] City Council, Minutes, January 13, 1861.
[99] Ibid.
[100] For example, the Dispatch reported (December 11, 1861) that in 1861, 68 fewer vessels visited the Richmond docks than in 1860, and that canal tolls were down 46½%.
[101] J. B. Jones (Rebel War Clerk's Diary, p. 92) noted, "It is sickening to be-

Sometimes Richmond's commercial community could find new domestic sources to supply the city's needs for consumer goods and creature comforts. Those businesses which did not, or could not, meet the demands of change failed. And as the war progressed, the challenges of consumer commerce multiplied.

However much the civilians clamored for shelter, clothing, and food, Richmond's army remained her largest consumer. War industries profoundly affected her economy throughout the war period. The Confederacy manufactured everything from cannon to currency in the city. With the Tredegar Works in the lead, Richmond's iron industry converted to war production. Machinery from the old Federal arsenal at Harpers Ferry found a new home in the state armory at the foot of Seventh Street and began turning out a thousand muskets per month.[102] Richmond's flour mills and bakeries flourished with the aid of government contracts. The Confederate government opened an ordnance laboratory on Brown's Island and employed numerous seamstresses at the quartermaster clothing department. These and other ventures made use of existing facilities in the city and added still more. However in industry, as in commerce, wartime wrought other changes. Richmond's iron makers and flour millers prospered; her tobacconists floundered. Many tobacco factories and warehouses became hospitals and prisons.[103] Nor was the situation entirely owing to the demands of an open market, since the government determined which industries were "necessary" and favored them with contracts, transportation priorities on the railroads, and, later, draft exemptions for key personnel.[104] More than this, the government bureaus and private enterprises often worked out exchange of various commodities. For

---

hold the corruption of the commercial men, which so much wounds our afflicted country." They "breathe fire" at Yankees and then import merchandise from the North to sell at a "fabulous profit." See also Ludwell H. Johnson, "Commerce between Northwestern Ports and the Confederacy, 1861–1865," *Journal of American History* 54 (June, 1967): 30–42.

[102] *Enquirer*, October 11, 1861.

[103] J. Malcolm Bridges, "Industry and Trade," in *Richmond, Approaches to Its History by Various Hands*, p. 74.

[104] Charles W. Ramsdell, "Control of Manufacturing by the Confederate Government," *Mississippi Valley Historical Review* 8 (December, 1921): 231–249.

example, in September, 1864, Haxall and Crenshaw, flour millers, swapped corn for wheat seed with a representative of the commissariat.[105] This arrangement benefited both parties, and demonstrated the advantage of doing business in Richmond in a vital commodity.

Very few average citizens recognized these shifting economic currents. They did notice the scarcity of life's necessities and the rapid rise in their cost. Refugees from occupied areas of Virginia swelled an already expanded population. One of the displaced recorded in her diary: "Spent this day in walking from one boardinghouse to another, and have returned fatigued and hopeless. I do not believe there is a vacant spot in the city. A friend, who considers herself *nicely* fixed, is in an uncarpeted room, and so poorly furnished, that, besides her trunk, she has only her wash-stand drawer in which to deposit her goods and chattels; and yet she amuses herself at it, and seems never to regret her handsomely furnished chamber in Alexandria."[106] Next day the woman found a place, but the rent she had to pay was only three dollars less than her husband's salary.

Government jobs and expanded industry yielded greater employment opportunities for the poor, but the inflated Confederate currency often reduced people living on fixed salaries to dire circumstances. During the four months between September, 1861, and January, 1862, all grades of flour advanced at least $1.00 per barrel. Butter rose from 26 to 40 cents a pound. The Union blockade doubled the cost of coffee in the same period,[107] and Richmonders were already using compounds of sorghum seed, corn, sweet potatoes, chestnuts, and chicory as substitutes.[108] Common whiskey advanced from 65 cents to $1.50 per gallon, and the local Sons of Temperance became more successful in recruiting new members.[109] The blockade, lack of sufficient transportation facilities, wartime

[105] D. W. Haxall to Captain P. A. Wellford, September 8, 1864, Haxall and Crenshaw Papers.
[106] Judith W. McGuire, *Diary of a Southern Refugee during the War*, p. 88.
[107] *Dispatch*, September 14, 1861, January 4, 1862.
[108] Putnam, *Richmond during the War*, pp. 78–79.
[109] *Dispatch*, January 14, 1862.

disruption of farming, and the presence of an ever-consuming army were the basic causes of these high prices. Distraught Richmonders, however, blamed speculators and extortioners. Certainly this class existed, but, relative to food prices, they were more symptom than cause of the city's economic ills.

While the majority of Richmond citizens stoically accepted war's privations, others seemed actually to enjoy themselves amid the suffering. For a time amusements and social gatherings were shunned by all and sewing and knitting for the soldiers came first. Mrs. Chesnut recorded, "I do not know when I have seen a woman without knitting in her hand."[110] But then, to the delight of Tucker DeLeon, "human nature and inclination still held their own; and there were many defections from the ranks of the elect, to those of more practical—and probably equally well intentioned—pleasure seekers."[111] Many social activities, such as sewing circles, combined self-sacrifice with enjoyment. After attending benefit concerts the audience often had the "jolliest little suppers" until the "wee small hours."[112] Mrs. Chesnut recorded in her diary a trip to Pizzini's, "that very best of Italian confectioners," followed by a visit to Miss Sally Tomkins' Hospital to distribute delicacies to the wounded soldiers.[113]

The coming of fall intensified social activity in Richmond. The theater reopened; minstrels appeared in Metropolitan Hall; a benefit lecture series began; the Fairfield Race Course held a three-day meet.[114] Among the socially prominent were native-born Richmonders and government officials. The Mallorys, MacFarlands, Randolphs, Chesnuts, and Clays were some of the most active members of society. Mrs. Clement Clay, wife of an Alabama senator, smiled when recalling her maid's insistence on packing ball gowns *in case* they might be needed.[115]

---

110 Chesnut, *Diary from Dixie*, p. 121.
111 DeLeon, *Four Years in Rebel Capitals*, p. 148.
112 *Ibid.*, p. 149.
113 Chesnut, *Diary from Dixie*, p. 119.
114 *Dispatch*, October 25, 26, November 2, 1861; *Whig*, September 21, 1861, January 23, 30, February 6, 1862.
115 Mrs. Clement C. Clay, *A Belle of the Fifties: Memoirs of Mrs. Clay, of*

The President was so wearied by his duties that Mrs. Davis remembered, "We ceased to entertain except at formal receptions or informal dinners and breakfasts given to as many as Mr. Davis's health permitted us to invite. In the evening he was too exhausted to receive informal visitors."[116] Hetty, Jennie, and Connie Cary were Richmond's brightest belles of the Season, and soon admirers termed the cousins "Cary's Invincibles."[117] The *Whig* reported Christmas Day in the city:

The sidewalks were thronged all day by the crowds whom the sunshine and pursuit of pleasure attracted to the streets. The boys "kept Christmas" by firing crackers and torpedoes, the supply of which seemed as interminable as on any preceding Christmas. . . . Indoors, the day was spent in receiving calls and dispensing hospitality. Egg nog and other creature comforts were provided in many households, for the entertainment of visitors, and the grand feature of the day—a sumptuous dinner—was enjoyed by thousands at the numerous family reunions which take place every Christmas.[118]

Robert E. Lee exemplified the median in Richmond's attitude toward pleasure-seeking and creature comforts. Lee never allowed himself frivolity and to one who did he looked "so cold, quiet, and grand."[119] But even in the grim winter days of 1864 the general encouraged dances in the city, that his officers might find release and relaxation.

Alabama, Covering Social and Political Life in Washington and the South, 1853–66, ed. Ada Sterling, p. 169.

[116] Varina Howell Davis, *Memoir*, II, 161.

[117] Constance Cary Harrison, *Recollections Grave and Gay*, p. 67.

[118] *Whig*, December 27, 1861.

[119] Chesnut, *Diary from Dixie*, p. 95.

The Yankees Are Coming

URING THE FIRST MONTHS of 1862 as the nation began to tot-
ter, Richmonders' anxieties shifted from fretting about the
price of food and the propriety of attending the theater. Death and
defeat gave the city something more substantial about which to
worry. On January 18 John Tyler died in his room at the Ballard
House.[1] Richmond had recently chosen the ex-President of the
United States to represent her in the Confederate Congress, and his
death dissolved a link with the past.

In February, Forts Henry and Donelson fell and opened the Tennessee River to Federal gunboats, and the road to Nashville to
Union armies. Also in February, Roanoke Island in North Carolina fell to the Yankees. Henry A. Wise had commanded a numerically inferior force on the island (the *Enquirer* gave the numbers
as 450 against 5,000).[2] Wise's son, O. Jennings Wise, who had been
editor of the *Enquirer*, died in the futile defense. Richmonders

[1] *Richmond Daily Dispatch*, January 20, 1862.
[2] *Daily Richmond Enquirer*, February 25, 1862.

filled St. James Church for the funeral and many more watched the somber procession to Hollywood Cemetery.[3] A minister's wife noticed that the chaplain wore his uniform and wrote in her diary, "It was strange to see the bright military buttons gleam beneath the canonicals. Every thing is strange now!"[4]

Feeling sure that the disasters were not the soldiers' fault, the capital began to wonder about her leaders. High-placed carping and quarrels there had been. During the few months of the Confederacy's existence, rifts had been spawned between the "starving" army and Commissary General Northrop,[5] between General Joseph Johnston and President Davis, Mrs. Johnston and Mrs. Davis,[6] Senator Wigfall and President Davis,[7] Attorney General Judah Benjamin and General Beauregard,[8] General John Winder and Benjamin,[9] and between a host of other officials. As early as August, Mrs. Chesnut noted that her friend Mrs. Davis "is utterly upset. She is beginning to hear the carping and fault-finding to which the President is subjected."[10]

George William Bagby, editor of the *Southern Literary Messenger*, scribbled his thoughts on a blank page in the rear of his journal: "We have reached a very dark hour in the history of this struggle. I do not say the cause will fail, but the chances are all against us. . . . Cold, haughty, peevish, narrow-minded, pig-headed, *malignant*, he [President Davis] is the cause. . . . While he lives, there is no hope for us. God alone can save us. Will He?"[11] During the February adversities Richmond's press divided sharply on the merits of Davis's administration. The *Whig* screamed for an investigation of the Roanoke Island debacle.[12] On February 19 the

[3] Sallie Brock Putnam, *Richmond during the War: Four Years of Personal Observation*, p. 98; W. Ashbury Christian, *Richmond, Her Past and Present*, p. 238.
[4] Judith W. McGuire, *Diary of a Southern Refugee during the War*, p. 93.
[5] Mary Boykin Chesnut, *A Diary from Dixie*, ed. Ben Ames Williams, p. 99.
[6] *Ibid.*, p. 106.
[7] *Ibid.*, p. 109.
[8] J. B. Jones, *A Rebel War Clerk's Diary at the Confederate States Capital*, ed. Howard Swiggett, I, 89–90.
[9] *Ibid.*, p. 99.
[10] Chesnut, *Diary from Dixie*, p. 108.
[11] George W. Bagby, Diary, 1860–62, George William Bagby Papers.
[12] *Richmond Daily Whig*, February 15, 1862.

Examiner thundered: "The game we are in is no child's play. We must fight our best; we must persist in the struggle to the last, or consent to a fate too miserable to contemplate. We must go to work with greater earnestness than we have yet shown. We must discard luxury and ease. We must put down incompetence; cease to put our trust in pigmies, and listen no longer to pedants."[13] The *Enquirer* and the *Dispatch* rallied behind Davis. The *Dispatch* termed the President the "impersonation of the principles and spirit of the free and valiant people over whom he has been called to preside."[14] The *Enquirer* struck to the heart of the matter: "The press has its duty. The people have theirs. That duty consists not in cynical fault-finding, in illiberal suspicions, in useless criminations—but in encouraging a union of hands in maintaining the independence of our beloved country!"[15]

On February 22, the anniversary of George Washington's birth, Jefferson Davis took his oath as permanent President of the Confederate States, while rain soaked the onlookers in Capitol Square. Davis's inaugural address was heartening. After some remarks about Yankee tyranny, the President faced the issues confronting his own government. Frankly, honestly, he admitted that there had been mistakes. He resolved to correct them and earnestly sought the assistance of his countrymen.

The umbrellas and carriage roofs hid temporarily the reactions of Richmond's citizens. Since the wild joy of Manassas, Richmonders had experienced confusion and frustration. They had asked why the victory at Manassas had not been pressed. They had agonized over the wounded men in their homes and had "adopted" patients in the hospitals. Drunken soldiers, gamblers, and thieves had disturbed their peace. Richmonders had sacrificed to support the Cause and to feed their families, and in time they had begun to wonder if others were doing the same. They believed in the gallantry of the Southern soldier, and they could not comprehend

[13] *Richmond Daily Examiner*, February 19, 1862, quoted in Frederick S. Daniel, ed., *The Richmond Examiner during the War; or, the Writings of John M. Daniel with a Memoir of His Life*, pp. 39–41.

[14] *Dispatch*, February 22, 1862.

[15] *Enquirer*, March 7, 1862.

military disaster. They were still bewildered by new people, new expedients, and new pressures. But in the midst of their anxiety was the knowledge that Richmond had faced the war's challenges and endured its discomforts. On this rainy inaugural day, the President said that this was the country's "darkest hour," but then he invoked the blessing of God and of his countrymen upon his government that the Cause might prevail. And Richmond answered with soggy, determined, cheer after cheer.

Rain continued to fall in Richmond until far into the night.[16] Inauguration ceremonies ended in the early afternoon; and as soon as the President had finished his address, the members of Congress trooped back into the Capitol wondering if they would ever again be warm and dry. The Senate quickly adjourned. In the House, Tennessee Congressman Henry S. Foote seized the floor and began calling for a committee to investigate the Secretary of War's preparations for the nation's defense. More important considerations prevailed, however, as the representatives responded gratefully to Virginia Congressman William Smith's motion to adjourn in order to remedy the sodden state of feet and clothing.[17] That night the President and Mrs. Davis held a Washington-style levee in the executive mansion. Jefferson Davis, though haggard and worn, acted well the part of a gracious host. His wife charmed the guests and lent a personal air to the large gathering. The foul weather outside did not dampen the visitors' spirits, and those in attendance pronounced the permanent government a social success.[18]

Outside the brightly lit executive mansion, the capital's war went on. Back in January, Abraham Lincoln had issued the President's General War Order No. 1 directing that Federal armies would commence a general forward movement on February 22. Although

---

[16] Good accounts of the inauguration ceremonies are in "Proceedings of the Confederate Congress," *Southern Historical Society Papers* 44 (June, 1923): 38–41; *Dispatch*, February 24, 1862; Jones, *Rebel War Clerk's Diary*, I, 111; Kate Mason Rowland, Papers.
[17] "Proceedings of Congress," *Southern Historical Society Papers* 44 (June, 1923): 40–41.
[18] Jones, *Rebel War Clerk's Diary*, I, 111; McGuire, *Diary of a Southern Refugee*, p. 96.

the commander of the Army of the Potomac, George B. McClellan, had put off his execution of the grand advance, he had faced General Johnston's army at Manassas with a force three times as large.[19] Labeling a government permanent would not reverse the military disasters of the winter, and spring would surely bring McClellan's assault on Richmond.

By Monday, February 24, two days after the inauguration, the capital had resumed in earnest the task of conducting a war. On the morning of the twenty-fourth, the *Examiner* concluded its enthusiastic editorial coverage of the inauguration with an attack on Judah Benjamin, now Secretary of War, and Secretary of the Navy Stephen Mallory. "It is the fervent hope of every rational man and distinguished patriot," the *Examiner* stated, "that he [Davis] will with all speed create a cabinet of the ablest, best informed, most experienced, and especially of the most active and energetic men."[20]

Later in the day, the House of Representatives paid some attention to Henry Foote's fulminations against the administration's conduct of the war. The House adopted Richmond Representative James Lyons's resolution requesting the President to furnish it information on the state of the James River defenses.[21]

When the city council met at four o'clock in the afternoon, Thomas H. Wynne presented a caustic preamble to a series of resolutions creating a Committee of Safety of the City of Richmond.

Whereas it is evident that neither the state nor the Confederate authorities are, either of them, doing, or likely to do, any thing for the Cities of Richmond and Petersburg, and it is palpable that they are, for want of protection, in imminent danger of an attack, against which we are at present incapable of making any resistance, it behooves the corporate authorities and people of these two cities to adopt some meas-

19 James G. Randall and David Donald, *Civil War and Reconstruction*, p. 210.
20 *Examiner*, February 24, 1862, quoted in Daniel, *Examiner during the War*, pp. 41–43.
21 "Proceedings of Congress," Southern Historical Society Papers 44 (June, 1923): 46.

ures by which prompt and efficient action will secure at least a delay from, if we cannot effectually prevent, the capture of our city.[22]

The council adopted the resolutions and appropriated fifty thousand dollars for the city's land and river defense.[23] Two days later the *Examiner* echoed the prevailing mood: "The Government must do all these things by military order, and without consulting anybody. The President is looked to for the call to arms, to order the mounting of batteries, the blockading of channels and the enforcement of the necessary though disagreeable laws. To the dogs with Constitutional questions and moderation! What we want is an effectual resistance."[24] Almost overnight Richmonders had forgotten their concern for maintaining their city's provincial integrity through unsettled times. Apprehension over distant military reverses had yielded to fear for Richmond's physical safety. Let the soldiers come and governments multiply. The Yankees were coming in earnest.

On March 1 President Davis proclaimed martial law in Richmond.[25] The Confederate Congress had granted Davis authority to suspend the privilege of habeas corpus on February 27.[26] General John G. Winder, commanding the Department of Henrico, assumed responsibility for administering military rule in the city and within a ten-mile radius.[27] Winder appointed Colonel John G. Porter to be provost marshal for Richmond and divided the city into two administrative districts. Porter's assistant provost marshals, A. C. Godwin and J. C. Maynard, commanded the eastern and western districts respectively.[28] Winder's first general order

[22] Richmond City Council, Minutes, February 24, 1862.

[23] *Ibid.*

[24] *Examiner*, February 26, 1862, quoted in Daniel, *Examiner during the War*, p. 43.

[25] James D. Richardson, ed., *A Compilation of the Messages and Papers of the Confederacy including the Diplomatic Correspondence, 1861–1865*, I, 220.

[26] James M. Matthews, ed., *Statutes at Large of the Confederate States of America, Commencing with the First Session of the First Congress*, 1862, chap. 1.

[27] Richardson, *Messages and Papers*, I, 220.

[28] Department of Henrico, General Order No. 5, printed in *Whig*, March 7, 1862.

forbade liquor sales in the city and required all citizens to surrender their private firearms to the Confederate Ordnance Department.[29]

During the first half of March the general tightened his control on the capital. By March 15 the military had placed twenty-eight men and two women in Castle Godwin for suspected disloyalty to the Cause.[30] Most conspicuous among the inmates of the improvised political prison was John Minor Botts. After nearly two months' confinement, the old Whig nationalist secured his release only on the condition that he would reside far from the capital and say nothing against the Confederacy or its government.[31]

Hotels were required to deliver a list of new arrivals to the Provost Marshal's Office each morning. Soldiers allowed no one to enter or leave the city without a military pass.[32] Railroads were not permitted to transport liquor into the city, and the names of all passengers carried into Richmond by the railroads had to be reported. Winder prohibited apothecaries from buying liquor without an order from his headquarters and required a doctor's prescription for each druggist's sale of spirits.[33] The general even tried to enforce the city's Hack Ordinance governing the rates charged for hired carriages[34]—a feat which for some years had frustrated city police.

However ambitious Winder's actions might have been, Confederate martial law involved a unique blend of civil and military sovereignty. From the first the Mayor's Court remained open.[35] On March 8 the President reopened Hustings Court, and in response to a question from Davis, Attorney General T. H. Watts instructed

[29] Richardson, *Messages and Papers*, I, 221.

[30] *Dispatch*, April 3, 1862.

[31] Adjutant and Inspector General's Office, General Order No. 28, April 25, 1862, in U.S., Congress, House, *War of the Rebellion: A Compilation of the Official Records of the Union and Confederate Armies*, ser. II, vol. 2, p. 1547.

[32] Department of Henrico, General Order No. 4, printed in *Whig*, March 14, 1862.

[33] Department of Henrico, Special Order No. 43, printed in *Whig*, March 14, 1862.

[34] Department of Henrico, Special Order No. 48, printed in *Whig*, March 14, 1862.

[35] Richardson, *Messages and Papers*, I, 220.

the President, "Let the *general* rule be that the civil jurisdiction of the courts shall be exercised as usual; and the exception prevail only when a necessity for the departure is manifest."[36] Richmond police still functioned, and Winder primarily employed troops in enforcing his own orders. The military authorities tried violators of the general's orders by courts-martial, but a month's hard labor was the maximum penalty allowed.[37] And in April, Congress restricted military arrests of civilians to those committing crimes against the government.[38] However, some features of martial law, such as the passport system, lingered in Richmond throughout the war.

General Winder's reign in the capital was not without excesses. In exhaustive search for contraband liquor, his troops even seized Elijah Baker's patent medicine "Baker's Bitters."[39] The general recruited many of his civilian detectives from his fellow-refugee Marylanders. Critics resented the manners and questioned the integrity of these "aliens," who often earned the sobriquet, "Plug Uglies."[40] The detectives' zeal reached alarming proportions when they themselves forged prescriptions for brandy and arrested four Richmond druggists for filling them.[41] One citizen complained of Winder's force: "The Baltimore detectives are the lords of the ascendant. They crook a finger, and the best carriages in the street pause, turn around, and are subject to their will. They loll and roll in glory. And they ride on horseback, too—government horses, or horses 'pressed' [impressed] from gentlemen's stables. One word of remonstrance, and the poor victim is sent to Castle Godwin."[42] However, few Richmonders would have agreed with war clerk

[36] T. H. Watts to Jefferson Davis, April 25, 1862, quoted in Rembert W. Patrick, ed., *The Opinions of the Confederate Attorneys General, 1861–1865*, pp. 73–75.
[37] Richardson, *Messages and Papers*, I, 220.
[38] Matthews, *Statutes at Large*, 1st cong., 2d sess., chap. 40.
[39] *Whig*, March 17, 1862.
[40] Jones, *Rebel War Clerk's Diary*, I, 91, 141, 309.
[41] *Whig*, March 25, 27, 1862. To Winder's alleged dismay a court martial found the four druggists innocent of a crime (Jones, *Rebel War Clerk's Diary*, I, 116).
[42] Jones, *Rebel War Clerk's Diary*, I, 123.

diarist J. B. Jones that martial law "is, indeed, a reign of terror!"[43]
In April the *Dispatch* reported happily:

Men, women, and children now sleep the sleep of security; their
dreams are not disturbed by visions of Yankee cannons; by the paddle
of Yankee gunboats, or worse, by the vile rows of drunken soldiery.
Our streets are quiet. Brawls are rare. Pistol-shots do not disturb the
unstrung nerves of delicate or antique dames. . . . The streets are
morning, noon, and night being patrolled by guards, who arrest all
loiterers, vagabonds, and suspicious-looking characters. . . . And the
consequences are peace, serenity, security, respect for life and property,
and a thorough revival of patriotism and enthusiasm.[44]

Despite her enforced domestic tranquility, the Confederate capital remained in imminent danger from McClellan's hosts. On
February 27 General Winder received a discouraging report on the
field fortifications surrounding the city. These works encircled the
capital at roughly a twelve-mile radius. The eighteen batteries and
seven outworks already covered likely approaches to the city, but
some of the batteries contained three feet of water and very few
had guns.[45] Colonel Charles Dimmock, chief of ordnance for the
state of Virginia, was even less sanguine in his report to the Virginia House of Delegates on February 28. The whole system
seemed to Dimmock to be too close to the city. If a large enemy
force should invest the works, the city would be in a dismal state
of siege. Breastworks between the batteries would be necessary to
defend against assaults of infantry. Dense forests impeded the
gunners' field of fire, and only 25 of the 218 guns necessary to arm
the works were in place. "Richmond, as far as any reliance is to
be placed upon these batteries," Dimmock wrote, "is in no state of
defense against an enemy likely to approach."[46]

[43] *Ibid.*, I, 120.
[44] *Dispatch*, April 4, 1862.
[45] Colonel R. Tansill to John H. Winder, February 27, 1862, *War of the Rebellion: Compilation of Official Records*, ser. I, vol. 9, pp. 45–46.
[46] Report of Charles Dimmock, Colonel, Virginia Ordnance, to Virginia House
of Delegates, February 23, 1862, *War of the Rebellion: Compilation of Official
Records*, ser. I, vol. 9, pp. 47–48.

In March, Jefferson Davis answered the inquiry from the House of Representatives concerning the defense of the James River. Besides informing the congressmen about Richmond's defense systems, Davis revealed in his message some of the basic concepts of his military thinking. The President based his information on a report from Alfred L. Rives, acting chief of engineer bureau.[47] Listing five points of strength along the river, he pronounced Drewry's Bluff to be the key work in the defense system. This high promontory overlooking a narrow place in the river's channel lay seven miles below the city. Batteries of guns and river obstructions made the Drewry's Bluff position quite formidable against wooden ships. If the enemy came in ironclad ships, no one could predict the outcome. Significantly the President concluded by pointing out that defenses, no matter how impregnable, served only to gain time. He did not anticipate shutting his armies within a besieged city and watching them starve. Richmond must not become beleaguered. Johnston's army must strike McClellan and defeat or destroy him.[48]

Constructive action in Richmond's defense came from all levels and branches of government. The city council released the city engineer from all other duties, so that he might concentrate on the circle of fortifications.[49] Governor Letcher began enrolling as Second Class Militia all white males of ages sixteen to eighteen and forty-five to fifty-five.[50] By March 3 General Winder could report to the governor that two regiments for the capital's local defense were nearly complete.[51]

In the face of growing military crisis Richmond watched a significant cabinet shuffle take place. Since Secretary of State R. M. T.

---

[47] William Cabel Rives to Judah Benjamin, March 12, 1862, *War of the Rebellion: Compilation of Official Records,* ser. I, vol. 9, pp. 61–62.

[48] Richardson, *Messages and Papers,* I, 201–203.

[49] City Council, Minutes, March 5, 1862.

[50] "By the Governor of Virginia, A Proclamation," March 13, 1862, printed in *Dispatch,* March 14, 1862.

[51] John H. Winder to John Letcher, March 3, 1862, H. W. Flournoy, ed., *Calendar of Virginia State Papers and Other Manuscripts from January 1, 1836, to April 15, 1869, Preserved in the Capital at Richmond,* pp. 202–203.

Hunter's resignation on February 18, Jefferson Davis had pondered a replacement. Judah Benjamin, the Secretary of War, was perhaps the most capable man in the cabinet, but he was not popular. The affable Jew was a favorite of Richmond's hostesses who delighted in his ability to converse in French or English, but, charming though he was, Benjamin was a very direct soul. His facile mind had an affinity for cutting through red tape to get a job done and this tendency did little to aid in his understanding of the official language of military reports and orders. The generals resented this ignorance, and the public blamed him as Secretary of War for the Roanoke Island disaster.[52] Nevertheless, Davis, desperately seeking unity, now made Benjamin Secretary of State, and brought General George Wythe Randolph from the field to be Secretary of War.[53] Many of Benjamin's enemies were scathing in their anger. The *Examiner* commented: "Mr. Davis has sacrificed to popular clamor without yielding to public opinion. . . . The representation of the Synagogue [Benjamin] is not diminished; it remains full. The administration has now an opportunity of making some reputation; for, nothing being expected of it, of course every success will be clear gain."[54]

Generally, though, Richmonders could not help but be pleased. Randolph was a native, and he had proved himself as capable as he was charming. Since the Secretary of War had advanced to the ascendant position in the cabinet, Virginians were flattered to see the war portfolio go to one of their own. Indeed the Confederacy seemed obsessed with the old Commonwealth: Hunter was President pro tem of the Senate; Virginian Thomas S. Bocock was Speaker of the House; Lee was close to the President; and Johnston commanded in the field. The old Union had had its Virginia Dynasty, and now, with so many of their fellows in high places,

---

[52] See Jones, *Rebel War Clerk's Diary*, I, 118; Putnam, *Richmond during the War*, p. 99. Mrs. Putnam commented, "Although no complaints of want of efficiency as Secretary of State were made against Mr. Benjamin, he was ever afterwards unpopular in the Confederacy and particularly in Virginia."

[53] See Douglas S. Freeman, *Lee's Lieutenants: A Study in Command*, I, 116–117, 144–145; and Frank E. Vandiver, *Mighty Stonewall*, pp. 191–195.

[54] *Examiner*, March 20, 1862.

Virginians might hope for the Dynasty's reincarnation in the young Confederacy.[55]

Richmond had little time for pride; McClellan threatened from without. And within the city food prices soared ever higher. Finally, under the authority of martial law, General Winder sought to restore sanity to Richmond's market places. On March 31 he issued a general order which established maximum prices on fish, butter, eggs, and potatoes.[56] To enforce the schedule, military authorities confiscated produce offered at the higher rates and distributed it among the city's hospitals.[57] Unfortunately, the general's price-fixing resulted in disaster. After the schedule went into effect on April 7, the low prices and the unsettled state of the surrounding countryside greatly reduced the quantity of food brought into the city. In late April, under pressure of dwindling supplies and a citizens' committee, Winder lifted his price schedule.[58] Farmers resumed their trips to the markets, but the cost of food soared. In one month, eggs rose 400 per cent in price from Winder's schedule, to $1.00 per dozen.[59] In two days the price of butter climbed from a prescribed 50 cents per pound to $1.40.[60] No one starved, but Richmond's outlandish prices prompted French Consul Paul to write his superior, "The city has become a hell for all those who are forced to live here."[61]

Early in March McClellan's vast army had begun to move. Instead of assaulting Johnston's front, however, the Federals made preparations for an amphibious invasion of eastern Virginia. Mc-

---

[55] On the same subject Wade Hampton complained, "Of all the cavalry generals, one *Maj. Genl. and five Brigadiers are from Va.* So that if any other officers are to be appointed, I think some of the other states should be represented" (Wade Hampton to Louis T. Wigfall, May 17, 1863, Louis T. Wigfall Papers).

[56] Department of Henrico, General Order No. 12, printed in *Whig*, April 2, 1862.

[57] *Dispatch*, April 17, 23, 1862.

[58] Putnam, *Richmond during the War*, pp. 113–114; *Whig*, April 30, 1862.

[59] *Dispatch*, May 24, 1862.

[60] *Ibid.*, May 1, 1862.

[61] Cited in Gordon Wright, "Economic Conditions in the Confederacy as Seen by the French Consuls," *Journal of Southern History* 7 (May, 1941): 211 n.

Clellan sought to land his hundred thousand troops on the peninsula between the York and James rivers and move on Richmond from the east. The plan was sound, if a bit complicated. Union gunboats could cover the advance and perhaps shell the Confederate Capital while land forces conducted the probable siege. By March 24 advance columns of the ponderous Federal army were concentrating at Fortress Monroe.

In mid-April, while the Army of the Potomac massed men and materials on the new front, General Johnston evacuated his position on the Rapidan River and marched the bulk of his force through Richmond onto the peninsula. Lee, the President's chief military aide, as well as Johnston and Davis, agreed that Johnston's army should defend Richmond resolutely. The question was where to meet McClellan's impending advance. Johnston wanted to make a determined stand in front of the capital, but Lee supported President Davis's desire to meet the Federals farther down the peninsula. After a fourteen-hour meeting on April 14, Johnston yielded. He agreed to face McClellan at Yorktown. The strong-willed Virginian made no promises, however, and he clearly did not relish the prospect of fighting McClellan and his gunboats on the peninsula while General McDowell, who had commanded the Federals at Manassas, still had an army in northern Virginia.[62] Feeling that under the circumstances he could do little more than slow McClellan down, Johnston later wrote, "The belief that events on the Peninsula would soon compel the Confederate government to adopt my method of opposing the Federal army, reconciled me somewhat to the necessity of obeying the President's order."[63]

Fortunately, most Richmonders were unaware of division among their chiefs. The capital saw an army coming to its rescue and took heart. Troops and wagons poured through the city for several days during mid-March. One Sunday a trooper interrupted church services in the city and asked the ladies to prepare food for the men in transit. That afternoon women and girls lined the streets and

[62] See Freeman, *Lee's Lieutenants*, I, 145–151.
[63] Joseph E. Johnston, *Narrative of Military Operations Directed during the Late War between the States*, p. 119.

divided their Sunday dinners among the passing companies. However hungry and dirty the men were, to the nervous city the army seemed invincible.[64] And the weary troops responded to Richmond's generosity with cheers which occasionally swelled into the high-pitched rebel yell. The men chided any healthy-looking civilians they saw and invited them to come along. One youth waving a handkerchief from his window seemed an especially likely comrade.

"Come right along sonny! . . . Here's a little muskit fur ye!"

"All right, boys!" cheerily responded the youth, rising from his seat —"Have you got a leg for me too?" And Colonel F. stuck the shortest of stumps on the window sill.

With one impulse the battalion halted; faced the window, and spontaneously came to "present!" as the ringing rebel yell rattled the windows of the block.[65]

When the last gun carriage had rattled down the Williamsburg Road toward Yorktown, the city went to work renewing her efforts to support her defenders. Ladies filled a request for thirty thousand sandbags in thirty hours.[66] On March 24 Richmond women had formed the National Defense Association, and now they continued soliciting contributions to build an ironclad gunboat.[67] Work on the city's field fortifications went on. City council appropriated fifty thousand dollars for obstructing the river channel and an equal amount to equip Richmond volunteers in the Confederate service.[68] A citizens' meeting on April 18 adopted Virginia Attorney General

[64] Clara Minor Lynn, "A Scene in Richmond in 1862," Clara Minor Lynn Papers; T. C. DeLeon, *Four Years in Rebel Capitals: An Inside View of the Southern Confederacy from Birth to Death*, pp. 190–191; Mrs. Fannie A. Beers, *Memories: A Record of Personal Experience and Adventure during Four Years of War*, pp. 47–49.
[65] DeLeon, *Four Years in Rebel Capitals*, p. 192.
[66] *Ibid.*
[67] *Dispatch*, March 26, 1862.
[68] City Council, Minutes, April 30, 1862. Among the obstructions placed in the river were torpedoes [mines] manufactured by Matthew Fontaine Maury (Col. Richard L. Maury, "The First Marine Torpedoes Were Made in Richmond, Va., and Used in James River," *Southern Historical Society Papers* 31 [1903]: 326–333).

John Randolph Tucker's resolution to secure quarters for the wounded. A committee of twelve men received pledges from householders and reported them to the surgeon general.[69] Beyond these actions, Richmond prayed for deliverance and hoped.

In the midst of the crisis, on April 16, the Confederate Congress authorized national conscription of men between eighteen and thirty-five for three years' service.[70] This legislative expedient represented the first nationwide draft in American history and a momentous departure from the government's state rightist origins.

Despite the vigorous preparations in the campaign for Richmond's life, the prospects appeared dim. The impending Federal advance even kindled nascent Unionist sentiments among a few Richmonders. "Union Men to the Rescue!" "God Bless the Stars and Stripes!" Residents of the capital awoke on several mornings to find such slogans chalked on walls and fences about the city.[71] Elizabeth Van Lew, the doughty Unionist spinster who had spent much of the previous fall aiding Yankee prisoners, now boasted in her journal that she had a room prepared for General McClellan in her mansion on Grace Street.[72] General Winder's passport office was crowded with people seeking to flee the threatened city. In the midst of growing apprehension, on April 22, Congress voted itself a raise in pay and adjourned. Making one of its few understatements of the war period, the *Examiner* commented: "To leave Richmond at the very moment of hazard is not the way to encourage the army or help a cause in peril."[73] Congressman Dupré of Louisiana expressed the spirit of some when he said, "People looked somewhere else than to this Congress for aid."[74] If Dupré referred to the army, Joseph Johnston was doing little to inspire the capital with confidence.

[69] *Whig*, April 19, 1862.

[70] Matthews, *Statutes at Large*, 1st cong., 1st sess., chap. 31.

[71] *Whig*, April 21, 1862; Putnam, *Richmond during the War*, p. 101.

[72] Miss Elizabeth Van Lew, Journal, quoted in Katherine M. Jones, *Ladies of Richmond, Confederate Capital*, p. 119.

[73] *Examiner*, April 21, 1862, quoted in Daniel, *Examiner during the War*, pp. 50–51.

[74] See "Proceedings of Congress," 44 (June, 1923): 178–83, for debate over the hasty adjournment.

Throughout most of April, McClellan had assembled his host on the peninsula and conducted siege operations against Yorktown. General John B. Magruder faced the cautious McClellan there with a small force and Quaker guns (black logs mounted to look like cannon). Magruder bluffed as long as he could. On May 3, shortly before the Federals were to open a massive artillery bombardment, Johnston began moving his entire Confederate army back up the peninsula toward Richmond. They paused only briefly to delay McClellan at Williamsburg, and by the second week in May Richmond's defenders were camped in front of the city.[75] Tucker DeLeon described their return: "They straggled into Richmond muddy—dispirited—exhausted; and, throwing themselves on cellar doors and sidewalks, slept heavily, regardless of curious starers that collected around every group. Never had a Southern army appeared half so demoralized; half so unfit to cope with the triumphant and well-appointed brigades pressing close upon it."[76] These were the same men who had seemed invincible only a few weeks before. Surely, somehow they would hold the capital. Yet New Orleans had probably felt the same desperate hope, and New Orleans had fallen a few weeks earlier.

[75] See Freeman, *Lee's Lieutenants*, I, 148–55.
[76] DeLeon, *Four Years in Rebel Capitals*, p. 194.

The Yankees Are Here

MORE AND MORE PEOPLE felt the urgent call to visit a sick aunt in the country or attend to some business affairs farther south. On the night of May 9 Varina Davis was entertaining a small company in the executive mansion when a messenger interrupted the party. He spoke briefly with the President. Davis took his wife aside and told her that a flotilla of Union gunboats had started up the James toward Richmond. When Mrs. Davis rejoined her guests, the evening went on as before, but the next day the President's family left for Raleigh, North Carolina.[1] A Richmond lady wrote in her diary, "It is said the President does not fear; he will send his family away, because he thinks it better for men, on whom the country's weal is so dependent, to be free from private anxiety."[2] However valid the President's reasoning, his wife's departure was hardly calculated to inspire confidence among Richmonders.

[1] Varina Howell Davis, *Jefferson Davis, Ex-President of the Confederate States of America: A Memoir by His Wife*, II, 268.
[2] Judith W. McGuire, *Diary of a Southern Refugee during the War*, p. 110.

The same day that Varina Davis left for Raleigh, Secretary of War Randolph sent a memorandum to his chiefs of bureau:

> Have such of your records and papers as ought to be preserved, and are not required for constant reference, packed in boxes, for removal and marked, so as to designate the bureau to which they belong. Books and papers necessary for constant reference may be kept in the presses, but boxes must be prepared for them. This is only intended as a prudent step, and is not caused by any bad news from the army. There is no need, therefore, for any panic in the city, and it should be prevented by the assurance that we have every reason to think that the city can be successfully defended.[3]

Randolph may have stretched a point when he said that the decision to pack the department archives did not result from "bad news from the army." Richmond's greatest threat seemed now to come from the Federal navy. As the Union ships steamed up the James, the Confederates reluctantly blew up the ironclad *Virginia* on May 11. The *Virginia* was actually the rechristened *Merrimac*. The Confederate navy had raised her from the bottom of Norfolk harbor and shielded her with iron plates from the Tredegar Works. For weeks she had held the Federal navy at bay, but because of her heavy draught, the presence of the Union ironclad *Monitor* compelled her abandonment.[4] When Richmond heard of the *Virginia's* fate on May 12, "it was a dreadful shock to the community."[5]

The first stirrings of organized resolution in the face of the crisis appeared in the distraught city on May 14. The Virginia General Assembly declared: "The General Assembly hereby expresses its desire that the capital of the state be defended to the last extremity, if such defense is in accordance with the views of the President of the Confederate States; and that the President be assured that whatever destruction and loss of property of the state or individuals

---

[3] Secretary of War to Adjutant and Inspector General, May 10, 1862, U.S., Congress, House, *War of the Rebellion: A Compilation of the Official Records of the Union and Confederate Armies*, ser. I, vol. 11.3, p. 504.

[4] For a full account of the *Virginia's* brief career see Harrison A. Trexler, *The Confederate Ironclad "Virginia" ("Merrimac")*; and *Richmond Daily Dispatch*, March 10, 11, 1862.

[5] McGuire, *Diary of a Southern Refugee*, p. 112.

shall thereby result, will be cheerfully submitted to."[6] Next day, May 15, Governor Letcher underscored the legislature's determination by calling Richmonders to meet at City Hall to organize companies of citizens for the city's defense. Guns were booming on the river when the mass meeting convened at five o'clock in the afternoon.[7] While Colonel Ellis was enrolling the volunteers, Mayor Mayo appeared. The *Whig* reported Mayo's reaction to the crisis: "Before God and Heaven he would say to one and all, that if they wanted the Mayor to surrender the city, they must get some other Mayor. 'So help me God, I'll never do it.' "[8] Three cheers rang out. Letcher's response, as described in the *Whig*, was similar. "He didn't know who is to surrender it [Richmond], but if the call was made upon him to surrender the city, or have it shelled, he should be tempted to reply, 'Shell and be d——d.' "[9] Uproarious applause signaled the people's determination to fight the Yankees amid the rubble of their homes.

Later that night the joyous news came. The batteries at Drewry's Bluff had repulsed the Federals' advance.[10] For the moment, at least, the capital was safe.

Jefferson Davis was not impressed. Next day, the sixteenth, he wrote his wife in Raleigh: "The panic here has subsided and with increasing confidence there has arisen a desire to see the city destroyed rather than surrendered. 'They lightly talk of scars who never felt a wound,' and these talkers have little idea of what scenes would follow the battering of rows of brick houses. I have told them that the enemy might be beaten before Richmond or on either flank, and we would try to do it, but that I could not allow the Army to be penned up in a city."[11] After contemplating the

[6] Virginia General Assembly, *Acts of the General Assembly of the State of Virginia, Passed at Extra Session, 1862, in the Eighty-sixth Year of the Commonwealth*, Resolution no. 16.

[7] Sallie Brock Putnam, *Richmond during the War: Four Years of Personal Observation*, p. 130.

[8] *Richmond Daily Whig*, May 16, 1862.

[9] *Ibid.*

[10] Douglas S. Freeman, *Lee's Lieutenants: A Study in Command*, I, 210–211.

[11] Dunbar Rowland, ed., *Jefferson Davis, Constitutionalist: His Letters, Papers, and Speeches*, V, 245–246.

situation, unbiased men would have agreed with Davis's military strategy. No political objective was worth sacrificing an entire army. But Richmond had neither the time nor the inclination for objective contemplation. The city was home and capital. She must not fall. The *Examiner* answered the President's letter on the same day he wrote it, almost as if an editor had looked over his shoulder. Concluding an editorial entitled "Virginia Is Not Dead Yet!" the paper stated: "When we speak of the people of Richmond, however, we do not include the Rats. We do not include the contemptible sneaks who care more about their own rickety carcasses, than for the independence, the destiny, the existence of the Confederacy. . . . If the authorities have not the energy, decision, firmness and resources to keep their grip on Richmond, then may God help the South!"[12]

During the last half of May the capital grimly made ready for the worst. Ladies gathered at St. Paul's Church to prepare bedding for the hospitals.[13] The General Assembly appropriated $200,000 for more river obstructions.[14] And then the solons voted another $200,000 for removing Richmond women, children, and the infirm in case of a general bombardment.[15] The legislature also voted to permit a temporary change in the seat of government "in a certain contingency,"[16] and authorized the Mayor's Court to convene outside the city limits.[17] Richmond's city council met almost daily. In the event of Richmond's capture the military authorities had ordered all tobacco and cotton to be burned, and the council feared that a warehouse fire in the heart of the city could spread and destroy the city. However, after much correspondence with the War Department, destruction by burning seemed the only meth-

---

[12] *Richmond Daily Examiner*, May 16, 1862, quoted in Frederick S. Daniel, *The Richmond Examiner during the War; or, the Writings of John M. Daniel with a Memoir of His Life*, p. 53.
[13] *Whig*, May 29, 1862; *Dispatch*, May 31, 1862.
[14] Virginia General Assembly, *Acts of General Assembly . . . Extra Session, 1862*, chap. 8.
[15] *Ibid.*, chap. 14.
[16] *Ibid.*, chap. 21.
[17] *Ibid.*, chap. 24.

od.[18] On May 28, Secretary Randolph had the boxes of War Department records moved to the railroad depot. He told his chiefs of bureau that "wagons will be ready tonight at 9 o'clock to commence the removal, which should be conducted quietly and from the rear of the building to avoid panic or excitement in the city."[19] Regardless of Randolph's precautions Richmonders saw the archives in transit. One citizen remembered, "It was evident to a casual observer that a removal of the government was contemplated."[20]

The ultimate defiance occurred on the night of May 29. Proprietors of the capital's gambling houses met and determined that the "Hells" were luring too many officers from their posts. Not only did they agree to close their establishments until the crisis passed, but the proprietors also pledged $20,000 to purchase items for the wounded![21]

A few weeks earlier the capital had faced the struggle with confusion and alarm. But the mettle displayed on the evening of May 15 had been genuine. Now there was no panic. In contrast to the mass exodus during the first half of May, people were coming into the city. Virginia's Episcopalians held their annual convention in Richmond during the third week in May as scheduled. The General Baptist Association met during the final week of the month. Government offices remained open, and citizens quietly went about their business. The *Whig* commented, "Upon the whole, the charge of apathy might be brought against Richmond with more apparent justice than that of panic."[22]

While Richmond's attention centered on the James River and Yankee gunboats, McClellan inched his way up the peninsula with

---

[18] Richmond City Council, Minutes, May 27, 28, 1862.
[19] Secretary of War to Chiefs of Bureau, May 28, 1862, *War of the Rebellion: Compilation of Official Records*, ser. I, vol. 11.3, p. 557.
[20] Putnam, *Richmond during the War*, p. 130.
[21] *Whig*, June 2, 1862.
[22] *Whig*, May 31, 1862. Also J. B. Jones (*A Rebel War Clerk's Diary at the Confederate States Capital*, ed. Howard Swiggett, I, 127) noted on May 19, 1862: "There is a sullen, but generally a calm expression of inflexible determination on the countenances of the people, men, women, and children. But there is no consternation; we have learned to contemplate death with composure."

his grand army. Poor roads and incessant rain combined with the general's caution to slow the advance. Johnston waited. Then McClellan made a mistake. The Federal commander threw two corps south of the Chickahominy River, and held the rest of his army on the north bank. The Yankee host straddled the sluggish stream. Johnston struck. On May 31 he advanced at Seven Pines and assaulted Little Mac's isolated corps.[23]

Thousands in Richmond lined the city's eastern hills to follow the progress of the battle by translating the sounds of the firing. They waited nervously through the morning and into the afternoon, "like an audience at a theater when some accident or disarrangement behind the scenes prevents the curtain from rising."[24] Toward the late afternoon cannon began firing in earnest. When the listeners heard in sequence the cannons, then muskets, and then silence, they knew that the attacking Confederates had carried a position with bayonets and "cheered accordingly."[25] Near sundown the firing told of a general Southern advance. McClellan's amoebic mass had yielded. Johnston's army had attacked and won. "The city had 'no language but a cry!' "[26]

Then for three days the ambulances came. Five thousand wounded men filled the city's sixteen army hospitals. They filled six private hosiptals and thirteen emergency hospitals and then overflowed into private homes.[27] Surgeon General Moore's facilities had increased, but the Confederates still needed the aid of Richmond ladies to care for the men. Servants darted through the streets with trays of food for the stricken. One woman remembered Seven Pines as the time when "our summer's work had begun."[28] Soldiers complained about the red tape and inconveniences of the government's hospitals,[29] but the individual heroism of Richmond's ladies moved

[23] Freeman, *Lee's Lieutenants*, I, 201–24.
[24] Jones, *Rebel War Clerk's Diary*, I, 130.
[25] *Ibid.*
[26] Mrs. Roger A. Pryor, *Reminiscences of Peace and War*, p. 171.
[27] McGuire, *Diary of a Southern Refugee*, p. 119; *Dispatch*, June 4, 1862.
[28] Putnam, *Richmond during the War*, pp. 134–136.
[29] Rev. Nicholas A. Davis, *The Campaign from Texas to Maryland, with the Battle of Fredericksburg*, p. 69.

one Georgian to state, "I can say this for the *good women* of Virginia: There are *no better women* on this globe."[30]

Among the casualties at Seven Pines was the Confederate commander, Joe Johnston. On the night following his victory the general lay seriously wounded on Richmond's Church Hill. The confusion which followed his fall on the field at Seven Pines had allowed the Federals an orderly withdrawal and the near rout of McClellan's left flank had degenerated into a mere repulse. With Johnston wounded, the President placed Robert E. Lee in command. The Virginian went to work at once forging an army and planning strategy. During the next three years, Lee's army, like its commander, would achieve greatness. Its mission now and to the end of its life was the defense of Richmond. They called the force the Army of Northern Virginia, but in truth it was Richmond's army.

While Lee looked for an opportunity to fight McClellan, the Union commander called for reinforcements from Washington. His spies had told him fabulous tales of Southern strength, and the cautious McClellan believed them. Lincoln, however, refused to send more troops to the peninsula. The prime reason for Lincoln's reluctance to dispatch more men from Washington was the recent activity of Thomas J. Jackson. With eighteen thousand men Jackson had outmarched and outfought sixty thousand Federals in the Shenandoah Valley. The stern Presbyterian had outlived the nickname "Tom Fool," acquired during his days as a professor at Virginia Military Institute. Now he was "Stonewall" to the public and "Old Blue Light" to his hard-hitting, "new model" Army of the Valley.

Richmonders followed Jackson's campaign in the valley with delight. When J. E. B. Stuart's cavalry rivaled Jackson's fame by riding completely around McClellan's army, the capital was able to laugh at the baffled invaders.[31] Secretary Randolph brought the

---

[30] G. W. Nichols, *A Soldier's Story of His Regiment (61st Ga.) and Incidentally of the Lawton-Gordon-Evans Brigade, Army Northern Virginia*, p. 65.

[31] See Freeman, *Lee's Lieutenants*, I, pp. 225–469; Frank E. Vandiver, *Mighty Stonewall*, pp. 197–244.

War Department's archives from the railroad depot back to the offices.[32] By June 15 the war clerk, J. B. Jones, could record in his diary, "What a change! No one now dreams of the loss of the capital."[33] Seven Pines had been the city's baptism by fire. Now Richmond, determined and confident, waited for the next round.

On an intensely hot June 26, General Roger A. Pryor lay in Richmond recovering from an attack of malaria. While his wife fanned him, a knock came at the door. When the general read the message handed him, he called for his boots. General Longstreet had written, "In thirty-six hours it will all be over."[34] Lee was attacking.

Richmond's streets were deserted. Everyone, it seemed, had gone out to the surrounding hills to hear the cannon and watch the "aurora of death" on the horizon.[35] Amid the sounds of firing from the east came more noise from the northeast. Rumor swept through the throng. "Jackson is here!" "Stonewall is behind them." On the night of the twenty-sixth the hilltops remained crowded and from every tall building in the city people watched the flashes of the guns.[36] Next day the diminished sound of the guns told the story. Jackson had joined Lee, and the Federals were withdrawing before the Southern assaults. Lee struck McClellan at Mechanicsville, at Cold Harbor, at Savage Station, at Glendale, and in White Oak Swamp. On the seventh day of fighting, the Yankees beat off a furious Southern charge at Malvern Hill and retired to the James River. On June 26, McClellan had camped four miles from Richmond. After July 1 he lay inert beneath the cover of his gunboats at Harrison's Landing, over twenty-five miles away. The capital was safe.[37]

July, 1862, was an awesome month in Richmond. She saw the dead swell and burst their coffins before the overburdened grave-

[32] Jones, *Rebel War Clerk's Diary*, I, 136.
[33] *Ibid.*, I, 134.
[34] Pryor, *Reminiscences*, p. 174.
[35] *Ibid.*, p. 178.
[36] Jones, *Rebel War Clerk's Diary*, I, 136–138.
[37] See Freeman, *Lee's Lieutenants*, I, 489–604.

diggers could bury them.[38] In the hospitals, women looked on while
dying men were taken to the dead house to make room for more
wounded.[39] The city watched piles of amputated limbs grow in the
rear of the hospitals.[40] One matron remembered, "We lived in one
immense hospital, and breathed the vapors of the charnel house."[41]

George B. McClellan and his grand army left the Virginia Peninsula in mid-August, 1862. The departure opened a period of un-
paralleled success for Southern arms in the eastern part of the
Confederacy. Federal armies would not seriously threaten Richmond's security for many months, and for a time the Army of
Northern Virginia carried the fight to the Yankees. On August 9
Stonewall Jackson routed a Union force at Cedar Mountain. Later
in August, Generals Lee and Jackson struck and overwhelmed
John Pope's bluecoats at Manassas. By using Jackson's corps for
independent operations, Lee was breaking a cardinal principle of
war and dividing a numerically inferior force in the face of the
enemy. But he was winning battles. On September 5 the Confederates crossed the Potomac and carried the offensive into the
enemy's country. The Federals halted the advance near Sharps-
burg (Antietam Creek). After a bloody, drawn battle, Lee abandoned the field and recrossed the Potomac into Virginia. On December 13, 1862, the Army of Northern Virginia closed the year's
active campaigning on the slopes of Marye's Heights near Fredericksburg. General Ambrose E. Burnside's Army of the Potomac
charged the entrenched Confederates all day. Lee's position proved
impregnable, and the slaughter was terrible.[42]

Hearing news of Lee's victory at Fredericksburg, Joe Johnston
commented, "What luck some people have. Nobody will ever come
to attack me in such a place."[43] Whether by luck or genius, Lee,

---

[38] *Whig*, June 24, 1862.
[39] Jennie D. Harrold, "Reminiscences of Richmond from 1861–1865," quoted
in Katherine M. Jones, *Ladies of Richmond, Confederate Capital*, p. 134.
[40] *Daily Richmond Enquirer*, July 11, 1864.
[41] Putnam, *Richmond during the War*, p. 154.
[42] For accounts of the eastern campaigns in the late summer and fall, 1862,
see Freeman, *Lee's Lieutenants*, II; Vandiver, *Mighty Stonewall*, pp. 323–432.
[43] Joseph E. Johnston to Louis T. Wigfall, December 15, 1862, Louis T. Wig-

Jackson, and the Army of Northern Virginia had saved the capital and won great victories. Some time between the Seven Days in June, and Fredericksburg in December, Richmonders had adopted Lee's army as their own. The city lionized Jackson and Lee and began to think Lee's army invincible. The *Dispatch* summarized Richmond's admiration for Lee: "As modest and unpretending as the Yankee Generals are boastful and false, he quietly permits results to speak for him, and those results prove him one of the greatest military leaders of modern times. We congratulate the country that it has at the head of its armies this calm, self-poised, consummate soldier—one who both as General and gentleman is a worthy representative of the glorious South."[44] Lee led only one of the Confederacy's armies, but that army was defending the capital and winning the battles. Richmond did not ignore other armies and the situation in the western Confederacy, but Vicksburg and Corinth seemed far away, and the campaigns nearer the rival capitals appeared infinitely more important.

From McClellan's departure in August through the end of 1862 the Army of Northern Virginia's major battlefields had been at least fifty miles from Richmond. Relative quiet had settled on the city during these months. Activity in the capital became prosaic in contrast to the alarms of the previous spring when the fighting had been close at hand. Since the militia no longer had need of daily drilling, the War Office rescinded the order compelling the city's businesses to close at two o'clock in the afternoon.[45] City banks, which had been closed during McClellan's advance, reopened.[46] Although government hospitals remained well populated, the great demand for emergency service and volunteer workers was sharply relieved.[47] Fewer prisoners were housed in Libby, the only large

---

fall Papers. Reproduced by permission of The Huntington Library, San Marino, California.

[44] *Dispatch*, September 3, 1862.

[45] *Whig*, July 17, 1862.

[46] As a result the city chamberlain no longer kept the municipal treasury in his office, and Governor Letcher removed the state's funds from the old iron safe in the treasury building (City Council, Minutes, August 11, 1862); F. N. Boney, *John Letcher of Virginia: The Story of Virginia's Civil War Governor*, p. 162.

[47] Since the beginning of the war Richmond had received 99,508 hospital pa-

numbers being prisoners waiting to be exchanged. Now at times Richmond found her warehouse-prison almost empty.[48] This quiet was deceptive, however, for although the cannon were no longer heard, the war presented new challenges almost daily.

Richmond though was coming of age. She had stood firm against the enemy in a dark hour and survived her ordeal-by-combat. When the danger passed, Richmonders emerged a special breed; proud and confident, they accepted their success quite casually. "No powder was wasted in salutes over the victory, no bonfires blazed, no windows were illuminated, and the general appearance of Richmond was in all respects unchanged from what it had been a month before."[49] A few months before, the capital had been an adolescent. She had been unsure of her strength and had gravitated between poles of bravado and despair. Now the crisis was past; Richmond had prevailed. Joy and confidence coalesced quietly in a mood that smacked of maturity.

---

tients (figure quoted from Congressional report in *Whig*, September 23, 1862). See War Department Collection of Confederate Records, Hospital reports of the Medical Director at Richmond, vol. 151, chap. 6, for a month by month survey of Richmond's hospital patients. During the fall of 1862 the number treated at Chimborazo never fell below 4,300 for any month. At General Hospital No. 1 the number treated ranged from 376 to 600. However, Mrs. McGuire reported Richmond's emergency facilities "comparatively empty" in November (*Diary of a Southern Refugee*, p. 169), and Dr. Holloway wrote his wife on August 16, "I have very little to do, in the way of practice now—my hospital is almost clear of patients" (Holloway Papers).

[48] For details and subsequent history of the cartel of exchange see the statement of Robert Ould, Confederate Commissioner of Exchange, in "The Treatment of Prisoners During the War Between the States," *Southern Historical Society Papers* 1 (March, 1876): 125–131. The *Dispatch* reported 511 Federals in Libby on November 5, and 1,350 there on December 22, giving some idea of the fluctuation.

[49] Heros von Borcke, *Memoirs of the Confederate War for Independence*, I, 75.

PART III   REVOLUTIONIZED CITY

Challenge and Response

ICHMOND'S NEW-FOUND WARTIME MATURITY did not go un-
tested. From mid-summer 1862 through the following spring
the Confederate capital constantly fought the quiet battles of home-
front war.

General Winder spent an active year in command of the Department of Henrico. According to the *Whig*, "At times, he apparently
carries on conversation with two or three persons simultaneously,
whilst examining or signing papers, yet there is no confusion, and
so far as we have seen, no exhibition of ill-temper or official self-
importance."[1] In mid-July Winder again attacked the rising prices
in Richmond's markets. On July 12 he fixed a maximum price for
corn, and on the twenty-sixth he issued a schedule of maximum
prices for all types of livestock fodder and bedding.[2] However, the
general's second experiment in managing Richmond's commercial
economy was no more successful than the first. Farmers withheld

[1] *Richmond Daily Whig*, July 16, 1862.
[2] Department of Henrico, Special Order 110, July 12, 1862, printed in the
Whig, July 17, 1862; and General Order 45, July 26, 1862, printed in the *Whig*,
July 30, 1862.

shipments of the enumerated items, after which Winder was rebuked by the War Department which declared that martial law did not include price fixing.[3] By August 14 the general held 250 deserters, political prisoners, and disorderly soldiers in Castle Godwin.[4] Later in the month Winder transferred his motley guests to William Greaner's tobacco factory on Cary Street and it became known as Castle Thunder.[5] This institution and its commandant, Captain Alexander, soon achieved wide reputation among soldiers and would-be deserters. An army ballad proclaimed:

> I'd ruther be on the Grandfather Mountain
> A-taking the snow and rain
> Than to be in Castle Thunder
> A-wearin' the ball and chain.[6]

Stories of prisoners hung up by their thumbs and forced to wear "barrel shirts" may have served as deterrents to insubordination in the army, but they also caused a congressional investigation in the spring of 1863.

During the fall and winter General Winder made further attempts to establish more order in his command. In October he dismissed all but one of his "Plug Ugly" detectives for "malfeasance, corruption, bribery, and incompetence."[7] War clerk J. B. Jones was still not satisfied. "These are the branches," he wrote, "the roots should be plucked up, and General Winder and his Provost Marshall [sic] ought to resign."[8] To replace the civilian detectives, Winder had an armed soldier accompany each of the city's forty night watchmen.[9] By November 10 the *Whig* noted significant increase in law and order.[10] Later in the fall, Winder issued a general order forbidding the importation of more than 150 barrels

[3] Adjutant and Inspector General's Office, General Order 56, August 6, 1862, printed in the *Whig*, August 6, 1862.
[4] *Richmond Daily Dispatch*, August 14, 1862.
[5] *Daily Richmond Enquirer*, August 12, 1862; *Dispatch*, August 19, 1862.
[6] Cited in Arthur Palmer Hudson, *Folklore Keeps the Past Alive*, p. 27.
[7] J. B. Jones, *A Rebel War Clerk's Diary at the Confederate States Capital*, ed. Howard Swiggett, I, 178; *Enquirer*, October 31, 1862.
[8] Jones, *Rebel War Clerk's Diary*, I, 178.
[9] *Dispatch*, October 31, 1862.
[10] *Whig*, November 10, 1862.

(6,000 gallons) of liquor into the city. None of this was to be sold to soldiers.[11] As a result of the general's order and an act of the state legislature banning the manufacture of alcohol except for medicinal purposes,[12] whiskey commanded $22.50 to $23.00 per gallon by the beginning of 1863.[13] John Winder had a thankless task, and even his best-intentioned actions met with disapproval from most Richmonders.

The Virginia General Assembly and the Richmond City Council more than matched Winder's energy and resourcefulness in meeting Richmond's wartime needs. The council raised the salaries of city employees an average of $200 per year to meet the rapid inflation of the national currency. Attempting to slow the issue from Secretary of the Treasury Memminger's printing press, the council loaned the Confederate States $300,000 to bolster the treasury.[14] In September the council made a contract with Stuart, Buchanan and Co. of Saltville, Virginia, by which the company agreed to furnish the city one thousand bushels of salt every month. The council then sold the salt for five cents a pound, when the necessary item brought seventy to ninety cents in Richmond's markets.[15] To meet the probable scarcity of fuel during the coming winter, the city fathers authorized the gas works to sell coke to residents of the capital.[16] Virginia's legislature permitted the State Board of Public Works to require railroads to transport wood into Richmond, and Richmond's council appropriated $5,000 for the cost of cutting and hauling the needed fuel.[17] The legislature also authorized Governor Letcher to impress slaves for further work on Richmond's for-

---

[11] Department of Henrico, General Order 41, December 9, 1862, printed in the *Dispatch*, December 13, 1862.

[12] Virginia General Assembly, *Acts of the General Assembly of the State of Virginia, Passed at the Called Session, 1862 in the Eighty-seventh Year of the Commonwealth*, chaps. 11, 12.

[13] *Dispatch*, January 3, 1863.

[14] Richmond City Council, Minutes, July 11, August 11, 1862.

[15] *Ibid.*, September 8, 1862; *Dispatch*, December 10, 1862.

[16] City Council, Minutes, October 13, 1862.

[17] Virginia General Assembly, *Acts of the General Assembly of the State of Virginia . . . Called Session, 1862 . . .* , Resolution no. 3; City Council Minutes, October 23, 1862.

tifications.[18] In November, Richmond's council, "in view of the present large and unprecedented number of prisoners confined in the jail," appropriated $3,500 to construct six more cells. The municipal authorities also increased their support of the city's public schools to meet the higher wartime costs.[19]

In these and other actions, General Winder, the legislature, and the council sought to meet the war's demands on the Confederate capital. During a period of peace any government impressing slaves, fixing prices and quotas, and competing with free markets would have been labeled a tyranny. Richmond's general acceptance of these expedients gave some indication of the war's impact upon her and of the city's mature dedication to the war effort.

During the final months of 1862, official and individual relations with the national authorities underwent a series of crises involving the competence of the Davis regime. The resultant friction accelerated the city's transfer of her first allegiance from Jefferson Davis's government to General Lee's army.

In November Richmonders looked from their windows and saw barefoot soldiers marching through the snow on the city's streets.[20] Great was Richmond's outrage over the mistreatment of her defenders. The disgraceful situation did not appear to be the fault of the Clothing Bureau, for Major Walker's ladies had produced over 300,000 pairs of boots and shoes during the past twelve months.[21] Naturally, criticism focused on Quartermaster General Myers and the President.[22] The *Whig* exhorted the citizens, "Come and shame the government as you have shamed it before. The naked soldier, who is fighting for your freedom, is shivering in your streets. Help him."[23] Richmonders did help. But, as they had contributed six to

18 Virginia General Assembly, *Acts of the General Assembly of the State of Virginia . . . Called Session, 1862 . . .* , chap. 2.
19 City Council, Minutes, November 10, 1862.
20 Jones, *Rebel War Clerk's Diary*, I, 186; *Whig*, November 10, 1862.
21 *Whig*, November 22, 1862.
22 General Henry A. Wise wrote in the *Enquirer* (quoted in the *Whig*, November 29, 1862) that the quartermaster general had answered a desperate plea for shoes for Wise's troops, "Let them suffer."
23 *Whig*, November 10, 1862.

eight thousand pairs of shoes,[24] they wondered why it was still necessary for them to clothe the national army.

While the citizens raged over a government which allowed its soldiers to suffer, Secretary of War Randolph resigned. Throughout the spring and summer of 1862 the popular Virginian had performed his duties in a creditable manner. Then in November he advocated his own scheme for a united command in the western theater of war, and advanced it to the point of ordering troops from one geographical command to another.[25] The President, preferring to be his own Secretary of War, sent Randolph a tactless letter pointing out the limitations of Randolph's official position.[26] When an exchange of notes between the two men yielded no satisfactory solution, Randolph, calling his position that of a chief clerk, resigned. Although Davis's next War Secretary, James A. Seddon, was also a Virginian, Richmonders could not condone the loss of Randolph. The Dispatch calling Randolph "one of the most popular men in Virginia" noted his "decided and acknowledged talent." "The regret at the resignation of Mr. Randolph," the paper concluded, "we are sure is general; yet if rumor as to the causes of his resignation, be true, he cannot be censured. On the contrary, his cause will be generally approved."[27] Richmond's approval became evident with Randolph's selection to the city council in the next election.

Later in the year a clash between Richmond's council and the Confederate executive branch further strained relations between the city and the national government. During the fall, the Confederate Congress passed another conscription bill,[28] and on December 20 Richmond's council made a routine request to exempt city

24 *Ibid.*, November 20, 1862.

25 See Clement Eaton, *A History of the Southern Confederacy*, pp. 128–129.

26 Dunbar Rowland, ed., *Jefferson Davis, Constitutionalist: His Letters, Papers and Speeches*, V, 371–372.

27 *Dispatch*, November 18, 1862. The *Richmond Daily Examiner* (November 17, 1862) stated, "Indeed, if cabinet ministers are to continue mere automatons, it matters little by what names those machines are called."

28 James M. Matthews, ed., *Statutes at Large of the Confederate States of America*, 1st cong., 2d sess., chap. 80.

officers from the expanded draft. Governor Letcher and Secretary of War Randolph had always been most cooperative in this matter, and the committee appointed to secure the necessary exemptions anticipated no trouble. Jefferson Davis was on an inspection tour in the western theater, so the committee called on War Secretary Seddon. The Secretary explained that he did not have the power to grant such exemptions and referred the councilmen to the President. The council's committee then had to procure from an enrolling officer a thirty-day stay in which to petition the President. Davis returned, refused the exemption, and referred the committee back to Seddon. The Secretary again refused, this time saying he lacked authorization from Congress, so the committee prepared a memorandum to Congress. However, before Congress could consider the matter, the thirty days would expire, and so the committee returned to Seddon for an extension. Seddon refused the extension and stated that should Congress leave the matter to him, he would not even exempt the city's fifty-one firemen who were eligible for military duty. Although the committee finally found an officer who did extend the thirty days, the harassed councilmen concluded their report: "If the gas works and water works are left without officers, and the fire brigade disbanded and between twenty and thirty millions of private property belonging to the Confederate Government are left unprotected, and the citizens and government left without water and light, upon the President and secretary of war must rest the mighty responsibility."[29]

Congress responded favorably, and the council's dire predictions were not realized. Afterwards, however, the city fathers' attitude toward their Confederate guests was, if not hostile, at least more formal. In February the council requested the Confederacy to remove its soldiers and other prisoners from the city's jail.[30] Later in the month they presented the national government with a $7,470 hospital bill for the treatment of soldiers in the city's hospital.[31]

[29] City Council, Minutes, January 14, 1863.
[30] Ibid., February 9, 1863.
[31] Ibid., February 17, 1863.

They also began charging the Confederacy rent for use of the Alms House as a general hospital.[32]

Hard times and growing impatience with Jefferson Davis and his government caused at least one Richmonder to say, "I am coming to Mr. Ruffin's [Major Frank G., Assistant Commissary] opinion. He says he used to think Jefferson Davis a *mule*, but a *good mule*. He has come to think him a jackass."[33] Ironically, it was President Davis himself who best expressed the relationship between capital and government. When he returned from his tour of the west on the night of January 5, several hundred people and a brass band turned out to meet him. The hour was late, but Davis was grateful. "I thank you my friends for the kind salutation tonight," he said. "It is an indication that at some future time we shall be better acquainted."[34] He had lived in Richmond over nineteen months, and still the city did not know him.

Richmond celebrated Christmas, 1862, with the usual popcrackers, calls, eggnog, and the like.[35] But winter was hard in the city. The council's committee on the destitute poor reported in December: "There can be no doubt that public charity will have a much larger field for its exercise this winter than heretofore and that the occasion calls for increased appropriations from the city treasury. It is one of the highest duties of every community to see that the necessities of life are provided for its poor. And your committee are satisfied that the people of Richmond will cheerfully bear any additional burden incident to this object."[36] The council appropriated twenty thousand dollars to the Union Benevolent Society to care for the needy during the winter.[37] Although the numbers of destitute poor grew, and the ranks of the needy expanded to include the wives, widows, and children of soldiers, the council provided relief

[32] *Ibid.*, February 23, 1863.
[33] Edward Younger, ed., *Inside the Confederate Government: The Diary of Robert Garlick Hill Kean, Head of the Bureau of War*, p. 31.
[34] *Enquirer*, January 7, 1863, quoted in Rowland, ed., *Jefferson Davis . . . Letters, Papers and Speeches*, V, 390–395.
[35] *Whig*, December 27, 1862.
[36] City Council, Minutes, December 8, 1862.
[37] *Ibid.*

as long as it could secure the funds. Besides supporting the unfortunate in Richmond, they dispatched ten thousand dollars in February to the Mayor of Fredericksburg to aid the citizens left homeless there by battle and Union occupation.[38]

During the last months of 1862 the influx of refugees became alarming. Some of these newcomers were wives of Confederate soldiers who could not work their family farms alone and sought employment in the city. Some were residents of the areas of Virginia occupied by Federals. Some fled from farms and towns which had been battlegrounds. And they all profoundly affected Richmond's economy. The refugees helped drive rent in the city "head and shoulders above the means of salaried men."[39] In February the council's finance committee declared that rents had quadrupled in two years.[40] To escape the high costs, a colony of refugees found quarters several miles away in the village of Ashland and commuted by railroad to jobs in the city.[41]

Both refugees and natives in Richmond depended greatly on the government and war industries for employment. The Tredegar Iron Works hired almost three times the number of men that had been on the payroll in 1861. By January, 1863, Joseph R. Anderson employed 2,500 men and operated a tannery, shoemaking shops, firebrick factory, sawmill, and nine canal boats in addition to his mills and furnaces.[42] Anderson even entered the food business. Throughout the winter of 1862–1863, Tredegar agents ranged as far as Alabama seeking livestock and Tredegar bought, transported, slaughtered, and sold the animals to employees at cost. Tredegar hands consumed one thousand company hogs that winter.[43] The Confederate Quartermaster Department Clothing Bureau employed two to three thousand women as seamstresses.[44] More women signed Confederate currency notes at the Treasury Office.

[38] *Ibid.*, February 23, 1863.
[39] *Whig*, November 27, 1862.
[40] City Council, Minutes, February 24, 1863.
[41] Judith W. McGuire, *Diary of a Southern Refugee during the War*, pp. 168–169.
[42] Kathleen Bruce, *Virginia Iron Manufacture in the Slave Era*, p. 386.
[43] *Ibid.*, pp. 377–379, 400.
[44] *Whig*, November 22, 1862.

Indeed, one of Richmond's refugee citizens felt that, "the *poor*, being well supplied with Government work, are better off than usual."[45]

Many people in the capital supplemented their income with the fruits of domestic industry. Several refugee ladies made soap and sold it for a dollar per pound. Another lady put an old family recipe for gooseberry wine to profitable use. Still another made pickles and catsup for restaurants.[46] Despite these and other projects, the mass of Richmond's immigrants and salaried people generally found it difficult to meet the ever-rising cost of life in the city. The Union blockade made dry goods particularly dear. Auction companies seemed to make scandalous profits on shipments run in from Europe by privateers or smuggled through the lines from the North. In April a Confederate congressman paid $120 for a suit and wondered, "What is to become of the Country?"[47] Women lost contact with styles in clothing, and one lady remarked: "The blockade has taught our people their own resources; but I often think that when the great veil is removed, and reveals us to the world, we will, in some respects, be a precious set of antiques."[48]

Food prices continued to rise. In January the *Dispatch* compared a small family's weekly grocery bill in 1860 with the same fare in 1863.

Article	Quantity	Cost 1860	Cost 1863
Bacon	10 lbs.	$1.25	$10.00
Flour	30 lbs.	1.50	3.75
Sugar	5 lbs.	.40	5.75
Coffee	4 lbs.	.50	20.00
Tea	½ lb.	.50	8.00
Lard	4 lbs.	.60	4.00
Butter	3 lbs.	.75	5.25
Meal	1 pkg.	.25	1.00
Candles	2 lbs.	.30	2.50

45 McGuire, *Diary of a Southern Refugee*, p. 198.

46 *Ibid.*, p. 196.

47 Mary S. Estill, ed., "Diary of a Confederate Congressman, 1862–1863," *Southwestern Historical Quarterly* 39 (July, 1935): 51.

48 McGuire, *Diary of a Southern Refugee*, p. 197.

Soap	5 lbs.	.50	5.50
Pepper and salt		.10	2.50
TOTAL		$6.65	$68.25[49]

Many people in the city now more than ever cherished friendships with those in the country. A senator's wife recalled, "When I had starved in the capital, I dropped down to 'Buxton Place,' whence I was sure to return laden with hampers of sweets and meats and bread made of the finest 'Number One' flour."[50] However scarce and expensive food became during the winter of 1862–1863, the resourceful among Richmond's population would not go hungry. Mrs. Chesnut wrote of her servant: "Lawrence has simple ideas, but effective. 'You give me the money, I'll find everything you want.' There is no such word as fail with him. 'There ain't nothing to eat in Richmond, not a bit of it; but you give me the money.' "[51]

During the winter an epidemic of smallpox raged among the poorer neighborhoods in the city. Prompt action by the city council effected quarantine of the afflicted and free vaccination of all people who were unable to pay for private immunization. The city secured three wards of Howard's Grove army hospital for Negro patients and utilized the city hospital for whites. Badges identified those houses infected with the disease. Although the total number of cases was relatively slight, smallpox constantly threatened the city from November to February.[52]

In the midst of the hardship and disease of these somber days, Richmonders sought release from the sober realities. The soldiers came to the city for enjoyment. One Alabamian described a typical

[49] *Dispatch*, January 29, 1863. These figures are only for comparison. Few Richmonders drank coffee or tea in 1863, and thus the average small family did not spend $68.25 per week for food.

[50] Mrs. Clement C. Clay, *A Belle of the Fifties: Memoirs of Mrs. Clay of Alabama, Covering Social and Political Life in Washington and the South, 1853–66*, ed. Ada Sterling, p. 185.

[51] Mary Boykin Chesnut, *A Diary from Dixie*, ed. Ben Ames Williams, pp. 281–282.

[52] City Council, Minutes, November 24, December 12, 1862, January 13, February 9, 17, 1863. Council paid for 734 vaccinations. The largest number of Negro patients at any one time was 102.

day in February, 1863: "I remained in the city all day, meeting with many officers and men at the hospitals, the Exchange Hotel and Ballard House, and Spotswood Hotel. At night I saw 'Lady of the Lake' acted. At its conclusion, while en route to camp, stopped with Capt. Hewlett and Lieut. Tate, of 3rd Ala., at a 'shindig,' and had an enjoyable time. Kissing games were popular, and some of the dancers were high kickers and not over graceful."[53] The same soldier celebrated St. Valentine's Day with a "glorious bath" at the Ballard House.[54] Richmond's parties, hospital visits, theaters, and loafing, as well as less reputable forms of entertainment, were pleasant changes from the routine of winter quarters.

Soldiers especially enjoyed the theater, which had always been popular in Richmond. To replace the Richmond Theater, which had burned in January, 1862,[55] the manger, D'Orsay Ogden, built the New Richmond Theater, and opened it in February, 1862, with As You Like It followed by Romeo and Juliet and Othello.[56] During February, entertainment in the capital also featured Harry Macarthy, composer of "Bonnie Blue Flag," at the Broad Street Theater. White, Wells, and Parrow's minstrels, judged the Confederacy's best by the Whig, played Metropolitan Hall. As the Whig commented, Richmond's residents and visitors had "no lack of resources with which to banish dull care."[57] Richmonders augmented public entertainments with private theatricals and charades.[58] The haunting "Lorena" was easily the most popular song in the city and nation during that winter. "Maggie Howell [sister of Varina Davis] says there is a girl in large hoops and a calico frock at every piano between Richmond and the Mississippi, banging on the out-of-tune thing and looking up into a man's face, singing that song.

---

[53] Robert Emory Park, "War Diary of Captain Robert Emory Park," Southern Historical Society Papers 26 (1898): 3.
[54] Ibid.
[55] Enquirer, January 3, 1862.
[56] Whig, January 26, February 19, May 16, 1863.
[57] Ibid., January 26, 1863.
[58] T. C. DeLeon, Belles, Beaux, and Brains of the 60's, p. 217; Clay, Belle of the Fifties, pp. 174–177.

. . . Well, the song has not had a fair chance. We hear it squalled so, and to banged accompaniments which are discord itself."[59]

By the second winter of war, Varina Davis had become the acknowledged leader of official society in the capital. Her circle was relatively small and excluded many native Richmonders. The ladies of Richmond in general resented Mrs. Davis's intrusion, but they could not ignore her. Mrs. Chesnut wrote in her diary: "I was asked wherever I turned: 'What did you do?' and more frequently: 'What did Mrs. Davis do?' Finally out of patience with so much idle curiosity I cried: 'We danced on the tight rope.' 'Have mercy, dear,' whispered Mrs. Davis. 'Never say that again. They will believe you. You do not know this Richmond. They swallow scandal with wide open mouths. Their easy credulity is such that next winter they will have the exact length of our petticoats and describe the kind of spangles we were sprinkled with.' "[60] Tucker DeLeon described another important institution of Richmond's high society of that time. "What came nearest to a salon in Richmond—and as far as I know in America—was held at Mrs. Robert C. Stanard's."[61] Wife of a Richmond judge, Mrs. Stanard entertained frequently and brilliantly.

In some contrast to the official society was the so-called Quiet Set which "made small pretense of entertaining in the lavish old way, but Hospitality sat on their front steps and invited the proper passer within. . . . If some good housekeeper fell heir to a large jug of sorghum, had a present of some real flour or acquired a tiny sack of 'true-and-true' coffee, then and there went forth the summons."[62] This group included John R. Thompson, poet and a former editor of the *Southern Literary Messenger*; John Esten Cooke, the romantic novelist; and Virginia Attorney General "Ran" Tucker.[63]

The first winter of total war had brought difficulty and privation —a harder life than the city had yet known. Winter and wartime had challenged Richmond daily in a thousand ways. Nor did the

[59] Chesnut, *Diary from Dixie*, p. 304.
[60] *Ibid.*, p. 283.
[61] DeLeon, *Belles, Beaux, and Brains*, p. 198.
[62] *Ibid.*, p. 201.   [63] *Ibid.*, pp. 203–210.

capital's crises ease with the coming of spring—indeed the pace quickened.

Spring, 1863, came with explosions, literally as well as figuratively. On Friday, March 13, Mary Ryan went to work as usual in the ordnance laboratory on Brown's Island. Her duties involved working with explosives, but she was older and more experienced than many of her coworkers and felt no apprehension. Mary worked on friction primers, the highly explosive devices used to ignite gunpowder in large field pieces. On this day other women and girls were breaking open paper cartridges nearby. In the course of her work, Mary encountered difficulty with one of her friction primers. The obstinate device stuck in a board, and she could not pull it loose. Impatiently, the young woman struck the board on the table hoping to drive out the primer. On the third blow the laboratory exploded. The initial blast blew Mary Ryan to the ceiling. As she came down, the gunpowder in the room ignited and blew her into the air once again. Mary Ryan and sixty-eight other employees were casualties. By March 15, thirty-four had died of burns. Mary Ryan lingered until March 16.[64]

Chief of Ordnance Josiah Gorgas conducted a thorough investigation of the accident and instituted more rigid safety precautions.[65] There were no more serious accidents in his shops. For Richmond the incident served as one more unnecessary reminder of the perilous times in which she lived. And there were other reminders.

Until the spring of 1863 Richmond blamed extortioners for the high prices in the markets. They could not identify the evil men by sight, but everyone knew they existed. People struggling to live on fixed incomes felt the ruinous inflation was probably the fault of some unprincipled speculators. They heard stories of vast profiteering and cursed the Yankee-like cupidity of some of their fellow citizens. In 1863 a readily identifiable class of villains entered the

[64] Frank E. Vandiver, ed., *The Civil War Diary of General Josiah Gorgas*, pp. 25–26; *Whig*, March 14, 16, 1863.
[65] Vandiver, ed., *Diary of General Josiah Gorgas*, p. 52 n. The *Examiner* (May 22, 1863) reported the Brown's Island laboratory again functioning.

market place. Army agents began impressing food, and Congress regularized the procedure in law.[66] The act to regulate impressment, passed in March, required the military to pay a fair price for articles taken. But farmers often set the price too high, and the army agents often insisted on too meagre a settlement.[67] In Richmond the impressment system immediately drained the markets and drove prices ever higher. The *Whig*, under the title "Our Worst Enemies," summarized the situation: "It is deplorable in times like these, when the country is bleeding from every pore, when there is wailing in nearly every household, and when the energies of the best portion of us are taxed to the utmost for the bare necessities of life, that we should be gouged by heartless extortioners and robbed by official rogues."[68]

By the end of March flour brought $30 to $35 per barrel in the city. Eggs sold for $1.50 a dozen and butter for $2.70 to $3.00 per pound.[69] The Secretary of War drew up a uniform schedule of prices, but the schedule could not keep pace with soaring costs. An official in the War Office analyzed the dilemma:

Farmers are making preparations for only so much corn as will suffice for their own use. They resent the Secretary's schedule prices which are often 50% below the market or neighborhood price. The instant impressment of flour, corn, and meat, as soon as they are brought to any of the inland towns to be put in market, is causing universal withholding of surplus—secreting and non-production. The army will be starved, and famine will ensue in the cities unless the Secretary changes his policy and buys in the market for the best price. The Government will have to outbid the traders; else *neither* will get anything of the present scanty stock, and no future stock will be produced.[70]

[66] Matthews, ed., *Statutes at Large of the Confederate States of America*, 1st cong., 2d sess., chap. 10.

[67] Chief of War Bureau Kean complained in his diary (April 13): "The new impressment law bids fair to ruin the country and cause. Appraisers in Powhatan the other day put the 'just compensation' for hay at $20 per cart and in Hanover wheat at $6.00 per bushel. The farmers are the worst we have to deal with and at this rate will wholly break up supply of the army" (Younger, ed., *Diary of . . . Kean*, p. 52).

[68] *Whig*, February 16, 1863.

[69] *Dispatch*, March 25, 1863.

[70] Younger, ed., *Diary of . . . Kean*, p. 41.

View of Richmond before the War. *Virginia State Library.*

Bell Tower and Capitol Square in the 1850's. *Virginia State Library.*

Confederate Navy Yard, Rocketts. *Virginia State Library.*

Main Street, Richmond in 1856. *Virginia State Library.*

Tredegar Iron Works. *Virginia State Library.*

Governor's Mansion in 1865. *Virginia State Library.*

Lee Home on Franklin Street. *Virginia State Library.*

Robert E. Lee. *Library of Congress.*

Henry A. Wise. *Virginia State Library*.

Governor John Letcher. *Virginia State Library*.

Governor William Smith. *Virginia State Library.*

Mayor Joseph Mayo. *Virginia State Library.*

Vice-President Alexander H. Stephens.
Virginia State Library.

President Jefferson Davis.
Virginia State Library, courtesy Confederate Museum.

Confederate Chief of Ordnance Josiah Gorgas. *Virginia State Library.*

General John Winder. *Virginia State Library.*

Evacuation of Richmond. *Virginia State Library.*

Federal troops entering Richmond. *Virginia State Library.*

Federal troops marching up Main Street. *Virginia State Library.*

View with ruins from Gambles Hill.
Library of Congress, photograph by Alexander Gardner.

Spotswood Hotel in April 1865.
Library of Congress, photograph by Alexander Gardner.

View from the Spotswood looking north up Eighth Street, St. Paul's
Episcopal Church steeple at right. *Virginia State Library.*

Chimborazo Hospital in April 1865. *Library of Congress.*

Libby Prison in April 1865.
Library of Congress, photograph by Alexander Gardner.

Ruins of Richmond arsenal. *Virginia State Library*.

Ruins of Virginia state armory (foreground) and Richmond and Petersburg railway bridge (left and center). *Virginia State Library*.

President Abraham Lincoln visits the captured capital on April 4, 1865.
Virginia State Library.

The same official noted ominously in his diary, "There is a manifest uneasiness in the public mind different from anything I have noticed heretofore."[71] Richmond's flour merchants could, and did, apply to state courts for injunctions preventing seizures.[72] But the city's consumers had no such legal recourse. They were forced to pay the high prices for available food or starve. In February the Virginia General Assembly authorized Richmond's city council to arm its police and take whatever measures were necessary to "suppress riots and unlawful assemblies."[73]

Nine inches of snow fell in Richmond on March 19 and 20. It thawed quickly and by the end of the month roads into the city were quagmires.[74] Even farmers willing to display their produce in Richmond's markets found it difficult to transport. Faced with even greater want than before, a group of women from Oregon Hill assembled in Belvidere Hill Baptist Church on the morning of April 2.[75] They talked for a time and shared their desperation, and then they decided to act. First the women called on John Letcher at the Governor's Mansion. The delegation explained their plight and sought redress, and the governor listened to their grievances and expressed his sympathy.[76] But sympathy would not suffice. Rapidly the delegation became a mob.

Boys and men loafing on Capitol Square joined the throng. Mary Jackson, "a tall, daring, Amazonian-looking woman, who had a white feather standing erect from her hat,"[77] led the procession down to Main Street. Some of the women bore hatchets or knives, and a few brandished pistols. On Main Street the riot began in earnest. Shouting "bread," women smashed store windows and took

[71] *Ibid.*

[72] *Ibid.*

[73] Virginia General Assembly, *Acts of the General Assembly of the State of Virginia . . . Adjourned Session, 1863 . . .* , chap. 74.

[74] Younger, ed., *Diary of . . . Kean*, p. 45.

[75] *Richmond Sentinel*, April 6, 1863.

[76] F. N. Boney, *John Letcher of Virginia: The Story of Virginia's Civil War Governor*, pp. 189–190.

[77] Varina Howell Davis, *Jefferson Davis, Ex-President of the Confederate States of America: A Memoir by His Wife*, II, 373.

food. Others shouted "bread," and seized clothing and shoes.[78] One merchant lost goods worth over $13,000, and the rioters carried off 310 pounds of beef from the City Hospital.[79] For a number of minutes it seemed that a revolution had begun. Thomas Mumford from the YMCA invited the mob on Cary Street to come to the association's army depot and receive food.[80] A few stopped their pillage and followed Mumford, but the riot went on unabated on Main Street. Mayor Mayo and Governor Letcher arrived and tried to reason with the looters. No one listened; the pillage continued.

Finally a column of troops appeared. A company from the Confederate Armory marched up Main Street driving looters before it. Captain Gay, a "no nonsense" officer, and his reserve troops halted before a horseless wagon around which milled a large crowd. Then, into the impasse strode Jefferson Davis. The President mounted the dray between the armed soldiers and the mob. Women hissed. His voice rising above din, Davis informed the crowd that such lawlessness must cease immediately. The crowd was unmoved. Then the President took out his watch, glanced at the troops, and gave the rioters five minutes in which to disperse. No one moved. Captain Gay commanded his soldiers to load and to shoot to kill when the five minutes had elapsed. Still the mob stood firm. The troops prepared their weapons, and Jefferson Davis studied his watch. Another five minutes and the President would have to carry out his promise. He steadied the hand which held his watch and pondered alternatives. Then the mob broke. The mayor, the governor, the President, and the troops stood alone in the empty street.[81]

Indignation prevailed when the city council met that afternoon. No informed citizen would deny that scarcity existed in Richmond. However, the plump rioters, while screaming for bread, had concentrated their pillage on dry goods and luxuries. Furthermore, the

[78] Sallie Brock Putnam, *Richmond during the War: Four Years of Personal Observation*, p. 208.

[79] City Council, Minutes, April 12, 13, 1863.

[80] McGuire, *Diary of a Southern Refugee*, p. 203.

[81] Varina Howell Davis, *Memoir*, II, 373–376; Mrs. Roger A. Pryor, *Reminiscences of Peace and War*, pp. 251–259; Vandiver, ed., *Diary of . . . Gorgas*, p. 289; Emory M. Thomas, "The Richmond Bread Riot of 1863," *Virginia Cavalcade* 18 (Summer, 1968): 41–47.

council had received no recent applications for expansion of its relief to the poor.[82] One lady recorded a typical sentiment in her diary: "I saw the Rev. Mr. Peterkin, who is perhaps more thoroughly acquainted with the state of the poor than any in the city. He says that they are admirably attended to. Large sums of money are put in the hands of the clergy for their benefit; this money is disbursed by ladies whose duty and pleasure it is to relieve suffering. One gentleman gave as much as $5,000 last winter. Besides this the industrious poor are supplied with work by the Government, and regularly paid for it."[83] The council declared that the disturbance was "in reality instigated by devilish and selfish motives," and resolved that Richmond's "honor, dignity, and safety will be preserved." The city fathers blamed outsiders and requested the committee on police to consider an ordinance requiring all who had lived in the city less than a year to post bond for their good behavior. The council also offered to pay for stolen property and posted a fifty-dollar reward for information leading to the conviction of any rioter.[84]

Secretary of War Seddon ordered the telegraph to send "nothing of the unfortunate disturbance of today over the wires for any purpose."[85] Acting for the Secretary, Assistant Adjutant General John Withers also sent a note to the city's newspapers. "The unfortunate disturbance which occurred to-day in the city is so liable to misconstruction and misrepresentation abroad that I am desired by the Secretary of War to make a special appeal to the editors and reporters of the press at Richmond, and earnestly request them to avoid all reference directly or indirectly to the affair."[86] On April 3 the *Dispatch*'s lead editorial concerned "Sufferings in the North,"[87] and the *Enquirer* gave prime space to an article on Poland.[88] The

[82] City Council, Minutes, April 2, 1863.
[83] McGuire, *Diary of a Southern Refugee*, p. 204.
[84] City Council, Minutes, April 2, 1863.
[85] John Withers to W. S. Morris, April 2, 1863, U.S., Congress, House, *War of the Rebellion: A Compilation of the Official Records of the Union and Confederate Armies*, ser. I, vol. 18, p. 958.
[86] Withers to the Richmond Press, April 2, 1863; *Ibid.*
[87] *Dispatch*, April 3, 1863.
[88] *Enquirer*, April 3, 1863.

Whig avoided mention of the riot, but it did sound a none-too-oblique warning: "If any class is suffering—if profligate commissaries or hoarding speculators have produced artificial wants, there is an appeal to the law and an appeal to the native benevolence of the proverbially hospitable, generous, open-handed people of the South. Violence before remonstrance is an unheard-of thing under the Southern sun. It will not be tolerated."[89]

The day following the riot a smaller crowd returned to the scene, but a cannon placed there during the night effectively discouraged renewal of the looting.[90] More than a week later, however, Mayor Mayo feared another outbreak and requested more troops. All of Winder's force and two battalions from the river defenses stood ready to suppress further demonstrations.[91]

Despite assurances from Richmond officials that the bread riot had originated in sheer lawlessness probably sparked by Yankee spies, there was want in the city. The courts sent convicted participants in the riot to jail for as many as three years.[92] However, the municipal authorities recognized that beneath the wanton looting of a few there lay genuine frustration and privation for many. A week after the incident, when the fear of anarchy had passed, the council appropriated twenty thousand dollars for free-food depots in the city. A committee of 24 men dispensed tickets to the deserving poor in each ward. The tickets were exchangeable for provisions at either of two depots.[93] For as long as food was available, this expedient removed any cause for further disturbance.

May brought a renewal of military hostilities. Federal General Joseph Hooker moved the Army of the Potomac out of winter quarters on the Fredericksburg front. Preparing to face Lee, Hooker dispatched General George Stoneman's Cavalry to the Confederate

89 *Whig*, April 4, 1863.
90 McGuire, *Diary of a Southern Refugee*, p. 203; Estill, ed., "Diary of a Congressman," p. 48.
91 S. Bassett French (Aide de Camp to Governor Letcher) to James A. Seddon, April 10, 1863, *War of the Rebellion: Compilation of Official Records*, ser. I, vol. 18, pp. 977–978.
92 *Whig*, May 28, 1863.
93 City Council, Minutes, April 9, 1863; *Whig*, April 9, 1863.

rear. Stoneman's mission was the destruction of supplies and communications. On Sunday, May 3, couriers reported that the Yankees were in Hanover County and advancing on Richmond. Richmonders heard the news from the pulpits of their churches. After the services George W. Randolph organized nine volunteer companies to man the city's fortifications. The confusion was enormous. General Arnold Elzey, commander of the Military Department of Richmond, told an official in the War Department he wished he were dead.[94] Mrs. Chesnut became so frightened over the city's imminent capture, that she burned her diary.[95]

Stoneman came within five miles of the capital on Monday the fourth. Bells rang in the city, and Randolph's improvised force again marched out to the batteries. Unfortunately they forgot to take any gunpowder with them. Randolph noticed the oversight and sent for powder. Then he discovered that none of the guns had friction primers with which to ignite the powder. Had Stoneman assaulted the works, not a single cannon could have fired against him. To the relief of all, the fifteen hundred Yankees came no closer than Ashland.[96]

Explosion, riot, and raid caused severe consternation in the city. Yet these did not compare in effect with the death of General Thomas J. Jackson. While the residents of the capital were quaking before Stoneman's advance, Lee and Jackson had performed brilliantly. The Army of Northern Virginia doubly enveloped Hooker at Chancellorsville and thoroughly foiled his projected assault on Richmond. But Jackson was wounded by his own troops while returning from an evening reconnaissance. He died May 10.[97]

Richmond learned of Jackson's death the next morning. Business

---

[94] Younger, ed., *Diary of . . . Kean*, pp. 55–56.

[95] Chesnut, *Diary from Dixie*, p. 306. Mrs. Chesnut's servant Molly told her, "Missie, listen to the guns. Burn up everything. Mr. Lyons say they sure to come, and they'll put in their newspapers whatever you write here every day." Mrs. Chesnut later recalled, "When Mr. Chesnut rode up and told me if Mrs. Davis left Richmond I must go with her, I confess I lost my head."

[96] Younger, ed., *Diary of . . . Kean*, p. 56.

[97] See Frank E. Vandiver, *Mighty Stonewall*, pp. 455–494.

ceased at ten o'clock, and people began walking to the railroad depot. The body arrived in mid-afternoon. Perhaps the largest crowd ever assembled in the city followed the coffin to the Governor's Mansion.[98] The city council met to adopt resolutions of respect. The men found that they had to "refrain from an attempt at eulogy which no language can express."[99] One resident remembered, "Nothing in the war, perhaps, excepting the surrender, ever struck Richmond with such stunning force."[100] The *Examiner* added, "There was the stuff of Cromwell in Jackson, Hannibal might have been proud of his campaign in the Valley, and the shades of the mightiest warriors should rise to welcome his stern ghost."[101]

On the morning of May 12 Jackson's body passed through Richmond's streets. Three brass bands went before the hearse, and the general's riderless horse followed.[102] "The whole people stood bareheaded and mute. . . . It was no mocking pageant. No holiday soldiery, spruce and gay, followed that precious bier—no chattering crowds pointed out the beauties of the sight. Solemn and mourning the escort passed; sad and almost voiceless the people turned away and, going to their homes, sat with their sorrow."[103] At noon the body lay in state at the Capitol. A visitor wrote, "If I had not learned of the Nation's great loss; I should think that every person in the City of Richmond had today buried their nearest and dearest friend."[104] The day after the funeral procession the general's body was taken to Lexington for interment.[105] Very few Richmonders

98 *Whig*, May 12, 1863.

99 City Council, Minutes, May 11, 1863.

100 Constance Cary Harrison, *Recollections Grave and Gay*, p. 138.

101 *Examiner*, May 11, 1863, quoted in Frederick S. Daniel, ed., *The Richmond Examiner during the War: Or The Writings of John M. Daniel With a Memoir of His Life*, p. 83.

102 *Whig*, May 13, 1863.

103 T. C. DeLeon, *Four Years in Rebel Capitals: An Inside View of the Southern Confederacy from Birth to Death*, pp. 251–252.

104 William W. Heartsill, *Fourteen Hundred and 91 Days in the Confederate Army: A Journal Kept by W. W. Heartsill, for Four Years, One Month, and One Day or Camp Life; Day-by-Day of the W. P. Lane Rangers, from April 19, 1861 to May 20, 1865*, 2d ed., Bell I. Wiley, ed., p. 126.

105 *Whig*, May 14, 1863.

ever knew Jackson personally. But he had defended them. His deeds and his character made him one of them, and they felt his loss deeply.[106]

The previous spring Richmond had met the clear and present challenge of McClellan's invasion. Since that period of acute danger the capital had dealt with the strains of home front war. She had found food, faced riot, and improvised local defense. Although the city quarreled with her national government, she sacrificed dearly for the Cause. Her reaction to Jackson's death indicated the depth of her total commitment. In turn she had faced squarely the various challenges of war—overt and subtle, internal and external. Although she never found final solutions, Richmond kept adjusting and continued seeking. And in this steadfastness was her glory.

[106] Mrs. Wigfall wrote her son on May 11, "I feel more disheartened about the war now than I have ever felt before. It seems to me, it is to be interminable, and what a wretched life of anxiety it is to look forward to! I suppose the death of Jackson has affected us all, and I can't help thinking it will put new life into the enemy and give him courage to make another attempt very soon" (Mrs. D. Giraud Wright, *A Southern Girl in '61: The War-Time Memories of a Confederate Senator's Daughter*, p. 126).

⊫Ⓢ⊫

Apogee

WO DAYS AFTER JACKSON'S FUNERAL the *Whig* printed an editorial about the "Revolutionized City." Lamenting the influx of undesirable aliens, the editor hoped that no one thought Richmonders responsible for the crime and vice prevalent in the capital.[1] Earlier he had written: "Richmond has had to pay through the nose for her greatness. With the Confederate government came the tag, rag and bobtail which ever pursue political establishments. The pure society of Richmond became woefully adulterated. Its peace was destroyed, its good name defiled; it became a den of thieves, extortioners, substitutes, deserters, blacklegs and cyprians. The glory and shame of a great city was its heritage."[2] War indeed made a strong impression upon the city. Her ante-bellum past seemed so absurdly simple compared with the complexities wrought by this Confederate war. Hospitals, prisons, government offices, and war industries occupied once familiar buildings. And so many were strangers. A native could walk from one end of Frank-

[1] *Richmond Daily Whig*, May 14, 1863.
[2] *Ibid.*, April 30, 1863.

lin Street to the other and not recognize a single face. Richmond's first citizen was a general who rarely visited the city; her martyred hero lay in Lexington; and her President was known to most of his fellow-Richmonders only by sight.

Ironically some of the best descriptions of the two-year-old capital were given by the strangers who crowded her streets and hotels. During the summer of 1863 a number of Europeans, attracted by the Confederacy's military success, came to see the American rebellion firsthand. Some were newspaper correspondents; many were soldiers. All of these travelers were curious about this new nation and the prospects of its survival. Some of these who visited Richmond left a vivid account of their impressions.

The visitors' first impressions chronicled the city's wartime development. If they approached from the south, they noted that field fortifications now guarded the Richmond and Petersburg railroad.[3] As trains reached the James River, visitors had the opportunity for a long look at Richmond's panorama on the opposite bank. The cars now crossed the James with extreme slowness because of the rickety condition of the much-used bridge.[4] Once inside the city:

The idleness and business of war are instanced, on the one hand, by the belted and spurred bragarts who lounge about the hotels; the closed shops, the schools that keep perpetual holiday, the old men that gather in the shady side walks to gossip and bewail, and the negro women that scream delightedly at the peals of music. On the other, by the thousands of workmen that frame oddly-constructed floating batteries at the waterside, and forge great guns at the Tredegar works: the medley of transportation teams that rumble over bridges and file along the turnpike roads; the gangs of negro men that are marched under guard to work at entrenchments and government buildings; the regiments in homespun gray and "butternut," that trail dustily through the high streets to swell distant camps. War looks at you from hospital churches and through the bright eyes of fever; it thrills you

---

[3] Arthur James Lyon Fremantle, *The Fremantle Diary, Being the Journal of Lieutenant Colonel Arthur James Lyon Fremantle, Coldstream Guards, on His Three Months in the Southern States*, ed. Walter Lord, p. 163.
[4] Charles Girard, *A Visit to the Confederate States of America in 1863: Memoir Addressed to His Majesty Napoleon III*, p. 47.

in the limp of cripples that beg at the wayside; it whispers sadly in the rustle of crape, and shouts its discontent in the yells of newsboys.[5]

When the traveler sought hotel accommodations, he realized that, "Richmond was never intended to hold as many inhabitants as it does now."[6] Most of the estimates placed the city's population at 100,000 souls.[7] Frenchman Charles Girard noticed the prevalence of homespun and uncolored clothing. "Today," he wrote, "master and slave wear almost identical clothing." Perhaps the sympathetic Girard exaggerated a bit when he continued, "at Richmond, however, they have begun to manufacture fabrics which promise to rival those of France and Belgium in beauty and quality."[8]

In the course of his comings and goings about the city, Fitzgerald Ross, a captain of the Austrian Hussars, perceived the war's impact upon Richmond's economy. "Planters, and those who have anything to sell, are nearly as well off as before, as they get proportionately high prices for their goods. For those who can command gold or exchange upon England, living is exceedingly cheap. ... But as Richmond is crowded with Government officials, most of whom have only their salaries, and with refugees from parts of the country occupied by Yankees, who have little or nothing at all, the war is much more severely felt here than anywhere else in the Confederacy."[9]

M. Girard saw permanence in the political structure at the new capital. He insisted that "it is no longer a trial Government, which is seated now at Richmond, but really a normal Government, the expression of popular will."[10] Lieutenant Colonel Fremantle of the Coldstream Guards noted further "normal" indications. "I found,"

[5] This quote, originally appearing in the *Cornhill Magazine* (a British periodical), was reprinted in the *Record of News, History and Literature*, I (1863), pp. 41–42, and again in Fitzgerald Ross, *Cities and Camps of the Confederate States*, ed. Richard B. Harwell, p. 23 n.

[6] Ross, *Cities and Camps*, p. 93.

[7] *Ibid.*; *Whig*, December 30, 1863.

[8] Girard, *A Visit to the Confederate States*, pp. 51–52.

[9] Ross, *Cities and Camps*, p. 94.

[10] Girard, *A Visit to the Confederate States*, p. 62.

he recorded, "at least as much difficulty in gaining access to the great men as there would be in European countries."[11]

Military observers Ross and Fremantle hurried to join the van of Lee's army as it began the second major invasion of the North. Captain Justus Scheibert, a Prussian officer, joined them on the journey which ended at Gettysburg. Before he left the capital, however, Scheibert visited the fields of the Seven Days. He described the country to the east of Richmond: "Although almost a year had passed since this land had been the scene of battle, the whole country still looked as if it had been sown with debris—knapsacks, articles of leather, and broken weapons—while unpleasant miasmata lay over the deserted landscape. Only grunting swine wandered around on level ground, often rooting at the shallow graves and gnawing on bodies which stared with distorted horrible expressions at persons who rode by. Where was the time in those days to bury the many thousands of dead deep enough."[12]

Most enlightening of the foreigners' comments were those dealing with morale. Although Richmonders sometimes criticized the Davis administration and often complained of the riffraff which had accompanied the Confederacy to its capital, the city's identification with the Cause was well demonstrated to Charles Girard. After witnessing Richmond's reaction to the defeats of 1863 he wrote: "In the midst of the most serious reverses, when in the eyes of a foreigner, their cause seemed to waver most, they showed an ardor, a warlike spirit that nothing, not even the fear of death, could daunt. In all ranks of the people there was the same rallying cry, to fight an abhorred enemy to the death."[13] Captain Scheibert was equally impressed. "The moral force of the resistance," he stated, "was also centered in Richmond, the capital of the rebellion. . . . The energy of the Confederate resistance that was typified in

[11] Fremantle, *Diary*, p. 164.
[12] Captain Justus Scheibert, *Seven Months in the Rebel States during the North American War, 1863*, trans. Joseph C. Hayes, ed. William Stanley Hoole, p. 33.
[13] Girard, *A Visit to the Confederate States*, p. 92.

Richmond impressed me almost as much as the great efforts of the army later to hold the field against an overwhelming adversary."[14]

The institutions which buttressed the "moral force of the resistance"—churches, schools, and the press—continued and even flourished in the wartime capital. Religion in Richmond underwent transition; some of the less conventional protestant sects declined but the more traditional churches grew in members and enthusiasm. The Universalist congregation disbanded early in the war.[15] The Cedar Creek Quaker congregation, disliked for its opposition to both slavery and the war, made itself even less popular by holding services for Federal prisoners. Richmond's Friends, though, muddled along and kept their religious community alive throughout the war period.[16] All of Richmond's churches experienced material hardships. By the summer of 1863 most of them had donated their bells to the Confederate army to be melted down and recast as cannon. Some had offered their buildings as hospitals. One church had sold its pew cushions to the army to be used as bedding. Shortages of fuel oil canceled night meetings. When the state government and the military imposed heavy restrictions on the making and sale of ardent spirits, one Baptist pastor secured communion wine for his flock on a visit to North Carolina.

In spite of, or perhaps because of, such demands of war, organized religion thrived in the Confederate Capital.[17] Richmond's churches, almost without exception, grew in members during the Confederate period. In 1862 St. Paul's rector, Charles Minnegerode, had baptized and confirmed Jefferson Davis and Josiah Gorgas on

[14] Scheibert, *Seven Months in the Rebel States*, p. 31.
[15] Frank W. Pratt, "The History of the Unitarian Church of Richmond, Virginia," in Sketches of Societies and Institutions Together with Descriptions of Phases of Social, Political and Economic Development in Richmond, Virginia, comp. Virginia Capital Bicentennial Commission, pt. 38, p. 2.
[16] Cedar Creek Friends, Minutes.
[17] G. McLaren Brydon, "The Church," in *Richmond, Approaches to Its History by Various Hands*, pp. 98–99; Blanche Sydnor White, *First Baptist Church, Richmond, 1780–1955: One Hundred and Seventy-Five Years of Service to God and Man*, pp. 67–70; W. C. James, *Leigh Street Baptist Church, 1854–1954: A Brief History of its First One Hundred Years in the Service of Christ*, p. 64; Mrs. John B. Harvie, ed., *Beacon on a Hill: A Brief History of 100 Years of Christian Service, 1855–1955*, p. 18.

the same day. Richmond ministers were also active in the army encampments around the city.[18] During 1862, Moses D. Hoge of the Second Presbyterian Church had run the blockade and secured in England over 300,000 Bibles and portions of scripture for distribution in the Confederacy.[19] The Baptists carried on an extensive colportage campaign from Richmond. Also, tracts, such as *Are You Ready?*, *The Brown Jug*, and *True Conversion: A Dialogue between Hopeful and Christian* . . . , went to the armies from the Presbyterian Committee of Publication in Richmond.[20] Groups of ladies from almost every church in the city served as hospital volunteers and as seamstresses.

The increased numbers and activities paralleled an increase in the influence of Richmond's churches. From the city's pulpits came patriotic propaganda exhorting the hearer to sacrifice for the Cause. Yankees became latter-day Philistines whom Jehovah would surely smite down. On one of many days of national fasting and prayer, William Norwood thundered at St. John's:

Oh! Shall the blessing of God on our noble cause, shall our independence, shall our lands, shall our happy homes, shall the freedom of our sons, and the honor of our daughters, be offered as a sacrifice on the altar of mammon? Yes! Unless the food of the country is wrested from the grasp of the speculators; unless the wealth of the country, instead of being hoarded for purpose of selfish gratification and aggrandizement, be laid on the altar of patriotism; unless our armies be increased and sustained; unless the hands of the government be upheld by the people; unless the voice of the factious . . . be silenced; . . . unless all of every age, profession, and pursuit, rally, in one united, great, self-sacrificing, patriotic effort to support the army, and sustain

[18] *Ibid.*; Dover Baptist Association, *Minutes of the Dover Baptist Association*; Manchester Baptist Church, *A Century of Service: A History of Bainbridge Street Baptist Church 1857–1957*, p. 39.

[19] *Fifty Years a Pastor: An Account of the Observance of the Semi-Centennial Anniversary of the Installation of Rev. Moses Drury Hoge, D.D., L.L.D. in the Pastorate of the Second Presbyterian Church, Richmond, Virginia*, pp. 7–8.

[20] For the titles and locations of these and other tracts, see Marjorie Lyle Crandall, *Confederate Imprints: A Check List Based Principally on the Collection of the Boston Athenaeum*, vol. II, *Unofficial Publications*, pp. 220–828; and Richard Harwell, *More Confederate Imprints*, vol. II, *Unofficial Publications*, pp. 283–296.

the government. Oh! how easy it is to find fault, how hard to act
well.[21]

In the fall of 1863 the Dover Baptist Association, to which Richmond Baptist churches belonged, resolved "that nothing that has
occurred in the progress of the present war has weakened our con-
viction of the justice of our cause or our confidence in its final
success."[22]

Throughout the war, in times of individual and corporate crises,
the churches served as havens of peace and bastions of hope. In
satisfying these emotional needs of a people at war, Richmond's
churches lost some degree of theological sophistication. It is not too
surprising that the less emotional groups, like the Universalists,
should break up, or that the less liturgical forms of worship, like
that of the Quakers, should not prosper. It would appear that wartime Richmonders, like most people under stress, expressed their
religion emotionally. Like most people undergoing change, the
majority of Richmonders sought the timelessness of liturgy and
ritual.

Education in Richmond suffered from the effects of the war, but
endured. Private tutors and academies still educated most of the
capital's children. In 1862 the state suspended its aid to Richmond's
public schools, and the municipal government assumed the entire
cost of operating the Lancasterian School, and the three public
primary schools which survived the war. The Medical College of
Virginia was the only Southern medical school to remain open
during the war. That Richmond offered any public instruction or
higher education at all during the Confederate period was no small
accomplishment.[23]

Richmond's press continued to thrive. In March of 1863 the
Alexandria Sentinel wearied of almost continuous Federal occupation and sought refuge in Richmond.[24] For the rest of the war Rich-

[21] William Norwood, *God and Our Country—A Sermon*.

[22] Dover Baptist Association, *Minutes*.

[23] Richmond City Council, Minutes, November 10, 1862, March 26, 1863,
March 14, 1864; F. W. Boatwright, "Education," in *Richmond, Approaches to
Its History by Various Hands*, pp. 210–211.

[24] The *Sentinel* first appeared in Richmond March 13, 1863.

mond boasted five major daily newspapers. Though these dailies differed violently on the merits of the Davis administration and its policies, all of them professed intense loyalty to the Cause. The differences among these newspapers involved not the justice of the Cause, but how best to defend it.

In addition to her active newspapers, Richmond was also the home of a lively periodical press. Besides the *Southern Literary Messenger*, Richmonders published *The Southern Punch*; *Smith and Barrow's Monthly*; *Bohemian*; *Record of News, History* and *Literature*; *Southern Illustrated News*; *Magnolia: A Southern Home Journal*; and *Age: A Southern Eclectic Magazine*. Some, notably the *Southern Illustrated News* and the *Magnolia*, became popular throughout the Confederate South. Others quickly folded. The *Bohemian*, for example, ran only one issue. Most of these journals were intensely patriotic and carried pictures and character sketches of Confederate generals as well as tributes to "Our Martyrs" in every issue. The literary quality of Richmond's Confederate periodicals was uneven at best. The *Magnolia* offered installments of a previously unpublished story by William Gilmore Simms, that probably should have remained unpublished. Nevertheless, Richmond's periodical press, like her newspaper press, her religious establishment, and to some extent her educational system, supported the city's claim to be the "moral force of the resistance."[25]

In June of 1863 Richmond's European guests saw her at the peak of her powers. The capital felt the stimulation of Lee's victories. Her army had repulsed the invader and now readied for an offensive in Pennsylvania. In the war's eastern theater, Richmond's army was supreme.

On the home front also, the capital had prevailed; Richmond had adapted to total war. McClellan had come, and the city had shouted defiance and stood fast. Hunger and crime had increased, and Richmond sought remedies. New frictions, new expedients, and

[25] The Virginia State Library, Richmond, has good runs of all these periodicals except the *Southern Punch* for which the best file is in the Confederate Museum, Richmond.

new people had strained the old town, but she absorbed and sifted
the newness and survived the transformation. Richmond the capital had matured.

While two years as the Confederate capital had made great
changes in Richmond, the city in turn had exerted considerable influence upon the character and policy of the Confederacy. Richmond
had had rather set ways before the advent of Jefferson Davis's government. The resident national government made accommodation
to her characteristics and idiosyncrasies in untold instances—from
the boarding habits of congressmen to Varina Davis's management of official society. More important were the effects of the capital's location and military significance on the conduct of the war.
Richmond had psychological importance as the capital, and logistical importance as the center of many Confederate war industries.
She was the key to military strategy in the eastern theater of the
war, and concern for her security provided the Davis government
with a strong temptation to emphasize victory in the East at the
expense of success in the West.

It was not, however, only her adjustment to the trials of wartime, nor her military significance that made Richmond a great
capital. Her claim to greatness in June, 1863, rested upon her "warlike spirit that nothing, not even the fear of death, could daunt."
The city had faced her assailants, dealt with her problems, and
endured. Amid the stress of total war Richmond still danced and
laughed. As long as she continued the moral force of the resistance,
she would prevail.

But Richmond's tragedy lay in the revolution's inconclusiveness.
The capital was constantly evolving. As the war continued, the
pace of events and crises would outstrip Richmond's capacity to
meet the challenges of her revolution.

Challenge and No Response

URING MAY AND JUNE of 1863 an atmosphere of expectancy pervaded the city. No one doubted that the Yankees would return. But Lee and his army still barred the way, and the *Dispatch* assured its readers that the enemy's ninth "on to Richmond" drive would go the way of all the rest.[1] Richmond waited quietly. The sword would decide her fate soon enough.

Even the May 28 election proved quiet. There were a few fights and some tippling, but these were common on election days.[2] Richmond voters rejected incumbent James Lyons, and chose Colonel Williams C. Wickham for the Confederate House of Representatives. The *Enquirer* had tried to label Wickham a Unionist, because of his opposition to secession in 1861 at the convention.[3] However, the forty-three–year–old ex-Whig had satisfied all doubts about his patriotism by forming a cavalry company for the Cause.[4] Richmond seemed delighted to resume her prewar political persuasion

[1] *Richmond Daily Dispatch,* June 29, 1863.
[2] *Ibid.,* May 29, 1863.
[3] *Daily Richmond Enquirer,* May 29, 1863.
[4] Lyon G. Tyler, ed., *Encyclopedia of Virginia Biography,* III, 45.

and vote for the more conservative of two ex-Whigs; she gave Wickham 61 per cent of the vote. In the same election Richmonders supported their local gubernatorial candidate, Thomas S. Flournoy.[5] However, a sizable army-vote elected ex-Governor William Smith. The colorful soldier would succeed John Letcher on January 1, 1864.[6]

Late in June Lee put his army on the road north. Aside from the strategic and diplomatic advantages of a successful invasion of the enemy's territory, Lee realized that northern Virginia was agriculturally exhausted. He determined to let Pennsylvania farmers feed his troops. Virginia had been too long a battleground.[7] The capital's hopes went with its army. The *Dispatch* likened the Army of Northern Virginia to "the sword of the Lord and of Gideon."[8]

For a time Richmond focused her attention on every rumor of Lee's advance. However, Federal troops compelled the capital to narrow its vision and look to nearer fronts. While the Southern army marched through Maryland and into Pennsylvania, Union General John A. Dix threatened Richmond from the east. On June 28 the War Office learned that 25,000 Yankees were at Williamsburg and 5,000 more had landed at White House on the Pamunkey River.[9] Once again volunteer companies in Richmond took up arms. Two thousand government clerks and mechanics began drilling. George W. Randolph commanded the city council's latest attempt at creating effective militia force.[10] When only about three hundred men enlisted (besides the government employees), Governor Letcher called out the second class militia.[11] On July 2 the Federals were reported in New Kent County, eighteen miles from Richmond. The

[5] *Richmond Daily Whig*, May 29, 1863.
[6] See Alvin Arthur Fahrner, "The Public Career of William 'Extra Billy' Smith," Ph.D. Dissertation.
[7] See Douglas S. Freeman, *Lee's Lieutenants: A Study in Command*, II, 714 and n.
[8] *Dispatch*, June 22, 1863.
[9] Edward Younger, ed., *Inside the Confederate Government: The Diary of Robert Garlick Hill Kean, Head of the Bureau of War*, p. 77.
[10] Richmond City Council, Minutes, May 19, 1863.
[11] Younger, ed., *Diary of . . . Kean*, p. 77.

same day the city's volunteer troops marched out to support General D. H. Hill's regulars.[12]

Businesses closed in the capital. The Confederate Treasury and Post Offices, as well as ordnance shops, suspended operations. Provost marshals combed the city for stragglers and escorted every able-bodied man remaining in the city to Castle Thunder.[13] The *Whig* noted:

> Richmond shows her teeth. Her guardian, Robert E. Lee, having gone off with the boys on a little summer tour of Maryland and Pennsylvania, she has been forced to take care of herself. A party of Yankee rapscallions, hearing of her unprotected condition, have crept up to the White House [landing], with the intention of insulting and robbing her. They don't know the old lady. . . . We saw her when she went out—She looked very unlike the quiet and genteel dame whom we have known for some years past. . . . She looked glorious in her anger. In fact she looked dangerous.[14]

The assemblage of clerks, laborers, and officials marched eight miles east on Darbytown Road on Thursday the second. In the evening two of D. H. Hill's brigades repulsed three Yankee regiments below Bottoms Bridge over the Chickahominy. Then it appeared that the Bluecoats had slipped around to the north of the city. Reports placed the enemy in King William and Hanover counties. On Friday, July 3, Richmond's militia marched back toward the city and took up positions at Meadow Bridge about six miles north of the city limits. Next day the force moved to cover Brook Road. On Monday the sixth Richmond's militiamen returned to their normal occupations.[15] One of their number stated that their weekend campaign compared favorably with one of Stonewall Jackson's famous marches.[16] General Elzey, commander of the Department of Richmond, published a general order tendering his thanks for their efforts. He found no difference between these vol-

---

12 *Dispatch*, July 3, 4, 1863.
13 *Ibid.*, July 4, 1863; *Whig*, July 17, 1863.
14 *Whig*, July 6, 1863.
15 Younger, ed., *Diary of . . . Kean*, p. 78.
16 *Whig*, July 7, 1863.

unteers and the regulars.[17] The *Examiner* termed the volunteers and second class militia the "bulwarks" of Richmond's defense.[18]

Around midnight of July 7 Yankee cavalry swept down on Ashland, burned the railroad depot, and ripped up some track. After destroying some crops in King William County, the Federals withdrew down the peninsula.[19] But they did not cease their raids about the capital. Each threat, no matter how small, cost the Confederacy productive hours of the mechanic-soldiers. And the destroyed crops made winter that much harder. By August a company of "Silver Grays," men over fifty-five, were drilling in Richmond to guard the capital while the militia was away.[20]

On July 4, while Richmond's men guarded Meadow Bridge, an extra edition of the *Dispatch* announced that Lee was marching on Washington.[21] Three days later an extra of the *Sentinel* carried the headlines, "Important from Gettysburg, The Enemy Routed on Sunday, Forty Thousand Prisoners Captured."[22] The *Dispatch*, on July 7, told Richmonders that Johnston was in Grant's rear at Vicksburg, and that the city would surely be saved.[23] Then slowly Richmonders learned the worst. Lee was retreating. Perhaps he had not been beaten, but he was retreating. Vicksburg had surrendered. The Mississippi was a Yankee river, and Lee's invincible army had suffered a bloody repulse.

Richmond's reaction to the double disaster, Vicksburg and Gettysburg, took many forms and lasted several months. On July 14 the *Dispatch* still claimed a victory for Lee at Gettysburg.[24] Most Richmonders, however, sensed the significance of the defeat. A lady remembered, "Every countenance was overspread with gloom, and doubt took the place of hope."[25] Josiah Gorgas wrote in his diary,

[17] Department of Richmond, General Order No. 27, July 7, 1863, printed in *Enquirer*, July 10, 1863.
[18] *Richmond Daily Examiner*, July 6, 1863.
[19] Younger, ed., *Diary of . . . Kean*, p. 78; *Dispatch*, July 1–4, 6, 7, 1863.
[20] *Dispatch*, August 12, 1863.
[21] *Ibid.*, "Extra," July 4, 1863.
[22] *Richmond Sentinel*, "Extra," July 7, 1863.
[23] *Dispatch*, July 7, 1863.
[24] *Ibid.*, July 14, 1863.
[25] Sallie Brock Putnam, *Richmond during the War: Four Years of Personal Observation*, p. 242.

"yesterday we rode on the pinnacle of success—today absolute ruin seems to be our portion. The Confederacy totters to its destruction."[26] Gorgas later revived his hopes for the Confederacy, but he had not overstated. July, 1863, proved a turning point for the nation and its capital. Richmond had expended energy, resources, and life in the struggle for independence. Now spirit and flesh alike began to falter. The city's decline was gradual, and she rallied from time to time. But the military defeats of a single week had drained her confidence and accentuated her material weakness. From this point the capital was dying.

General Lee tendered his resignation to President Davis on July 8. The Virginian questioned the nation's confidence in his ability to lead one of its armies and offered to step aside gracefully. Davis rejected the offer.[27] No such courtesy occurred between the President and Joe Johnston, commander in the western theater. Davis had given Johnston authority over virtually all Confederate forces in the west;[28] and Vicksburg, it seemed, fell because Johnston sent no force to relieve its besieged garrison. Josiah Gorgas recorded an exchange with the President: "When I said that Vicksburg fell, apparently, from want of provisions, he remarked: 'Yes, from want of provisions inside, and a general outside who wouldn't fight.' "[29] Johnston blamed John C. Pemberton, commander of Vicksburg's garrison. Closing a twenty-five–page report Johnston wrote, "in his short campaign General Pemberton made not a single movement in

[26] Frank E. Vandiver, ed., *The Civil War Diary of General Josiah Gorgas*, p. 55.
[27] Varina Howell Davis, *Jefferson Davis, Ex-President of the Confederate States of America: A Memoir by His Wife* I, 393–399.
[28] Johnston did not grasp the advantages of his enlarged command, and he failed to see how he could coordinate dispersed forces directly commanded by other generals. (See Vandiver, "Jefferson Davis and Confederate Strategy.") Also, Johnston was a bit jealous of Lee. In March he had written to Senator Wigfall of Texas: "I am told that the President and Secretary of War think that they have given me the highest military position in the Confederacy, that I have full military power in all this western country. . . . If they so regard it, ought not our highest military officer to occupy it? It seems so to me that principle would bring Lee here. I might then, with great propriety, be replaced in my old command." Joseph E. Johnston to Louis T. Wigfall, March 8, 1863, Louis T. Wigfall Papers.
[29] Vandiver, ed., *Diary of . . . Gorgas*, p. 50.

obedience to my orders, and regarded none of my instructions; and finally did not embrace the only opportunity to save his army— that given by my order to abandon Vicksburg."[30] Johnston, Davis, and Pemberton kept the controversy alive throughout the winter. Mrs. Chesnut wrote of Johnston, "His hatred of Jeff Davis amounts to a religion. . . . Being such a good hater, it is a pity he had not elected to hate somebody else than the President of our country."[31]

Nor was all the carping confined to the military. Reverses in the field seemed to open the way for quarreling and dissidence at the capital. The fall elections of 1863 strengthened opposition in Congress to the Davis administration.[32] Mrs. Chesnut wrote of Texas Senator Louis T. Wigfall, a former friend of the President, "Wigfall was here last night. He began by wanting to hang Jeff Davis."[33] Virginia's R. M. T. Hunter also turned against the President. While visiting the executive mansion on business one December day, Hunter was forced to listen to a tirade by Davis against Virginia and Virginians. The senator left in a rage without even mentioning the purpose of his visit.[34] Although Confederate politics never developed an actual opposition party, the congressional hostility of men like Hunter and Wigfall damaged the Davis administration more than a rival political organization. Lacking the unity and leadership of party, Davis's opponents could never be a "loyal opposition."

While the Congress, the President, and the generals wrangled, confidence in the civil authority waned. As early as April, 1863, South Carolina politician James H. Hammond expressed a significant sentiment when he wrote Hunter regarding Congress, "Some malign influence seems to preside over your councils. Pardon me, is the majority always drunk? The People are beginning to think

[30] Joseph E. Johnston to General S. Cooper, November 1, 1863, Louis T. Wigfall Papers.

[31] Mary Boykin Chesnut, *A Diary from Dixie*, ed. Ben Ames Williams, p. 317.

[32] See Wilfred B. Yearns, *The Confederate Congress*, pp. 49–59.

[33] Chesnut, *Diary from Dixie*, p. 229.

[34] Younger, ed., *Diary of . . . Kean*, p. 127.

so."[35] For a time Richmonders had crowded the galleries in the Capitol's legislative halls.[36] They came to see the nation's great men debate key issues. But now whenever a crucial debate ensued, the legislators invoked the privilege of secrecy and barred the doors. In the House of Representatives visitors often heard, not the reasonable debate of learned men, but the shrill invective of Henry S. Foote. One Georgia congressman wrote his wife during one of Foote's lengthy fulminations: "Governor Foote of Tenn. is now speaking on the currency bill, and is rather *poking* Perkins [John Perkins, Jr., of Louisiana] in the ribs. Foote does not pretend to argue the merits of the bill; but is simply replying to and criticising the remarks of others."[37] A Richmond lady who admired the Tennessean's audacity, if not his statemanship, recalled: "It was amusing to watch the shade of angry resignation that would steal over the faces of the members, and of vexation that would mantle the brows of visitors to the hall of the House of Representatives, when, upon almost every bill introduced, they were condemned to listen to the ever ready tirade of invective that seemed always to pour from the lips of this remarkable man. . . . his speeches, which might have been spirited and interesting, were usually quarrelsome and disgusting."[38]

Many legislators seemed to transfer their contrariness in the United States Congress to its Confederate counterpart. Even so, the Confederate Congress did much constructive work for the Cause. Unfortunately, some of its soundest legislation violated the popular sacred cow of state rights. And residents of the capital saw first-hand the pettiness which often prevailed in their national councils.

During the summer and fall of 1863 Richmond's press divided

[35] James Henry Hammond to R. M. T. Hunter, April 9, 1863, Hunter Papers, quoted in Clement Eaton, *A History of the Southern Confederacy*, p. 63.

[36] Virginia General Assembly, *Acts of the General Assembly of the State of Virginia Passed in 1861–62, in the Eighty-sixth Year of the Commonwealth*, chap. 90.

[37] Bell I. Wiley, ed., *The Letters of Warren Akin, Confederate Congressman*, p. 41.

[38] Putnam, *Richmond during the War*, p. 173.

sharply on the government's conduct of the war. The *Sentinel* and the *Enquirer* became veritable bulwarks of the Davis administration though both papers denied being administration organs. Said the *Sentinel*'s editor, "We support the Administration because duty demands—not because we have received, or hoped for, its favors."[39] In July the *Sentinel* said of the anti-Davis press: "These critics include the one or two really bad, treasonable sheets in our Confederacy, and other journals that have surrendered themselves to personal prejudices, and to the sentiment of opposition to the Administration."[40] In the same issue the editor wrote in defense of Davis:

President Davis is devoting himself to the affairs of the country with a zeal and devotion that almost wear out his physical frame, and keep his health ever in a delicate condition. . . . He asks no one to pay better obedience to the laws than he pays himself. He sets us the example in this of a good citizen and a faithful officer. And while thus keeping within the limits of his official powers, he conducts our affairs with a transcendent ability, and fills his high station with honor to himself and to his country. Let us encourage him with our sympathies and sustain him with our generous support! This, we are sure, is the sentiment of the *people*; and it is just, and right, and wise, and politic.[41]

The *Dispatch* usually maintained a benign neutrality on issues touching the government. The paper occasionally criticized the administration, but amid the disillusion which followed Gettysburg and Vicksburg, the *Dispatch* concentrated its venom on Yankees abroad and "croakers" at home.[42] The *Whig* and *Examiner* remained outspoken critics of Davis's policies. These papers accused the President and his administration of despotism at home, sloth in the field, and favoritism in appointments.[43] If popular approval of an editorial policy had an effect on circulation, it was significant that the *Dispatch*, moderate in her views of the administration, led her four competitors in numbers of copies sold.

[39] *Sentinel*, September 21, 1863.
[40] *Ibid.*, July 21, 1863.
[41] *Ibid.*
[42] *Dispatch*, July 16, 1863.
[43] For example, see *Examiner*, October 7, 1863; and *Whig*, May 30, 1863.

When Jefferson Davis returned from his first major tour of the western Confederacy in January, 1863, Richmond greeted him with a brass band. In November, 1863, the President came back from a second tour very quietly. Not even the newspapers knew exactly when he had returned.[44] While politicians and press lauded or abused Davis, the ordinary Richmonder seemed to ignore him. Citizens in the capital had long since looked to Lee's army for national salvation, and in 1863 the carping and lack of vision among the officials in Richmond confirmed that view. Devotion to the Cause and its defenders transcended the seeming dearth of political leadership. Military adversity in 1863 drew most Richmonders together—behind the war effort, if not the war government.

Rather than criticizing their government, the majority of Richmonders transferred their anger to the enemy. The tide of Federal victories in 1863 created intense bitterness on the home front. The *Sentinel* expressed amazement that the Yankees in Libby Prison were actually praying.[45] A hospital matron wrote her sister in September: "The feeling here against the Yankees exceeds anything I could imagine, particularly among the good Christians. I spent an evening among a particularly pious set. One lady said she had a pile of Yankee bones lying around her pump so that the first glance on opening her eyes would rest upon them. Another begged me to get her a Yankee skull to keep her toilette trinkets in. All had something of this kind to say."[46] Among Richmond's children the epithet "Yankee" became an invitation to violence. One youngster regularly called ticks, "Yankees." And a little girl would not play

---

[44] *Whig*, November 9, 1863.

[45] *Sentinel*, July 29, 1863.

[46] Bell I. Wiley, ed., *A Southern Woman's Story: Life in Confederate Richmond by Phoebe Yates Pember including Unpublished Letters Written from the Chimborazo Hospital*, p. 168. In contrast to the bitterness on the home front, Confederate soldiers seemed to share a mutual respect with their enemies. According to Mrs. Pember this good nature lasted until the Federals employed Negro troops in the summer of 1864, and attempted to break Southern lines by tunneling beneath them and exploding a charge of powder. "In no instance up to a certain period did I hear of any remark that savored of personal hatred."

with her doll, because she feared the toy's hair might be from a Yankee.[47]

Amid the personal and national trials of 1863 a fervid religious revival swept through Richmond and its army.[48] Reacting to temporal circumstance and material hardship, the Confederates sought divine justification. During July and August an intense revival brought hundreds into Richmond's Negro churches.[49] That fall, Clay Street Methodist, Centenary Methodist, Grace Street Baptist, and Trinity Methodist held large revival meetings. Between September, 1863, and September, 1864, First Baptist Church gained 147 new members.[50]

During the winter of 1863 and 1864 even the staunchest patriot needed reassurance that God sided with the South. Throughout the fall, Lee, straining to rebuild his shattered army, feared for Richmond's safety. The general wrote President Davis in September that Colonel Gorgas "should commence at once to enlarge his manufacturing arsenals, etc., in the interior, so that if Richmond should fall we would not be destitute."[51] Toward the end of October Lee touched another somber chord in a letter to Secretary of War Seddon. Pointing out that Richmond was quite unsuitable for impounding prisoners, Lee explained, "Our capital is the great point of attack of the enemy in the eastern portion of the Confederacy, and the emergency might arise in which it would be exceedingly inconvenient to have Federal prisoners within its limits."[52] Lee's fears were unfounded. Despite the absence of direct Union pressure, however, that winter of 1863–1864 proved the war's hardest.

Richmond's supply problems began during the summer. On June

[47] Putnam, *Richmond during the War*, pp. 102–104.
[48] For the religious awakening in the army see John Shepard, Jr., "Religion in the Army of Northern Virginia," *North Carolina Historical Review* 25 (July, 1948): 341–376.
[49] *Dispatch*, July 17, 1863.
[50] *Sentinel*, October 23, 24, 27, November 3, 1863; *Whig*, December 14, 1863; Blanche Sydnor White, *First Baptist Church, Richmond, 1780–1955, One Hundred and Seventy-five Years of Service to God and Man*, p. 240.
[51] R. E. Lee to Jefferson Davis, September 11, 1863, Clifford Dowdy, ed., *The Wartime Papers of R. E. Lee*, p. 599.
[52] R. E. Lee to James A. Seddon, October 28, 1863, Dowdey, ed., *Wartime Papers*, p. 617.

1 Josiah Gorgas recorded in his diary, "The weather is very fine, but unless we can have rain soon our crops will suffer sadly, and without good crops what will become of us?"[53] In mid-July he wrote, "The weather is disheartening, for three or four weeks it has rained constantly. All the crops in this part of the country will be lost—a sad loss to us."[54] By the end of July Gorgas had counted about forty-five days of rain within the last fifty days.[55]

The miserable growing season kept many crops from ripening. And the desolation of war destroyed many yields before the harvest. In October the *Examiner* termed the countryside between the Potomac and the Rapidan rivers a desert.[56] Rival armies had lived in, and off, this land for three summers. Yankee raids like that in early July had compounded the destruction of food. Southern stragglers and brigands wearing Confederate uniforms performed depredations greater than the Federals.[57] Those farmers who were able to produce were quick to take advantage of the general scarcity in Richmond. One enterprising agriculturist, for example, realized a profit of $52.65 from the sale in the capital of a single cartload of ducks, chickens, and eggs.[58] In August the *Dispatch* proposed establishing a cavalry company to protect the fields in neighboring counties from marauders, Northern and Southern.[59] In Richmond much attention focused on such a contrasting event as the serving of the granddaddy of all turtles in Congress Hall by Jim Cook, a popular chef and julep-maker.[60] Refugees like Mrs. McGuire consoled themselves with stories of their forefathers' greater hardship in that other war for independence.[61] But in the markets the cheapest grade of flour advanced in price from $32 per barrel in June, to $42 per barrel in August.[62] On October 30 the *Dispatch*

[53] Vandiver, ed., *Diary of . . . Gorgas*, p. 42.
[54] *Ibid.*, p. 50.
[55] *Ibid.*, p. 56.
[56] *Examiner*, October 30, 1863.
[57] *Dispatch*, July 18, 1863.
[58] Jacqueline Taliaferro Papers.
[59] *Ibid.*, August 4, 1863.
[60] *Whig*, August 15, 1863; *Sentinel*, August 14, 1863.
[61] Judith W. McGuire, *Diary of a Southern Refugee, during the War*, p. 242.
[62] *Dispatch*, June 27, September 1, 1863.

reported no flour at all in the markets or mills. An occasional available barrel brought $65 to $75.[63] The *Whig* on October 30 blamed a breakdown in distribution facilities for the grim prospects: "It is useless to mince words: it were folly to remain silent, when we see every day evidences of an approaching *bread famine* in this city, whilst within the limits of the state, it is believed, there is food enough for all the people for twelve months. The population of Richmond cannot live upon air, and whilst the majority would be willing, we are sure, to subsist on half rations of bread, there is, at present, no prospect of obtaining this much during the winter."[64] The *Whig*, as early as August, had impressed upon its readers the advantage of leaving Richmond and going to the country.[65]

Given ample warning of the coming winter's severity, Richmond's city council prepared to meet the crisis. Between July 13, 1863, and April 11, 1864, the council appropriated over $150,000 for relief of the poor.[66] Within the same period, the municipal authorities raised city salaries twice, so that a city watchman's pay, for example, jumped from $4 per night to $6.25.[67] On October 15 the Committee on Supply recommended that the city enter the food business on a large scale. The council appointed a Board of Supplies to secure food in the country, arrange for transportation into the city, and establish warehouse depots for distribution.[68] By the first of November, the council had an agent combing the central and western Virginia countryside for food. Assurances were received from the Secretary of War that army impressment agents would not interfere with the collection of food for Richmond.[69] The first floor of Dunlop, Moncure and Company's warehouse was fitted out for a storage and distribution point.[70]

[63] *Ibid.*, October 30, 1863.
[64] *Whig*, October 30, 1863.
[65] *Ibid.*, August 12, 1863.
[66] City Council, Minutes, July 13, August 10, September 22, October 15, December 14, 1863, March 20, April 11, 1864.
[67] *Ibid.*, July 20, November 9, 1863, March 9, 1864.
[68] *Ibid.*, October 15, 1863.
[69] *Whig*, October 30, 1863.
[70] *Ibid.*, October 29, 1863.

In spite of these energetic preparations, the council's Board of Supplies failed to secure adequate provisions. Alexander Garret, the city's agent, found little for sale in rural Virginia.[71] With the aid of the YMCA, the council's supply store accommodated around one thousand families until the end of January, when the public supply ran low.[72] Although the board withheld some salted meat until spring,[73] the leanest season of the year, its program never fulfilled the council's ambitious hopes. There simply was not sufficient food in the state.[74] The chief of the Bureau of War recorded in his diary:

> The Commissary General of Subsistence [Northrop] was at the Secretary's office this morning before 10 o'clock urging him to retract the license to the city council to purchase for the city warehouse provisions to be retailed to the destitute. The Secretary declined and went out. Colonel Northrop then came to me and asked me to urge the thing on the Secretary. I told him I did not agree with him, that I thought it of very great importance that the city should be fed. He said very earnestly that the alternative was between the *people* and the army, that there is perhaps *bread* enough for both but not *meat* enough, and that we had to elect between the *army* and the *people* doing without.[75]

In accord with Northrop's prediction both city and army suffered a meat panic in January, 1864. Beef brought $1.25 per pound, and poultry $1.50–$1.75.[76] The *Examiner* called the frantic commissary general a "distinguished vegetarian" and declined further comment.[77]

The Virginia General Assembly did its part to prepare for winter's worst. The legislature passed an act in October requiring railroad companies to transport immediately all fuel shipments of

[71] *Ibid.*, October 30, 31, 1863, January 11, 1864.

[72] *Sentinel*, January 13, 23, 1864.

[73] *Whig*, January 13, 1864.

[74] The *Whig* noted that the agent for Petersburg was having some success in North Carolina (October 31, 1863). The agent for the Tredegar Iron Works covered many states in search of food supplies.

[75] Younger, ed., *Diary of . . . Kean*, p. 116.

[76] *Dispatch*, January 8, 1864.

[77] *Examiner*, January 19, 1864.

more than eight cords of wood or eight tons of coal to cities and
towns in the state.[78] The assembly also outlawed all "unnecessary
consumption of grain by distillers and other manufacturers of
spiritous and malt liquors." Not even a contract with the Confederate government provided a legal excuse for brewing or distilling.[79]

Throughout the fall of 1863 the legislators debated a state-wide
price-fixing bill. Many Richmonders remembered General Winder's fiasco in the spring of 1862 and became greatly alarmed. The
Enquirer stated: "It is beautiful in theory to talk of adjusting
prices, of making all things square by the schedule; but when the
Legislature has got its law fairly under way, the empty market
houses of the cities and towns may present an awful commentary
upon the wisdom of its action."[80] The proposed law provided for a
periodic review and adjustment of food prices. "But," wrote one
observer, "they have pretty well settled on the policy of making
little change as the currency declines. Flour they put at $22.50 to
$28 according to quality. When it is selling on the street here for
$40 . . . Production and movement will be so cut off and curtailed
that there will be great danger of famine here."[81]

While the legislators debated, Richmond divided on the merits
of the expedient. The *Enquirer* and *Dispatch* opposed price fixing
as fervently as the *Sentinel* supported it.[82] A workingman's mass
meeting on September 18 urged the general assembly to adopt
stringent laws respecting the market places.[83] Because State Senator
George W. Randolph declared that he would vote against the price-
fixing bill, unless otherwise instructed by his constituents, the
workers convened again on October 10.[84] A very large crowd filled
City Hall and adopted resolutions in favor of the proposed legislation. Resolution number seven evidenced real awareness of class

[78] Virginia General Assembly, *Acts of the General Assembly of the State of
Virginia . . . Called Session, 1863 . . .* , chap. 33.
[79] *Ibid.*, chap. 35.
[80] *Enquirer*, October 7, 1863.
[81] Younger, ed., *Diary of . . . Kean*, pp. 107–108.
[82] *Enquirer*, October 1, 1863; *Dispatch*, October 9, 1863; *Sentinel*, September
30, 1863.
[83] *Whig*, September 21, 1863.
[84] *Dispatch*, October 12, 1863.

among Richmond's laborers: "That as free men we do abhor and detest the idea that the rich must take care of the poor, because we know that without labor and production the man with his money could not exist, from the fact that he consumes all and produces nothing: and that such a dependence would tend to degrade rather than elevate the human race."[85] Property owners, along with the *Enquirer*, feared mob violence and called the workers "candidates for the penitentiary."[86] At this juncture, however, the city council conducted a poll of the electorate on October 22.[87] Richmond's voters overwhelmingly rejected the proposition.[88] Ultimately the General Assembly also rejected the expedient, and Richmond's markets, for better or worse, remained free of state control.

Rapid inflation of Confederate currency added to the burdens of salaried people in the capital. In August, clerks in the Post Office threatened to strike for an increase in their $700 to $800 annual salary.[89] One government official noted gloomily in October: "The wages of a journeyman saddler are from $10 to $12 per day, more by 30% than the salary of a head of bureau or assistant secretary in one of the departments. There is already great suffering among the clerks who get $1500. Those who have families are reduced to the most desperate straits; yet Congress is afraid to increase salaries."[90] Finally in late January the Confederate Congress recognized the special hardship imposed upon the government's civil servants in the capital. In Richmond all government salaries below two thousand dollars were increased 100 per cent; all between two and three thousand were raised 50 per cent.[91]

Secretary of the Treasury Memminger tried to help his foundering currency. Beginning in the fall of 1863, he argued for a repudiation of one-third of the issue. Memminger hoped to remove inflated paper from circulation and restore value to the remaining

---

[85] *Sentinel*, October 12, 1863.
[86] Quoted in the *Sentinel*, October 22, 1863.
[87] City Council, Minutes, October 19, 1863.
[88] The division was 867 to 296. *Whig*, October 23, 1863.
[89] Younger, ed., *Diary of . . . Kean*, p. 98.
[90] *Ibid.*, p. 108.
[91] James M. Matthews, ed., *Statutes at Large of the Confederate States of America*, 1st cong., 3d sess., chap. 16.

currency. However, his repudiation proposals, even long before they were enacted, greatly damaged public confidence and accelerated the inflationary spiral.[92] Richmond bankers met in September and agreed to take all Confederate notes at face value.[93] But such examples of financial confidence were rare.

Somehow the city survived. At Christmas the *Sentinel* calculated that one gallon of eggnog cost a minimum of $100. The *Whig* was more lugubrious:

Christmas

Old Style

Christmas cakes and English beer, Christmas comes but once a year.

New Style

Bald-faced whiskey, sour beer—Christmas, will it come next year?[94]

A good dinner for one resident of the capital consisted of "a piece of fat shoulder Capt. Warner let me have at $1 per pound—it is selling for $2.50—and cabbage from my garden, which my neighbor's cow overlooked when she broke through the gate last Sunday."[95] Mrs. McGuire struggled through an arithmetic examination and secured a job in Colonel Northrop's office. She also made canvas shoes at home to supplement her husband's salary.[96] By January, 1864, flour brought $125 per barrel, and corn meal $15 per bushel in Richmond's markets,[97] and many Richmonders went hungry.

In spite of scarcity, impressment, and inflation the capital carried on. She even found sardonic humor in her privation. War clerk Jones was grimly optimistic. "We look for a healthy year," he

---

[92] For a more complete coverage of this gloomy aspect of the Confederate statecraft see John C. Schwab, "Prices in the Confederate States, 1861-65," *Political Science Quarterly* 14 (June, 1899): 281-304; Richard C. Todd, *Confederate Finance*; and Henry D. Capers, *Life and Times of Christopher G. Memminger*.

[93] *Dispatch*, September 17, 1863.

[94] *Whig*, December 30, 1863; *Sentinel*, December 28, 1863.

[95] J. B. Jones, *A Rebel War Clerk's Diary at the Confederate States Capital*, ed. Howard Swiggett, II, 78-79.

[96] McGuire, *Diary of a Southern Refugee*, pp. 244-251.

[97] *Dispatch*, January 8, 1864.

wrote, "everything being so cleanly consumed that no garbage or filth can accumulate. We are all good scavengers now, and there is no need of buzzards in the streets."[98] Mrs. Chesnut repeated a standard remark about inflated currency: "You take your money to market in a market basket, and bring home what you buy in your pocketbook."[99]

During 1863 the *Southern Punch* began publication in Richmond.[100] Claiming to be a legitimate son of the *London Punch*, the periodical lampooned any and all in the capital. *Punch*'s "Hospital Catechism" defined as the duties of a military surgeon, "to physic soldiers according to the rules of defunct writers" and "to cut, slash, and saw off as many arms and legs as possible in one day."[101] "Judge Punch" was particularly severe with Mr. Hardflint, who was accused of charging Mr. Ref. Eugee $100 monthly rent.[102]

Unhappily the *Southern Punch* adopted the common practice of blaming Richmond's high prices and scarcity on the city's Jews. The magazine proposed a new name for the capital, "Jew-rue-sell-'em," and it spoke of the Jews as "Richmond Yankees."[103] Some of the anti-Semitic feelings in Richmond even transcended color and class, for on September 18, 1863, three boys—a white, a free black, and a slave—were arrested for throwing rocks through the windows of a synagogue.[104] In reality Richmond's small but influential Jewish community served the Southern Cause well. Jewish soldiers in the Army of Northern Virginia numbered 110.[105] In February the *Dispatch* stated: "We are thoroughly disgusted, in this era of universal speculation and extortion, with the slang of 'Jew, Jew,' a cry akin to that of the practiced pickpocket, when he joins the hue and cry of 'Stop Thief,' to divert attention from himself."[106]

[98] Jones, *Rebel War Clerk's Diary*, II, 156.
[99] Chesnut, *Diary from Dixie*, p. 368.
[100] The *Southern Punch* first appeared on August 15, 1863. The Confederate Museum in Richmond has a good file of this periodical.
[101] *Southern Punch*, August 29, 1863.
[102] *Ibid.*, October 10, 1863.
[103] *Ibid.*
[104] *Examiner*, September 19, 1863.
[105] Herbert T. Ezekiel and Gaston Lichtenstein, *The History of the Jews of Richmond from 1769 to 1917*, pp. 176–188.
[106] *Dispatch*, February 6, 1864.

The paper also pointed out that Richmond's Jewish businessmen were for the most part jewelers and dry-goods merchants. Extortioners or no, at least they had no part in the high cost of food and shelter.[107]

In February the *Whig* surveyed Richmond's social activity, which seemed to thrive even in the midst of privation.

> One of the least hopeful "signs of the times" is the prevailing mania for parties and frivolity in this city. There has never been a gayer winter in Richmond. Balls and parties every night! One night last week there were *seven parties*. . . . Go on, good people. It is better to be merry than sad. The wolf is far away from your doors, and it signifieth nothing to you that thousands of our heroic soldiers are shoeless and comfortless; or that a multitude of mothers, wives, and children of the gallant defenders of our country's rights are sorely pinched by hunger and want—aye, starving, or dying from broken hearts.[108]

Mrs. Chesnut answered a similar comment, "I do not see how sadness and despondency would help us. If it would do any good, we could be sad enough."[109]

Mrs. Chesnut recorded perhaps the most revealing illustration of social contrasts when she described visiting the capital's two "first ladies." Mrs. Lee arrived in Richmond during the peninsula campaign while Mrs. Davis was in North Carolina.[110] Richmond's city council had appropriated $60,000 to buy a house and lot for the Lees, but the general had declined the council's offer.[111] Mrs. Lee was living on Franklin Street when Mrs. Chesnut paid her respects.

> Her room was like an industrial school, with everybody so busy. Her daughters were all there, plying their needles, and also several other ladies. When we came out, I said: "Did you see how the Lees spend their time? What a rebuke to the taffy parties."[112]

[107] *Ibid.*
[108] *Whig*, February 10, 1864.
[109] Chesnut, *Diary from Dixie*, p. 357.
[110] Jefferson Davis to Varina Howell Davis, June 13, 1863, Dunbar Rowland, ed., *Jefferson Davis, Constitutionalist: His Letters, Papers, and Speeches*, V, 277–278.
[111] City Council, Minutes, November 9, 1863.
[112] Chesnut, *Diary from Dixie*, p. 385.

[In January:]

Mrs. Davis gave her "Luncheon for Ladies" on Saturday. Many more persons were there than at any of those luncheons which have gone before. We had gumbo, ducks and olives, lettuce salad, chocolate cream, jelly cake, claret cup, champagne, etc.[113]

In early January it seemed that the entire city entertained General John H. Morgan. The Southern cavalry commander had recently escaped from a Yankee prison, and Richmond honored him with an official reception. For days Morgan and his Kentuckians were the toast of the capital.[114] Later in the month, President and Mrs. Davis began holding weekly receptions on Tuesdays, and Virginia's new governor, William Smith, entertained officially every Friday night.[115] A guest of the Davises wrote: "President and Mrs. Davis gave a large reception last week, and all the ladies looked positively gorgeous. . . . We should not expect suppers in these times, but we do have them! Champagne is $350 a dozen, but we sometimes have champagne! The confectioners charge $15 for a cake, but we have cake!"[116]

Most Richmonders settled for less lavish entertainment. "Starvation parties" were quite popular among visiting soldiers and their belles. Musicians were the only expense at these gatherings. The guests danced, and laughed, and quenched their thirsts from a large pitcher of vintage 1864 James River.[117] The Mosaic Club united Richmond's literary and musical talent. The group provided music for charitable functions, and at impromptu gatherings the members entertained each other with essays, poems, songs, and

[113] *Ibid.*, pp. 366–367.

[114] *Ibid.*, p. 355; City Council, Minutes, December 31, 1863; *Whig*, January 9, 1864.

[115] *Sentinel*, January 18, 1863; *Whig*, January 11, 1864.

[116] "Agnes" to Mrs. Pryor, January 30, 1864, Mrs. Roger A. Pryor, *Reminiscences of Peace and War*, pp. 263–264.

[117] Putnam, *Richmond during the War*, p. 270. A member of the Washington Artillery wrote of the attractions of Richmond, "I don't believe there ever were so many pretty girls to the square inch as there are now in Richmond; it is remarkable" (William Miller Owen, *In Camp and Battle with the Washington Artillery of New Orleans: A Narrative of Events During the Late Civil War From Bull Run to Appomatox and Spanish Fort*, p. 295).

spontaneous wit.[118] As Mrs. Chesnut exclaimed, "There is life in the old land yet!"[119]

Richmond's troubles seemed always to increase with the coming of spring. In 1862 McClellan had threatened. Stoneman's raid, the bread riot, and Jackson's death had rocked the capital in 1863. And as the difficult winter of 1863–1864 waned, the city's security again became imperiled.

General Winder's problems had started to increase the previous fall. As commander of the Department of Henrico he had appointed as one of his new detectives, Augustus Simcoe, a native of Norfolk, who was, according to the *Sentinel*, "spoken of as being well fitted for the position."[120] But in October Simcoe disturbed the peace of a house of ill fame. When the proprietor accused the detective of being a rowdy, he shot her. The spectacle of a wounded madam shouting deserved insults at Simcoe in a Richmond courtroom did little to increase confidence in Winder's administration. The *Whig*, however, found nothing unusual in the event. "This circumstance excites no surprise in Richmond, where it has long been understood that detectives are, in not a few cases, not only *habitués* of bawdy and gambling houses, but the allies of the keepers of such establishments."[121]

In December another Winder appointment, Captain Alexander of Castle Thunder, was arrested for malfeasance in office.[122] Perhaps the crowning blow to confidence in Winder had occurred on the night of November 18. General John Winder, charged with protecting life, law, and property in Richmond suffered the supreme humiliation. A gang of thieves burglarized his home.[123]

In January and February Richmond's chronic problem of cap-

---

[118] T. C. DeLeon, *Belles, Beaux, and Brains of the 60's*, pp. 201–210.
[119] Chesnut, *Diary from Dixie*, p. 341.
[120] *Sentinel*, August 17, 1863.
[121] *Whig*, October 8, 1863.
[122] *Whig*, December 18, 1863. See Confederate States of America, Congress, House, *Evidence Taken before the Committee of the House of Representatives to Enquire into the Treatment of Prisoners at Castle Thunder*, for the disclosures leading to Alexander's arrest.
[123] *Whig*, November 21, 1863.

tive population—Yankee and slave—reached crisis proportions. By 1864 Richmond was the headquarters of a ring of "Negro runners," who charged $200 to $300 for smuggling slaves through the lines to the North.[124] As President Davis was only too well aware, the city's slave population represented potentially dangerous allies of the enemy. In February, in a message to Congress advocating suspension of habeas corpus in Richmond, he wrote:

I have satisfactory reasons for believing that spies are continually coming and going in our midst. . . . Yet however accurate and reliable such information might be, it was not competent testimony; and it was idle to arrest them only to be discharged by the civil authorities. . . . Apprehensions have more than once been entertained of a servile insurrection in Richmond. The Northern papers inform us that Butler [General Benjamin F.] is perfecting some deep-laid scheme to punish us for our refusal to hold intercourse with him. If, as is not improbable, his designs should point to servile insurrection in Richmond, incendiarism, and the destruction of public works so necessary to our defense, and so impossible to be replaced, how can we hope to fathom it and reach the guilty emissaries and contrivers but by incompetent negro testimony?[125]

Jefferson Davis had always had trouble keeping his servants. He blamed Federal bribes for the frequent runaways. Two more decamped on January 8. Then on the night of January 19, one of Davis's Negroes attempted to burn the President's home. Occupants of the executive mansion discovered the fire in time and confined it to a basement room.[126] When Mrs. Chesnut visited two days later, she found, "It was sad enough. Fancy having to be always ready to have your servants set your house on fire, to know they are

124 See *Dispatch*, March 10, 1864, and Bell I. Wiley, *Southern Negroes, 1861–1865*, p. 10.
125 James D. Richardson, ed., *A Compilation of the Messages and Papers of the Confederacy including the Diplomatic Correspondence*, I, 397–398.
126 One resident recalled, "We were compelled to keep up a rigid practice of barring and bolting and locking; yet all precautions proved ineffectual to prevent the thievish depredations of the negroes, demoralized by the various contending influences which served to develop such propensities in them" (Putnam, *Richmond during the War*, p. 266). See also, Chesnut, *Diary from Dixie*, p. 354; *Whig*, January 22, 1864.

bribed to do it. Such constant robberies, servants coming and going daily to the Yankees, carrying over silver, etc., does not conduce to make home happy."[127]

Black Richmonders, free and slave, were indeed more restive. The previous summer Richmond's city council had passed an ordinance forbidding free blacks to enter the city for any purpose except to trade in the market, without a certificate of good behavior from someone who knew them.[128] In the fall the council had amended the ordinance concerning Negroes to deny slaves the right of operating any business or of selling anything on the streets.[129]

The irony of the fears and repressive action of white Richmonders lay in that fact that black Richmonders rendered invaluable service to the Cause. Free and bonded blacks worked in war industries, replaced white labor at the municipal gas works, nursed wounded soldiers in Richmond's hospitals, and dug everything from trenches to graves.[130]

A classic example of how the city "used" her black population occurred in August, 1864. White gravediggers struck for higher wages and walked off the job in Shockoe Cemetery. The municipal authorities promptly replaced the white laborers with blacks. Whereupon the whites returned, beat up the blacks, and resumed their toil. The blacks, then, on the same day had been "scabs" and "whipping-boys" for the city.[131] In the end, no doubt, the white gravediggers blamed their black replacements for the entire incident.

It seemed that as the Confederate capital's military fortunes worsened, black Richmonders assumed more and more of the burdens of sustaining a cause which kept them in bondage. Only when

[127] Chesnut, *Diary from Dixie*, p. 363.

[128] City Council, Minutes, July 13, 1863 (Ordinance printed in Louis Manarin, ed., *Richmond at War: The Minutes of the City Council 1861–1865*, p. 349).

[129] City Council, Minutes, October 10, 1863 (Ordinance printed in Manarin, ed., *Richmond at War*, p. 519).

[130] City Council, Minutes, March 10, 1861, October 23, 1862. A list of nurses at Winder Hospital reveals that about one-half were blacks (Kate Mason Rowland Papers).

[131] *Examiner*, August 5, 1864.

the Confederacy required the ultimate sacrifice of the blacks—that
of actively fighting for the Cause—did any significant percentage
of Southern leaders recognize that, should the Confederacy become
independent, her social mores would have to change.

For months Yankee officers had picked away at the clay under
Libby Prison. Starting from a basement storeroom they had hewn
a tunnel to freedom. Using spoons as shovels and secreting the dirt
under a pile of straw, the resourceful inmates extended the shaft to
a vacant lot across the street from their prison. During the early
morning of February 10, a Federal prisoner of war emerged from
the ground. After he looked for sentinels, 108 other prisoners followed him into the streets of Richmond. Wholesale escape![132]

The *Whig* termed the group of escapees a "large odiferous rat"
but joined many Richmonders in praise of the prisoners' ingenu-
ity.[133] Five days later Confederate soldiers, unarmed boys and a
Negro brandishing a hoe had recaptured forty-three of the Federals.[134] Security precautions increased to such a degree that in
March an overzealous sentinel shot and killed one of his fellows, as
the unfortunate soldier peered from a window at Castle Thunder.[135]

Major prison escapes and possible servile insurrections constituted genuine threats to the capital's security. But the designs of
the Federal troops were infinitely more alarming. Late in February the city learned that a force of Yankees had penetrated Lee's
lines. The *Whig* confidently explained on March 1: "The movement, as far as we can learn, is confined to the enemy's cavalry
and artillery, and the object is believed to be merely a raid to cut
our communication by the Central [Rail] Road, the column moving by way of Charlottesville diverting attention in favor of one
moving on Frederick Hall. The enemy will hardly remain long
enough to do much damage, and it is hardly probable they will

---

132 *Whig*, February 11, 1864. The best account of the escape is in Captain I.
N. Johnston, *Four Months in Libby and the Campaign against Atlanta*, pp. 46–
112.
133 *Whig*, February 12, 1864.
134 *Ibid.*, February 15, 1864.
135 *Ibid.*, March 2, 1864.

make their escape as easily as they came in."[136] In Richmond people scarcely had time to read the *Whig*'s account before the Federals contradicted it. Early that raw March afternoon Yankee cavalry appeared on the Brooke Turnpike. General Judson Kilpatrick's three thousand veteran troopers appeared poised to dash into the capital. Alarm bells sounded. Local defense companies manned the capital's defenses and answered the Union fire. What was the Yankee commander waiting for? Just as a major charge seemed imminent, the Federal force withdrew.[137]

The capital did not have long to ponder the Union strategy. Later the same afternoon a smaller column of Yankees advanced on the city from the west. The Westham Plank Road became filled with excited farmers fleeing before the Federal cavalry. Rain and sleet muffled the sound of the muskets as the Yankees came on. Finally in the early darkness the Armory Battalion, reinforced with clerks and boys, halted the enemy two-and-a-half miles from the city. The concentrated fire of mechanics, old men, and furloughed officers was enough to convince the weary Bluecoats that a regular Confederate force guarded the capital.[138]

Both Federal columns were soon in full retreat. General Wade Hampton's cavalry harried Kilpatrick's troopers all the way to the Yankee lines at Williamsburg. The other Yankee force recoiled from the repulse on Westham Road, skirted Richmond on the north, and circled to the east in an effort to reach friendly lines. On March 2 Lee's Rangers (Company H, Ninth Virginia Cavalry) joined bodies of local defense troops in the pursuit. Lieutenant Pollard, commanding Lee's Rangers, hounded the fleeing raiders and by eleven o'clock held his small band in ambush near Mantapike on the Mattaponi River.[139]

The Federals came within twenty or thirty paces of the hidden

[136] *Ibid.*, March 1, 1864.

[137] Vandiver, ed., *Diary of . . . Gorgas*, p. 85; Virgil Carrington Jones, *Eight Hours before Richmond*, pp. 62–65.

[138] Jones, *Eight Hours*, pp. 75–82; Vandiver, ed., *Diary of . . . Gorgas*, p. 85; John M'Anery, "Dahlgren's Raid on Richmond," *Confederate Veteran* 29 (January, 1921): 20–21.

[139] Jones, *Eight Hours*, pp. 84–90.

Southerners. "Halt!" came from the darkness. The Yankee commander spurred his horse. "Disperse, you damned Rebels!" The
first volley cut him down. His troopers fled, and the Confederate
horsemen dashed after them. Next morning the Rebels would capture 350 of the luckless raiders and dispatch them to Richmond.
Meanwhile, when the confusion died about the point of ambush,
young William Littlepage slipped from a place of concealment.
The little schoolboy had always wanted a gold watch for his teach-
er, Edward Halbach, and that dead Yankee officer might have one.
Cautiously he felt for the lifeless enemy in the darkness. The
Yankee had no watch, but William Littlepage did take his cigar
case and present it to Halbach.

Halbach received the gift appreciatively and opened the case.
He found not cigars, but personal papers of the Yankee officer.
They identified him as Colonel Ulric Dahlgren, son of a distin-
guished naval admiral,[140] and they disclosed the true depths of
Yankee treachery. "We hope to release the prisoners from Belle
Island first, and, having seen them fairly started, we will cross the
James River into Richmond, destroying the bridges after us, and
exhorting the released prisoners to destroy and burn the hateful
city, and do not allow the Rebel leader, Davis, and his traitorous
crew to escape."[141]

In an age that still recognized war as a civilized institution, the
Dahlgren papers were regarded as a veritable bombshell. Varina
Davis could hardly believe the disclosure. "Once Commodore Dahlgren had brought the little fair-haired boy to show me how pretty
he looked in his black velvet suit and Vandyke collar," she wrote,
"and I could not reconcile the two Ulrics."[142] Richmond newspapers were unanimously in favor of hanging the 350 captives of

[140] *Ibid.*, 91–93; and the statement of Edward W. Halbach in relation to The
Dahlgren Papers in J. William Jones, comp., "The Kilpatrick-Dahlgren Raid
Against Richmond," *Southern Historical Society Papers* 13 (January–Decem-
ber, 1885): 546–551.

[141] *Examiner*, March 5, 1864. There is still question about the authenticity
of the Dahlgren papers. In April, 1864, General Meade responded to an official
inquiry from Lee and denied that Colonel Dahlgren gave any such orders. A
later writing on the raid (Jones, *Eight Hours*) accepts the papers as genuine.

[142] Varina Howell Davis, *Memoir*, II, 472.

the raid. The *Examiner* called them "robbers."[143] The *Sentinel* fumed: "We have some of these men in our hands. What shall we do with them? —What do they deserve? Tried by the rules of war of what are they guilty? They are murderers, incendiaries, outlaws, detected and arrested in the execution of their crimes. They have forfeited the character of soldiers, and they should not be treated as such."[144] General Lee termed the raid a "barbarous and inhuman plot" but advised against executing the prisoners. "I think it better to do right," he wrote the Secretary of War, "even if we suffer in so doing, than to incur the reproach of our consciences and posterity."[145] The prisoners were spared, but Richmond did not soon recover from her fury.

When the capital did regain her composure, she faced another year of campaigning. Grant and Meade threatened. At the surface, Richmond's prospects appeared no worse than in the past. Some of the soaring confidence had faded from the hearts of Richmonders, but determination remained. The Federals concentrating at the Rapidan River seemed far away, and Lee's army still barred the way to the capital.

In reality, however, the proud capital had declined noticeably. The reverses at Gettysburg and Vicksburg had shaken Richmond's faith—Confederate arms were not invincible. The crises of the previous summer had produced carping bitterness. Then a harder winter than ever before demonstrated the city's material deficiencies. Worse still, the capital rejected the maximum-price bill and tried to solve heightened problems with last year's remedies. The city still laughed at troubles, but even humor had developed a sour, sarcastic tone. Finally Richmond's security was imperiled. The city's poise faltered. Richmond's glory lay in the past.

143 *Examiner*, March 9, 1864.
144 *Sentinel*, March 5, 1864.
145 R. E. Lee to James A. Seddon, March 6, 1864, Dowdey, ed., *Wartime Papers*, pp. 678–679.

PART IV FINAL ILLNESS

"If It Takes All Summer"

THE OX WAS OLD AND DEBILITATED. As the beast plodded up Marshall Street late in March of 1864, his cadaverous frame bore witness to the hardship of the winter just past. Still, the butcher who led him was pleased; meat was scarce, and even this gaunt specimen would yield a fair profit. Then the lead rope went taut; the ox had fallen to his knees. Urging and a swat on the animal's spare rump had no effect. The ox groaned, lay down, and appeared ready to die in the street. Leaving the crumpled animal, the butcher hurried away to get the tools of his trade. He had to slaughter the ox before nature cheated him of his investment. Several passers-by stopped to speculate about whether the butcher would return in time. The dying beast made a piteous spectacle. But next day Richmonders would pay six dollars per pound for the frail remains.[1]

By the spring of 1864, at the age of three, the Confederate capital was old and failing. The Confederacy and its war were draining

---

[1] *Richmond Daily Whig*, March 22, 1864.

life from Richmond along with the hope which sustains life. Intermittently during the last year of the war, Richmond rallied, but she never recovered. Crises came often. In attempting to meet these challenges, men and institutions in the city sometimes held the line. More often they failed.

For three years the city had lived by wit, sacrifice, and will. Now precious little remained to be sacrificed. Richmond discovered that even the most inventive minds could not feed the city when there was no food. Even a genius could not defend the capital without sufficient troops and supplies. As the city realized that no sacrifice within her power would be great enough, even her spirit faltered.

Richmond's last illness progressed through three rather well defined stages. The first of these, lasting throughout the spring and early summer of 1864, saw attempts to drive off the invader and to feed the capital both end in frustration. Not failure *per se*, but maddening cognizance of its own weakness plagued the city. Pain characterized the second stage of Richmond's decline. The long summer of 1864 saw the enemy open siege operations. Bloody fighting weakened not only Richmond's defenders but also the city's capacity to sustain further suffering. During the fall and winter of 1864–1865 frustration, pain, and material infirmity brought Richmond to a series of collapses. Conditions became intolerable. Institutions failed. Nothing remained but an anticlimactic death. And death was almost welcome when it came.

Throughout the last year of the war Richmond existed in constant danger of dying or being killed. Like the ox which lay in Marshall Street, Richmond awaited death or slaughter. And on the Rapidan a man who would earn the sobriquet of "butcher" assumed command of the city's foes.

Ulysses S. Grant was an incredibly uncomplicated man. He had been remarkably successful. When Abraham Lincoln appointed him General in Chief of the Armies of the United States in March of 1864, Grant left the western theater of the war and came east.[2]

---

[2] For good studies of Grant's ascendency see Kenneth P. Williams, *Lincoln Finds a General*, vol. II, and T. Harry Williams, *Lincoln and His Generals*.

The news of his coming started the Confederate capital talking to herself. Richmonders told each other that this new assailant would do no better than his predecessors. The *Dispatch* reasoned: "Whatever he has accomplished has been the result of overwhelming numbers and the weakness and imbecility of our own resistance. . . . The man and his tactics are thoroughly understood by the great chieftain whom he is now confronting, and the next time Grant visits Washington, the Yankees, who perched him on a sofa to receive their adorations, may feel more like elevating him to a scaffold."[3]

Grant's strategy was simple. Federal arms would encircle and crush the rebellion at its perimeters. At the same time Union columns would drive deep into the Southland and slash at the Confederacy's vitals. The navy tightened its blockade, and Yankee ground forces applied pressure on all fronts. General Sherman pushed his army into Georgia, seeking to run Joe Johnston's Rebels to ground, to lay waste productive farmland, and to break Southern morale. Grant oversaw the entire Federal effort, but his immediate concerns were Richmond and the army which defended her. General George G. Meade, the "savior of Gettysburg," retained command of the Army of the Potomac. Grant, however, established his headquarters with Meade's army and personally directed operations against the Confederate capital.[4]

The presence of the Union general in chief before Richmond offered ample evidence of the city's military importance in the coming campaign. Preparing to meet Sherman, Joe Johnston wrote from Georgia: "I fear that the government does not intend to strengthen this army. My reason for the opinion is that it has done nothing yet, in that way. I suppose that Grant's arrival on the Potomac will turn the eyes of our authorities too strongly in that direction to let them see in this."[5] Johnston was correct; he received no troops from Lee and something less than rapt attention from the

[3] *Richmond Daily Dispatch*, March 26, 1864.
[4] For detail see K. P. Williams, *Lincoln Finds a General* and T. Harry Williams, *Lincoln and His Generals*.
[5] Joseph E. Johnston to Louis Wigfall, April 5, 1864, Louis T. Wigfall Papers.

Richmond government. Richmond's somewhat provincial concentration upon the war's eastern campaigns had influenced her resident government in the past. The capital sensed that before her gates the Confederacy would win or lose independence.

For three years Richmond had served the Confederacy as a magnet attracting Yankee armies. The Army of Northern Virginia had conducted a vigorously aggressive defense before the capital. Knowing the Federals' objective, Lee had waited, chosen his field, and won great victories. Richmond's army had frustrated the designs and military careers of five commanders of the Army of the Potomac. In the spring of 1864, however, Richmond's strategic position changed radically. Lee's force no longer bore any numerical relation to its adversary. Men and horses were often hungry. And death had taken its toll of Southern military talent. The army and its commander faced Grant's legions resolutely; some of the Army of Northern Virginia's finest hours would come during the sunset of its existence. But valor was not enough. Numbers and logistics made Lee's troops a decidedly inferior force. Richmond's army, like the city, had passed its peak.[6]

During March and April the rival armies faced each other across the Rapidan, and Richmond awaited the campaign for her life. In his lull the capital's quiet confidence in Southern victory faltered. Her genuine optimism of previous springs yielded to blind hope mingled with despair. One sturdy maid recalled: "Defeat was nowhere written on our future prospects. Discouragement might be, but defeat nowhere! And we once more hugged to our bosoms the phantom of hope, and it sang a lullaby to our fears, and the Confederate metropolis pursued its usual busy routine, and contented itself with the thought that 'the end is not!' "[7] But Varina Davis felt the end was quite near. On April 1 Mrs. Chesnut recorded that the Confederate first lady was "utterly depressed. She said the fall of Richmond must come, and when it did, she would send her children to me and Mrs. Preston."[8]

[6] Douglas S. Freeman, *Lee's Lieutenants: A Study in Command*, III, 340–346.
[7] Sallie Brock Putnam, *Richmond during the War: Four Years of Personal Observation*, p. 288.
[8] Mary Boykin Chesnut, *A Diary from Dixie*, ed. Ben Ames Williams, p. 399.

In public most Richmonders would probably have supported the sentiments of Reverend Seth Doggett. Addressing his Centenary Methodist congregation on April 8, Doggett spoke on "The War and Its Close." He counseled no mediation or compromise, feeling that because the enemy was factious and nearly insolvent, the war would soon end victoriously.[9] Reverend Doggett's sermon was comforting. Yet when Richmonders took stock of opposing armies, they feared Reverend Doggett's bold protestations concealed, but did not allay, the city's anxiety.

In such a variable state of mind the capital faced the advent of a new season of campaigning. Physical conditions within the city did little to ease Richmond's fears.

As usual the coming of spring brought with it a greater shortage of food. The supplies stored for the previous winter were exhausted before farmers could harvest their early spring crops. This year much of the farmland would yield no food for the famished city. Much of the surrounding acreage lay despoiled by fighting, and many farms were now in possession of the enemy. In addition, spring meant renewed campaigning, and this in turn meant the concentrating of troops. Richmond faced the obligation of sharing with her army what limited sustenance there was available. "In Richmond we had never known such a scarcity of food—such absolute want of the necessities of life. . . . Our markets presented a most impoverished aspect. A few stalls at which was sold poor beef, and some at which a few potatoes and other vegetables were placed for sale, were about all that were opened in Richmond markets."[10] Clothing and fuel, too, were in critically short supply. During the spring of 1864, private citizens, the city council, the state of Virginia, and the Confederacy, each in turn, attempted to relieve the city's chronic shortage of life's necessities. And a bizarre set of expedients they created.

In early March Virginia's General Assembly resurrected the

---

[9] Davis Seth Doggett, "The War and Its Close," a sermon delivered in Centenary Church, Richmond, April 8, 1864, in *Political Pamphlets*, vol. 45, Virginia State Library.

[10] Putnam, *Richmond during the War*, p. 303.

domestic system of manufacturing cotton cloth. In the capital of
the "Cotton Kingdom" a state storehouse sold cotton yarn and hand
cards at cost. With these essentials, citizens made their own cloth
and clothing.[11] The legislators also established a virtual state mo-
nopoly on the sale of salt. To meet the critical shortage of this necessity, the assembly authorized the governor to impress the pri-
vately owned works at Saltville.[12]

Some private citizens met this "chronic crisis" with increased
self-sacrifice. Haxall and Crenshaw, flour millers, sold bread to the
city's poor at reduced prices. The *Dispatch* noted appreciatively
that "the liberality and timely charities of Haxall and Crenshaw
entitle that firm to a prominent place amongst those who deserve
to be held in grateful remembrance for their deeds during this trying period of war."[13] Characteristically, General Lee declined the
city council's offer to furnish him a residence in Richmond. He
suggested that the funds appropriated for this purpose be applied to
aid the families of his soldiers.[14] Others reacted not quite so nobly.
On April 4 the *Whig* entitled one of its articles "Look Out for Your
Meat House." The rash of petty thefts defied efforts by the police
to protect stored food, and rarely a night passed that one or more of
Richmond's meat houses or chicken coops was not violated.[15]

Richmond's city council reactivated its Supply Store and again
dispatched agents through the surrounding country in search of
food for the city's needy.[16] In May the concept of needy expanded
to include "such officers and citizens as are prevented by military
service from earning their usual support."[17] By June the council
was charging its Committee on Supplies to secure provisions "for
the city."[18] The city fathers, refusing to increase Richmond's

[11] Virginia General Assembly, *Acts of the General Assembly of the State of Virginia, Passed at the Session of 1863–64 in the Eighty-eighth Year of the Commonwealth*, chap. 28.
[12] *Ibid.*, chap. 6.
[13] *Dispatch*, March 14, 1864.
[14] Richmond City Council, Minutes, March 14, 1864.
[15] *Whig*, April 4, 1864.
[16] City Council, Minutes, March 23, 1864.
[17] *Ibid.*, May 14, 1864.
[18] *Ibid.*, July 11, 1864.

bonded debt, financed their food-finding activities by making temporary loans on the city's banks. The annual March tax ordinance provided for revenue which replenished the city treasury; by this time the council had borrowed over $120,000.[19] Yet the council could not feed the entire capital.

Virginia's Governor William "Extra Billy" Smith easily qualified as Richmond's most energetic food-finder during 1864. The new governor determined that the Commonwealth should feed her citizens, and he laid plans to buy, transport, and resell staple items on a grand scale. The state senate, however, rejected the appropriation bill on which Smith depended to finance the venture. Immediately the governor began seeking other sources of money. First he relieved the state's civic and military contingent funds of $40,000 apiece. Next Smith borrowed $30,000 from William H. MacFarland's Farmer's Bank. Then, having accumulated $110,000 capital, the governor launched his enterprise.[20]

"Extra Billy" hired the master of a blockade runner, furnished him cotton, and sent him abroad to exchange the cotton for supplies. Desiring still more state participation in the risky but profitable trade, Smith contracted for state control of at least five blockade-running vessels. Virginia's seagoing trade flourished briefly, then withered to insignificance as the Federals tightened their encirclement and captured the blockaded ports, Wilmington and Charleston.[21]

On June 8 the governor informed Alexander Dudley, president of the York River Railroad:

Corn can only be obtained at the South—and in reflecting upon the means of transportation, which will least interfere with the government in bringing supplies for our armies to this point, it has occurred to me that a train from your road will cause as little embarrassment as one taken from any other road in the state.

The object of this communication is therefore to request a train of

19 *Ibid.*, April 11, May 31, August 30, 1864.
20 John W. Bell, ed., *Memoirs of Governor William Smith of Virginia, His Political, Military, and Personal History*, pp. 57–59.
21 Alvin Arthur Fahrner, "The Public Career of William 'Extra Billy' Smith," Ph.D. dissertation, pp. 260–262.

cars from your road, complete in all its equipments and with the necessary officers and men to run it, for the purpose of transporting corn and other supplies from the South to Virginia.[22]

Smith went on to remind the railroad president that the state was the largest stockholder in his road. The governor felt he could thus demand obedience to his request, and three days later the train was his.[23]

Smith then dispatched an agent south with the train, and the Commonwealth entered another phase of the food business. Utilizing "borrowed" funds, a commandeered train, and state-controlled ships, Smith was remarkably successful. He recalled later: "Indeed, I put rice on the general market at Richmond at 50 cents [$3.00 retail], and practically drove the retailer out of the market. At these prices, I was enabled to preserve my capital and have a margin of 10 per cent also, with which to cover losses. My supplies were such that I was able to make occasional loans to the Confederate Government."[24] For example, in March of 1865 the army's Commissary Department borrowed 2,500 bushels of corn to feed Lee's army. Smith estimated, "At the time Richmond was evacuated, that Government [the Confederacy], at Confederate prices, was indebted to the state, on such accounts, at least $300,000."[25]

In his resourcefulness Virginia's governor placed the Commonwealth in businesses directly competing with private enterprise. Smith's measures, gravitating as they did toward state socialism, were as extraordinary as the circumstances which occasioned them. But Virginians were hungry, and the governor tried to feed them.

While the city council and "Extra Billy" Smith brought food into the city, the Confederate administration attacked the food scarcity by sending excess mouths out of the capital. Credit for the

22 William Smith to Alexander Dudley, June 8, 1864, Bell, ed., *Memoirs of Governor William Smith*, p. 178.
23 A. R. Lawton, Quartermaster General, to William Smith, June 11, 1864, Bell, ed., *Memoirs of Governor William Smith*, p. 178.
24 Bell, ed., *Memoirs of Governor William Smith*, p. 58.
25 *Ibid.*

idea belonged to General Braxton Bragg.[26] Made military advisor to the President after calamitous defeat at Missionary Ridge, Bragg strongly advocated removing the government's clerical force from the capital. The cabinet, after two lengthy sessions, determined to send three hundred ladies, whose job was to sign treasury notes, to Columbia, South Carolina.[27] War Bureau Chief Kean recorded scornfully, "Another reason, which the Secretary of War communicated to us, was the hope thereby to stampede the citizens of Richmond and this was the main *point*. . . . The idea was worthy of the hero of Missionary Ridge!"[28] On April 21 the ladies, and the one trunk apiece allowed them, left Richmond.[29] The *Examiner* waxed caustic. The departure of three hundred women would not appreciably increase the food supply of those remaining in the city. Furthermore, the editor informed Bragg and Secretary of the Treasury Memminger, these ladies were neither ducks who migrate nor soldiers to order from place to place. "Steady, then, Mr. Memminger. A little more brains, Captain Bragg!"[30]

Having decided that further dispersion of the executive departments would seriously impair the government's operation, Confederate authorities next renewed their efforts to get prisoners out of Richmond. From the hodgepodge of deserters and reprobates lodged in Castle Thunder emerged four companies of infantry for Lee's army—the "Winder Legion."[31] General Winder himself left Richmond in June to become commandant of Andersonville Prison near Americus, Georgia.[32] In accord with his program to strain the Confederacy as much as possible, Grant had suspended the exchange

[26] Bragg's popularity was quite low. Said the *Enquirer* on February 23: "We earnestly implore the President not to dampen the enthusiasm of the people and dishearten them this early in the spring by the appointment of Gen. Bragg to any important command, where he has no superior officer."

[27] Edward Younger, ed., *Inside the Confederate Government: The Diary of Robert Garlick Hill Kean, Head of the Bureau of War*, pp. 145–146.

[28] *Ibid.*, p. 146.

[29] *Richmond Sentinel*, April 20, 1864.

[30] *Richmond Daily Examiner*, April 25, 1864.

[31] *Dispatch*, May 16, 1864.

[32] *Examiner*, June 9, 1864.

of prisoners of war.[33] In late June the Confederate Adjutant and Inspector General's Office ordered all able-bodied prisoners to Lynchburg and thence to Andersonville.[34] Prison facilities at Danville in Virginia, and Salisbury in North Carolina, received the overflow from Richmond. However, Richmond was never able to evacuate her prisons with sufficient dispatch. In September an officer complained that he still held 6,000 Yankees on Belle Isle and had too few men to guard them.[35] One room on the third floor of Libby Prison held 270 Federal officers in June.[36]

During the last year of the war Richmond saw her widespread need reflected in her prison conditions. The Yankees consumed a portion of the capital's limited food supply, although Libby's commandant, Major Dick Turner, made sure that no prisoner thrived. A Maine volunteer wrote of Turner, "His heart was blacker than any brogans that he may ever have shined with a brush."[37] According to inmates a day's rations at Libby consisted of a small square of cornbread (containing cob and vermin) and a piece of bacon as "big as your thumb" served twice a day.[38] Even so, every ounce of

[33] See the statement of Robert Ould, Confederate Commissioner of Exchange, in "The Treatment of Prisoners during the War between the States," *Southern Historical Society Papers* 1 (March, 1876): 125–131.

[34] Adjutant and Inspector General's Office, Special Order No. 150, June 28, 1864, in U.S. Congress, House, *War of the Rebellion: A Compilation of the Official Records of the Union and Confederate Armies*, ser. II, vol. 7, 432.

[35] Garnett Andrews, Assistant Adjutant General, to the Secretary of War, September 27, 1864, *War of the Rebellion: Compilation of Official Records*, ser. II, vol. 7, pp. 870–871.

[36] John Harrold, *Libby, Andersonville, Florence, The Capture, Imprisonment, Escape and Rescue of John Harrold, A Union Soldier in the War of the Rebellion, with a Description of Prison Life among the Rebels—The Treatment of Union Prisoners—Their Privations and Sufferings*, p. 33.

[37] Abner R. Small, *The Road to Richmond: The Civil War Memoirs of Major Abner R. Small of the Sixteenth Maine Volunteers. Together with the Diary which He Kept When He was a Prisoner of War*, ed. Harold Adams Small, p. 160.

[38] Daniel N. Reynolds, "Memoirs of Libby Prison," ed. Paul H. Giddens, *Michigan History Magazine* 23 (Autumn, 1939): 393; George Haven Putnam, *A Prisoner of War in Virginia 1864–5; Reprinted, with Additions, from the Report of an Address Delivered before the N.Y. Commandery of the U.S. Loyal Legion, December 7, 1910. Third Edition* [1914], *with a List of Commissioned Officers Confined in Danville, Virginia, 1864–5, and an Appendix Presenting Statistics of Northern Prisons from the Report of Thomas Sturgis, 1st Lieut. 57th Mass. Vol.*, p. 22; Harrold, *Libby*, pp. 33–34.

food the Yankees ate in Richmond robbed the city of energy and brought the capital a little nearer to exhaustion.

Some of the capital's old resourcefulness and daring showed through the efforts to feed and clothe her people. Yet Richmonders were wanting and individual philanthropy was insufficient. The city council's depots and Governor Smith's enterprises helped the situation, but the task of feeding nearly 100,000 people was too great. The Confederate government had sought to remove some of Richmond's consumers, but the relocated three hundred women and the evacuated prisoners were never enough to balance the numbers of fresh captives brought into the city. The very novelty of these expedients betrayed the capital's desperation; resourcefulness blended with recklessness. And the sum total of the spring's activity was failure. As if to confirm the failure, early in June the 30th Virginia Regiment, Army of Northern Virginia, sent the women and children of Richmond a day's rations and did without themselves. In spite of all the civil authorities could do, the troops who had so long shielded the city now had to feed her as well.[39]

During the first week in May, Grant put his army in motion. Crossing the Rapidan he faced Lee in the Wilderness. During the three-day encounter Lee's army received the blow, delivered a counterstroke, and preserved the stalemate. On May 8 the Army of Northern Virginia again checked the enemy advance at Spotsylvania Court House. After the initial repulse four more days of bitter conflict proved inconclusive. In less than two weeks the Army of the Potomac had absorbed around thirty thousand casualties, roughly half the strength of Lee's entire force. Less tenacious Federal commanders would have suspended the carnage and retired northward. But Grant was determined—he put it this way, "I am sending back to Belle Plain all my wagons for a fresh supply of provisions and ammunition, and propose to fight it out on this line if it takes all summer."[40]

---

[39] Varina Howell Davis, *Jefferson Davis, Ex-president of the Confederate States of America: A Memoir by His Wife*, II, 496.

[40] Summary of fighting is from Freeman, *Lee's Lieutenants*, III, 342–410; casualty figure comes from Richard B. Morris, ed., *Encyclopedia of American*

While Union infantry cudgeled Richmond's defenders to the north, Yankee cavalry thrust at the city herself. General Phillip Sheridan's troopers slipped by the Confederate right on May 9 and headed south. General "Jeb" Stuart's gray cavalry began the pursuit.[41] On the tenth, War Secretary Seddon reported the capital "in hot danger."[42] Next day Ordnance Chief Josiah Gorgas wrote:

> The day has been one of the greatest excitement. I slept but a few hours last night having been called up by messages, and kept awake by the ringing of alarm bells and the blowing of alarm whistles most of the night. At five this morning I went to Mr. Seddon's office and found him laboring under the impression that the last hours of Richmond were at length numbered. —The entire cavalry force of Meade's army were reported to be rapidly approaching the devoted city from the direction of Ashland, with Stuart at their heels it is true, but having a good deal the start of him. All the city militia were transferred to that side of the city, and a brigade of old troops (Hunton's), from Chaffins Farm. —We breathe more freely now (11:00 p.m.), as Stuart is on their flank and the city defenses in their front.[43]

Stuart's weary force beat off the Yankees at Yellow Tavern, but the action cost the gay warrior a mortal wound. He was borne into the failing city he had done so much to defend, and Jefferson Davis came to his deathbed. Early on the morning of May 12 the general died. Richmonders crowded St. James Church for the funeral and mourned his passing. Richmond had rung with Stuart's laughter, and his daring had thrilled the city. When he died some of Richmond's heart went with him. Stuart himself, going into his last battle, had said, "I'd rather die than get whipped."[44] His passing left Richmond to ponder both death and defeat.

History, pp. 242–243; and the quote is from *War of the Rebellion: Compilation of Official Records*, ser. I, vol. 36.1, p. 4.

[41] Freeman, *Lee's Lieutenants*, III, 411–416.

[42] James A. Seddon to P.G.T. Beauregard, May 10, 1864, *War of the Rebellion: Compilation of Official Records*, ser. I, vol. 36.2, p. 986.

[43] Frank E. Vandiver, ed., *The Civil War Diary of General Josiah Gorgas*, pp. 100–101.

[44] Freeman, *Lee's Lieutenants*, III, 420–433; quote is on p. 426. See also Varina Howell Davis, *Memoir*, II, 499–503; City Council, Minutes, May 14, 31, 1864.

Increasingly the beleaguered capital lived with death. Nor was the dying confined to the battlefields. Little Jeff, the President's son, was puzzled. His four-year-old brother, Joe, was sleeping on the brick pavement in the middle of the afternoon, and he could not wake him. Kneeling beside his brother, Jeff shook him at first and called to him. Finally Mrs. Semmes, wife of the Louisiana senator, came. She would help. "Mrs. Semmes, I have said all the prayers I know how, but God will not wake Joe!"[45] Four doctors could do no better. Joseph Emory Davis never regained consciousness after his fall from the piazza of the executive mansion.[46]

Joe had been his father's favorite. For once the President ignored the war. He sent away government messengers: "I must have this day with my little child."[47] All that night he paced the floor.[48] Davis's personal tragedy and the cumulative pressure of his public responsibilities exacted a heavy toll from him. Gorgas wrote of the President in June, "He is looking quite well, but is growing not only gray but white with his cares."[49]

Too many had died. Daily the cadence of the "Dead March" sounded in Richmond's streets as the funeral processions passed. Great men and warriors died, and their passing brought public sorrow in Richmond. Newspapers lined their columns in black, and great crowds paid their homage. But nearly every family, high and humble, lived with personal loss. Husbands, brothers, fathers, and sons—even the President's son—filled the hillsides about the capital. A soldier predicted that regardless of the war's outcome, the graves of Richmond's defenders would make the city a Southern mecca, a holy place.[50] In quiet moments Richmond mourned her sacrifice and wondered how many more would die for her. Even

---

[45] Chesnut, *Diary from Dixie*, p. 405.
[46] *Dispatch*, May 2, 1864.
[47] Varina Howell Davis, *Memoir*, II, 497.
[48] Chesnut, *Diary from Dixie*, p. 405.
[49] Vandiver, ed., *Diary of . . . Gorgas*, p. 129.
[50] Benjamin Washington Jones, *Under the Stars and Bars: A History of the Surry Light Artillery: Recollections of a Private Soldier in the War between the States*, p. 212.

Mrs. Lee yielded to a rare despondency. "What will my poor husband do? It seems God has turned his face from us."[51]

Grant kept pounding at Lee. Swinging southeastward he crossed the North Anna River and occupied the same ground that McClellan had held two years previously. Cold Harbor was again a battlefield and the bloodletting was awesome. In just over fifteen minutes the Confederates inflicted seven thousand casualties upon the blue invaders. The gray line stood firm, and at length Grant suspended the futile contact. Failing to overrun or outrun Richmond's defenders north of the city, he crossed the James below the capital and renewed his assault from the south and east. The Federals invested the city of Petersburg in mid-June.[52]

Tactically the Confederates had won a victory. Lee had met and repulsed Grant at every turn. Richmond was secure and her army intact. The size of Yankee casualty lists moved Northern papers to call Grant a drunkard and a butcher. In Richmond the *Examiner* mocked the Union General in Chief: "But let Grant not be cast down too much: Impossibilities are not fairly to be expected of any man; let him not resign himself to despair, nor give himself up wholly to drink. A good man struggling with adversity is a spectacle for the Gods; and although he can by no means take Petersburg, not to speak of Richmond, yet let him remember that he who ruleth his own spirit is greater than he who taketh a city."[53]

As the possibility of a mobile campaign for Richmond lessened, Lee dispatched Jubal Early with ten thousand troops to the Shenandoah Valley. After ridding the valley country of Federals, Early marched into Maryland, and on July 11 the Confederates were at the gates of Washington. The Rebels even managed a shot at Abraham Lincoln as he surveyed his capital's defenses. Early's force was too weak to storm the rival capital, but the raid thoroughly frightened Washington and her government. As two corps from

---

[51] Quoted by Sally Nelson Robins in "Mrs. Lee during the War," from R. A. Brock, ed., *General Robert Edward Lee*, which is reprinted in Katherine M. Jones, *Ladies of Richmond: Confederate Capital*, p. 243.

[52] Freeman, *Lee's Lieutenants*, III, 496–556.

[53] *Examiner*, July 6, 1864.

Grant's army hastened to secure the Union capital, Richmond rejoiced in Early's audacity. His raid had eased the pressure on Petersburg and given notice that the embattled South was yet capable of offensive action.[54] And after surviving over three years behind Lee's army, some in Richmond yielded to habit. They "had begun to regard it [Richmond] as invulnerable."[55]

Strategically, however, the situation was far less sanguine. Jubal Early never rejoined Lee at Richmond. From Maryland he withdrew into the Shenandoah Valley and there watched his corps wither away before the energy and overwhelming numbers of Unionists under Sheridan. Early's Washington expedition gained a brief respite for Lee, but time was no longer a Southern ally. The slaughter in the Wilderness, at Spotsylvania, and at Cold Harbor had drained life and leadership from the gray army. When Grant lost nearly sixty thousand men in one month, he replaced them. As always the Army of the Potomac was well fed and adequately supplied. Lee had fewer losses, and his army was close to its base. But the South had little to offer its army in the way of men or provisions.[56] When the determined Grant began siege operations at Petersburg, the campaign degenerated into one of attrition—a static contest the Confederacy could not win. Lee had scant room for maneuvers and insufficient striking power to threaten seriously the Yankee mass. Richmond was no longer the magnet which lured Federals to their defeat. The capital was a millstone around Lee's neck. The defense of Richmond immobilized Lee's army while Grant bludgeoned it into impotence.

For three years the Confederacy and its war had made a tremendous impact upon the capital. The Confederate experience had continued to transform Richmond, and she had continued to greatly

[54] For a full account of Early's activities see Frank E. Vandiver, *Jubal's Raid: General Early's Famous Attack on Washington in 1864.*

[55] Putnam, *Richmond during the War*, p. 303.

[56] Not the least of Lee's problems (along with numbers of men and provisions) was the loss of competent subordinates. As Douglas S. Freeman pointed out with reference to May of 1864, "The battles of a single month had put 37 per cent of the general officers of the Army of Northern Virginia *hors de combat*. Except as Lee himself embodied it, the old organization was gone" (*Lee's Lieutenants*, III, 514).

influence the nation and the war. Now, in the spring of 1864, the war was so very close to the city that, more than ever, Southern independence seemed to hinge upon the campaign for Richmond. And so the exchanged influences—Richmond's upon the Confederacy and the Confederacy's upon Richmond—began to coalesce. The city identified herself evermore with the national Cause; the Confederacy associated Richmond's internal welfare and external security with the nation's survival. City and Confederacy were becoming one in their concern for Richmond's provisioning and defense. Richmond was becoming a Confederate polis.

But Richmond was dying. Frustration mocked her best efforts and drained hope from her heart. Seeking to administer the coup de grâce, Grant assailed from without. Eventual death was certain; the only question was what would cause it—nature or butcher.

Siege

ITH EVERY SKIRMISH the frustration and the pain increased. Fortunately, during the long summer of 1864, the second stage of Richmond's fatal malady, the city seemed numb. The *Examiner* said it best. "To write or to think now of anything whatever, save the marching or fighting of the day that passes, is plainly impossible."[1] Richmonders closed their minds to all but Lee's army fighting at Petersburg and the suffering in the city's hospitals.

William Mason Smith had been a cadet at the Citadel when the war commenced. His widowed mother was a Huger, and he came from the South Carolina low country.[2] On the morning of June 3 a gap opened between Kershaw's and Hunton's brigades near Cold Harbor. Lieutenant Smith was deploying skirmishers in the void, and Yankee sharpshooters were active.

Then William Smith was sitting down. Instinctively his hand clutched at his stomach. "I am killed." Moments passed, and Willie

[1] *Richmond Daily Examiner*, June 17, 1864.
[2] Daniel E. Huger Smith, Alice R. Huger Smith, Arney R. Childs, eds., *Mason Smith Family Letters 1860–1868*, xix–xxi.

felt better. "I believe I am not much hurt." He stood up testing his wound and straightening his blouse. He continued giving directions to his men, but the pain returned, and Willie became uneasy. He lay down and called for a surgeon. Doctor Cain examined the small, blackened opening, but he refused to give an opinion. At the brigade field hospital the doctors told Willie his wound was mortal. He might live three or four days. The division hospital was two miles away, and Willie was convinced that the road was the roughest in the world. Two young doctors wanted to probe for the musket ball, but Willie refused. His wound was mortal; he would not add more pain. All day he lay on the wet ground suffering shock and agony from his throbbing stomach and preparing to die. Toward evening a captain from his regiment found him, borrowed an ambulance, and started for Richmond with Willie and two other wounded South Carolinians.

The journey took four hours, and it was dark when the ambulance reached the city. One hospital, then another, refused to receive them. The men groaned and cried out to the driver to stop. They would rather die in the street than continue the torture of travel. Their cries attracted attention. A gentleman and some ladies directed the ambulance driver to Stuart Hospital. There, more than twelve hours after his wounding at Cold Harbor, Willie Smith found rest.[3]

It took Willie all summer to die. His mother came from South Carolina to look after him. He lived his last summer on morphine, and even so he felt the pain. He had the best of care, but he often woke up at night screaming. Near the end, on August 12, Willie was not much more than bones and bed sores. Even so, it took four delirious "dying days" to wear the life out of him. Finally he asked his mother if he was going to die. She said he was. And Willie said, "All right, God's will be done."[4]

Willie and Richmond, the dying capital, had a lot in common

[3] Willie Smith's account apparently dictated to Mrs. William Mason Smith and enclosed in letter to J. J. Pringle Smith, June 11 or 12, 1864, *Smith Family Letters*, p. 101.

[4] Mrs. William Mason Smith to Mrs. Allen S. Izard, September 12, 1864, *Smith Family Letters*, p. 139.

that awesome summer. Both lived in pain and watched life wear
away. Perhaps Willie Smith was the more fortunate; he could say
"all right" and die in peace. Richmond's agony persisted.

News that Fort Harrison had fallen reached Richmond shortly
after breakfast on September 29. Loss of the earthwork bastion
southeast of Richmond seemed to open the way for Yankee armies
to storm the capital. In his diary, war clerk J. B. Jones said the
excitement was "the greatest I have ever known here."[5] In the face
of the emergency, "all the local organizations were immediately
ordered out. Not only this, but squads of guards were sent into the
streets everywhere with orders to arrest every able-bodied man
they met, regardless of papers; and this produced a consternation
among the civilians. The officers and government shops were closed,
and the tocsin sounded for hours, by order of the Governor, fright-
ening some of the women."[6] Finally, militia troops and reinforcements from Lee blunted the Union thrust, but they could not re-
capture Fort Harrison. After two days of futile counter-attacks, the
Confederate army threw up fresh earthworks and awaited the next
Union assault.[7] Ultimately the fall of Fort Harrison was not decisive. In the weeks that followed, Richmond remembered the excitement and alarm in the city, but soon the details of the military
encounter merged with those of countless other engagements. The
fall of the eastern fort was only one of many emergencies that
occurred during the third stage of Richmond's last illness. In other
stages the city had been frustrated and pained. Now in the fall and
winter of 1864–1865 the capital crumbled, piece by piece.

Throughout the long summer Grant had pounded, probed, and
extended Lee's lines. He even tunneled beneath the Southern
trenches and exploded eight thousand pounds of powder in an attempt to make a decisive breach in the Rebel front.[8] With determination and luck, and often by a hair's breadth, the Gray army

[5] J. B. Jones, *A Rebel War Clerk's Diary at the Confederate States Capital*,
ed. Howard Swiggett, II, 295.

[6] *Ibid.*

[7] Douglas S. Freeman, *Lee's Lieutenants: A Study in Command*, III, 590–591.

[8] *Ibid.*, pp. 540–543.

hung on. Grant had fought all summer, and still Richmond eluded him.

The continuous marching and fighting, however, had been hard on Richmond's defenders. One recalled, "We are always hungry."[9] After reinforcing threatened sectors of the front all summer, one veteran wrote to a friend, "There is hardly an acre of ground from Richmond to Petersburg, or from the James to the Chickahominy, that we have not been over a dozen times."[10] By autumn the Army of Northern Virginia's capacity for successful offensive action was confined to cattle raids against the Union commissary.[11] Richmond and her defense confined the army to the the trenches. Although Yankees did not encircle the city, in truth the Confederate army lay besieged. Spirits sagged under the deadly monotony of defense.

The malady of siege set the tone of Richmond's existence. The sounds of alarm bells clanging and citizen-soldiers hastening to a threatened section of the line became all too familiar. Happily the reserve troops were better soldiers than poets.

> Like a beast of the forest, fierce, raging with pain,
> The foe in his madness, advances again;
> His eyeballs are glaring, his pulses beat fast,
> While the furies are hastening this effort, his last.
> But the seven-thorned queen[12] a calm presence preserves,
> For they've sworn to defend her—the "Richmond Reserves."[13]

However romantic the *Sentinel's* correspondent thought the home guard troops, each time the clerks and workmen marched out of the capital and into the trenches, the work of the war government ceased. Mail remained in the post office. The routine correspondence swamped the few old men left behind in the executive departments. The Confederate Armory and the Tredegar Iron

[9] W. L. Timberlake, "In the Siege of Richmond and After," *Confederate Veteran* 29 (November, 1921): 412.

[10] Benjamin Washington Jones, *Under the Stars and Bars: A History of the Surry Light Artillery: Recollection of a Private Soldier in the War between the States*, p. 215.

[11] Freeman, *Lee's Lieutenants*, III, 590–615.

[12] That is, Richmond, which was originally built on seven hills.

[13] *Richmond Sentinel*, October 15, 1864.

Works stood idle until mechanics returned from the field. Cabinet officials attended the most menial tasks. Chief of Ordnance Josiah Gorgas wrote in his diary during one period of alarm, "As all my officers and clerks are in the field I am obliged to attend to details myself and have trudged about the streets until I am thoroughly tired."[14]

Richmond's militia force performed creditably, but Lee needed more than a few thousand civil servants and mechanics to reinforce his thin ranks. In the capital a government official recorded: "The conscription is now being pressed mercilessly. It is agonizing to see and hear the cases daily brought into the War Office, appeal after appeal and *all* disallowed. Women come there and weep, wring their hands, scold, entreat, beg, and almost drive me mad."[15] On one occasion the conscripters lured large numbers of men into a warehouse headquarters on the pretense that they would receive passes. When the petitioners arrived they received not passes but rifles. The headquarters quickly became a prison whose only exit led to the war front. War clerk Jones chronicled the desperation: "From the age of fifteen to fifty-five, all were seized by that order —no matter what papers they bore, or what the condition of their families—and hurried to the field. . . . No wonder there are many deserters—no wonder men become indifferent as to which side shall prevail, nor that the administration is falling into such disrepute at the capital."[16]

However hard life became in the rest of the Southern Confederacy, it was probably a few degrees harder in Richmond. A hospital matron in the capital later recalled a trip south in October, 1864, "I noticed on my return a great difference in the means of living between Virginia and the Gulf States. Even in the most wealthy and luxurious houses in Richmond, former everyday comforts had about this time become luxuries, and had been dispensed

[14] Frank E. Vandiver, ed., *The Civil War Diary of General Josiah Gorgas*, p. 101.
[15] Edward Younger, ed., *Inside the Confederate Government: The Diary of Robert Garlick Hill Kean, Head of the Bureau of War*, p. 174.
[16] Jones, *Rebel War Clerk's Diary*, II, 303.

with earlier in the war."[17] During the winter Congress raised the salaries of governmental employees in Richmond above those of workers elsewhere.[18] Indeed Judge Halyburton, Judge of the District Court of the Eastern District of Virginia, received exactly twice the salary of any other District Court judge.[19] Only too well did the congressmen realize the difficulty for salaried people in the capital.

Late in November Warren Akin, newly elected representative from Georgia, arrived at his post.

I was just 9½ hours going from Greensboro N.C. to Danville Va. a distance of 48 miles, traveled in a box car in the night and slept on some corn sack, but as it was not very cold, I made out pretty well. I am boarding for the present at the American Hotel, and have to pay $25 per day for board, and one dollar every time my boots are blacked, and $10 per dozen or $30 per month for washing. So my board will be at least $810 per month, and if I am here long it will take all my pay to meet expenses traveling to and from this place and while here,—even if it will then. I know not how long I am to support my family, if this war continues long.[20]

Akin soon moved into a boardinghouse and decreased his expenses as much as possible. "I wear my flannels, drawers and night shirts two weeks, I have worn two shirts, all the past week. My handkerchiefs will get soiled, and I would wash them myself, but I have no iron to iron them. A dollar apiece for washing socks and handkerchiefs is certainly very severe."[21] The Georgian began eating two meals per day, and in just over two months at Richmond Akin lost fifteen pounds.[22]

Another Georgian who refugeed to Richmond revealed, "The

[17] Bell I. Wiley, ed., *A Southern Woman's Story: Life in Confederate Richmond by Phoebe Yates Pember including Unpublished Letters Written from the Chimborazo Hospital*, p. 122.

[18] Charles W. Ramsdell, ed., *Laws and Joint Resolutions of the Last Session of the Confederate Congress (November 7, 1864–March 18, 1865) Together with the Secret Acts of Previous Congresses*, no. 83.

[19] *Ibid.*, nos. 6, 7.

[20] Bell I. Wiley, ed., *The Letters of Warren Akin, Confederate Congressman*, p. 35.

[21] *Ibid.*, p. 43.

[22] *Ibid.*, pp. 64, 105.

one topic of conversation everywhere and on all occasions is 'eating,' even the ministers in the pulpit unconsciously preach of it."[23] To ease the food shortage Dr. Minnegerode, rector at St. Paul's, formed the Richmond Soup Association.[24] And the Confederate authorities impressed food to such a degree that the *Examiner* stated, "If Richmond starves it will not be the fault of the enemy, but of the Sec. of War & impressment."[25] Then the Davis administration allowed an ever-expanding number of its civilian employees to draw rations from government stores.[26] In attempting to feed not only the army, but also employees in the capital with impressed food, the Confederacy resembled a leviathan state.

Even in peacetime the redistribution of wealth would have been difficult to effect. By winter, 1864, it was well nigh impossible. Of all Southern cities, Richmond felt the war's privation most keenly. Her resources and her people's cooperation were nearly exhausted. In the final analysis, the expedients of Richmond's governments did little good during the war's last winter. More than one Richmonder asked with Mrs. McGuire, "What would we do without our country friends?"[27]

The most embarrassing shortage was that of money. During the eleven months from April, 1864, to February, 1865, Richmond's city government spent over $1,700,000; city taxes yielded just under $450,000. The sale of railroad stocks for almost one million dollars had reduced the deficit to $326,250.[28] Still the city foresaw no decrease in spending during 1865, and thus the council's finance committee recommended tripling the tax rate and demanded that the gas and water works be self-sustaining,[29] which they had not been since the war began. In 1864 the gas works alone accumulated a deficit of over $600,000, and this when gas sold for up to $50

[23] Mrs. William A. Simmons, Diary, cited in Katherine M. Jones, ed., *Ladies of Richmond: Confederate Capital*, p. 265.
[24] Richmond Soup Association, Journal.
[25] *Examiner*, September 19, 1864.
[26] Ramsdell, ed., *Laws and Joint Resolutions*, no. 8.
[27] Judith W. McGuire, *Diary of a Southern Refugee during the War*, p. 325.
[28] City Council, Minutes, February 13, 1865.
[29] *Ibid.*, February 23, 1865.

per 1,000 cubic feet.[30] If the city's utilities could for once sustain themselves, if the rapid inflation of the currency did not make the tax rates almost immediately obsolete, if hoarders of city notes did not decide en masse to redeem them, if the supply of railroad stocks held out, if Richmond's taxpayers could meet the tripled rates, if all these improbabilities should occur—then, barring the unforeseen, the city would remain solvent another year.

The physical hardship of the last months was severe. Its cumulative effect on Richmond was pitiful. The once-proud capital, racked by inner pains, nearly ringed by assailants, and grown quickly old, entered second childhood. Richmonders sought release preferring to ignore reality.

> Some persons in this beleaguered city seem crazed on the subject of gayety. In the midst of the wounded and dying, the low state of the commissariat, the anxiety of the whole country, the troubles of every kind by which we are surrounded, I am mortified to say that there are gay parties given in the city.
>
> There are those denominated "starvation parties" where young persons meet for innocent enjoyment, and retire at a reasonable hour; but there are others where the most elegant suppers are served—cakes, jellies, ices in profusion, and meats of the finest kinds in abundance, such as might furnish a meal for a regiment of General Lee's army.[31]

Tucker DeLeon pronounced the gatherings "not the brilliant and generous festivals of the olden days of Richmond, but joyous and gay assemblages of a hundred young people, who danced as though the music of shells had never replaced that of the old negro fiddler —who chatted and laughed as if there were no tomorrow."[32] One resident stated, "There seems to be a perfect mania on the subject of matrimony,"[33] and another wrote, "Every girl in Richmond is engaged or about to be."[34] She went on to understate, "There was

---

30 *Ibid.*, March 13, January 9, 1865.
31 McGuire, *Diary of a Southern Refugee*, p. 328.
32 T. C. DeLeon, *Four Years in Rebel Capitals: An Inside View of the Southern Confederacy from Birth to Death*, p. 351.
33 McGuire, *Diary of a Southern Refugee*, p. 329.
34 Phoebe Yates Pember to Mrs. J. E. Gilmer, February 17, 1865, Wiley, ed., *Southern Woman's Story*, p. 187.

certainly a painful discrepancy between the excitement of dancing and the rumble of ambulances that could be heard in the momentary lull of the music."[35] Now "the fiddles scraped and the music swelled for 'the dancers dancing in tune'; while they shut their ears and would not hear the minor key that wailed the ruin of our hopes."[36]

In keeping with the gay abandon of Richmond's second childhood was the wedding of General John Pegram to Hetty Cary. The people of the capital filled St. Paul's Church on January 19, 1865, for the event. One of Pegram's comrades wrote, "One of the handsomest and most lovable men I ever knew wed to the handsomest woman in the Southland—with her classic face, her pure complexion, her auburn hair, her perfect figure and her carriage altogether the most beautiful woman I ever saw in any land."[37] The candlelit service was elegant, and the popular young couple received congratulations from the Confederacy's notables. Jefferson Davis sent his carriage for the bride, and his horses set tongues in motion by balking on the way to the church. Those in search of omens also discovered that the bride had torn her wedding dress as she entered St. Paul's. The nuptials proved gossipy as well as gala, and the worn capital loved it. The Pegrams spent their honeymoon in a farmhouse near the groom's command at Petersburg.[38]

Meanwhile, in the saloon of a steamer in Hampton Roads, there was talk of peace. Vice-President Stephens, R. M. T. Hunter, and Judge James A. Campbell met Lincoln and his Secretary of State, Seward. Politely the Federal President described his terms; they amounted to unconditional surrender. The Confederate commissioners politely refused. The entire proceeding consumed one four-hour session. Jefferson Davis had expected as much. He would never cry for quarter.

Richmonders crowded the African Church on February 6 to hear the results of the Hampton Roads Conference. Davis, Hunter, Gov-

[35] *Ibid.*

[36] Mrs. D. Giraud Wright, *A Southern Girl in '61: The War-Time Memories of a Confederate Senator's Daughter*, p. 241.

[37] Cited in Freeman, *Lee's Lieutenants*, III, 629.

[38] Constance Cary Harrison, *Recollections Grave and Gay*, pp. 201–203.

ernor Smith, and others fired the throng with patriotic orations. The President's speech was perhaps the best of his career. He moved the people to renewed hope. Josiah Gorgas noted, "The war feeling has blazed out afresh in Richmond, and the spirit will I hope spread thro' the land."[39] Lee was finally General in Chief of all Confederate armies, and Davis had a new Secretary of War, John C. Breckinridge.[40] For a few days the desperate hope persisted: perhaps a union of all the Southern armies—a decisive battle—Lee would save them.

Sheridan was ravaging the Shenandoah Valley; Sherman knifing through the Carolinas. Grant renewed his assaults. And on February 6, a little while before Richmonders shouted their patriotism in the African Church, John Pegram fell dead in the snow. Exactly three weeks after his wedding day the young general's coffin lay at St. Paul's where he had stood a bridegroom. "Beside it knelt his widow swathed in crepe. Again Dr. Minnegerode conducted the ceremony, again the church was full. Behind the hearse, waiting outside, stood his war charger, with boots in stirrups. The wailing of the band that went with us on the slow pilgrimage to Hollywood will never die out of memory."[41] The next time Josiah Gorgas wrote of morale at the capital he said: "People are almost in a state of desperation, and but too ready to give up the cause, not that there is not patriotism enough to sustain it, but that there is a sentiment of hopelessness abroad—a feeling that all our sacrifices tend to nothing, that our resources are wasted."[42]

The last hours were desperate. In January the irascible Congressman Foote departed for Washington to negotiate peace personally. He failed.[43] Cabinet member Judah Benjamin offered to resign, if President Davis felt the action would restore confidence in the

[39] Vandiver, ed., *Diary of . . . Gorgas*, p. 168; Clifford Dowdey, *The Land They Fought For: The Story of the South as the Confederacy 1832–1865*, pp. 381–384; Jones, *Rebel War Clerk's Diary*, II, 410–412.

[40] Freeman, *Lee's Lieutenants*, III, 641.

[41] Harrison, *Recollections Grave and Gay*, pp. 303–305.

[42] Vandiver, ed., *Diary of . . . Gorgas*, p. 172.

[43] Dowdey, *Land They Fought For*, p. 378; Foote was censured in the legislature for negotiating and for running off to the enemy ("Proceedings of Congress," *Southern Historical Society Papers* 52 (1959): 176, 215–217.

administration. Davis rejected the offer.[44] Joseph R. Anderson, master of the Tredegar Iron Works, petitioned the government to take over his enterprise and manage it for the remainder of the war. The overburdened government declined.[45] On March 14 the President approved an act of Congress authorizing him to remove the archives and to assemble Congress elsewhere.[46] And on congressional authority Richmond's city council began raising a volunteer force of men over fifty years old.[47] These desperate measures were signs of the capital's death throes.

The Confederacy had yielded many of its founding principles in the name of wartime expediency. Finally, the most basic of Southern mores lay sacrificed to the phantom hope of independence. The Confederates determined to take Negro slaves out of the fields and put them into the army.

In the winter of 1864–1865 only one source of manpower remained to fill out Lee's decimated ranks. The Virginia General Assembly and the Confederate Congress debated long and often bitterly the question of arming the slaves. Wrote President Davis to Governor Smith, "My idea has been that we should endeavor to draw into our military service that portion of the negroes which would be most apt to run away and join the army of the enemy, and that this would be best effected by seeking for volunteers for our own army."[48] Finally, in March of 1865 Congress passed a law authorizing Negro enlistment, but not guaranteeing freedom for the slave soldiers.[49]

Negroes had dug trenches, driven wagons, and carried ammunition to release whites for the conflict. Although Negroes were still legally chattel, no intelligent statesman could foresee sending the Confederacy's defenders back into bondage. On March 22 the

[44] Robert Douthat Meade, "The Relations between Judah P. Benjamin and Jefferson Davis: Some New Light on the Working of the Confederate Machine," *Journal of Southern History* 5 (November, 1939): 477.

[45] Kathleen Bruce, *Virginia Iron Manufacturing in the Slave Era*, p. 421.

[46] Ramsdell, ed., *Laws and Joint Resolutions*, no. 175.

[47] *Ibid.*, no. 191; City Council, Minutes, March 15, 1865.

[48] Jefferson Davis to William Smith, March 25, 1865, Dunbar Rowland, ed., *Jefferson Davis, Constitutionalist: His Letters, Papers and Speeches*, VI, 522.

[49] Ramsdell, ed., *Laws and Joint Resolutions*, no. 148.

curious passer-by could watch field hands, worth ten thousand dollars in the inflated national currency, drill in Capitol Square.[50] Lee welcomed the new volunteers and urged President Davis "to carry it [the law authorizing enlistment of Negroes] into effect as soon as possible."[51] The *Sentinel* asserted that the slaves were better men than the "wretches the Yankees send against us,"[52] and the *Examiner* exhorted the government to let the slave beat back the foe and worry about our social mores after victory.[53]

Finally, having made the last sacrifice, the Confederacy and its capital could only vow with Lee, "I shall however endeavor to do my duty & fight to the last."[54] And at the last the Confederacy and its capital were one and the same. The campaigns in northern Virginia had always been crucial; Richmond's location and logistical importance had long dictated not only strategy and tactics, but also breadth of vision. Militarily, once the Confederacy made the decision in 1864 to defend Richmond with Lee's army on Grant's terms, the fortunes of city and state were identical. The siege narrowed the war to one campaign, one theater, one objective. And when Richmond fell the nation collapsed; Lee's army, the only viable force in the Confederacy, lasted one week after the evacuation of the capital. As one perceptive Richmonder recalled, "The tremendous efforts to capture the Capital; the superhuman exertions to defend it in the last four years, *had made Richmond the cause!*"[55]

From the time of her selection as the Rebel capital, the city had been metamorphosed by the Confederate experience, and the conditions within Richmond had greatly influenced the Confederacy. Responding to the city's problems, Jefferson Davis had proclaimed martial law, quelled a bread riot, and made countless other national

50 Bell I. Wiley, *Southern Negroes 1861–1865*, p. 89; W. Ashbury Christian, *Richmond: Her Past and Present*, p. 250.

51 R. E. Lee to Jefferson Davis, March 10, 1865, Clifford Dowdey, ed., *The Wartime Papers of R. E. Lee*, p. 914.

52 *Sentinel*, March 24, 1865.

53 *Examiner*, March 9, 1865.

54 R. E. Lee, Headquarters, to Mrs. Lee, February 21, 1865, Dowdey, ed., *Wartime Papers*, p. 907.

55 DeLeon, *Four Years in Rebel Capitals*, p. 348.

adjustments to local situations. Now Richmond was a city-state, and the distinctions between local and national were completely blurred. Congress as well as the city council sought means to feed the city's population. The President went to the people—Richmond people at the African Church—with his indignation over Lincoln's refusal to negotiate peace. The wires and rails leading from the capital were usually open, but somehow governmental communication between Richmond and the hinterland had broken down. It seemed that the problems, the crises, the people that really mattered were in Richmond.

In spirit, too, Richmond embodied the Confederacy. The nonchalance with which the city faced her perils, the contagious determination of Davis—these and other qualities were evident in the mind of Richmond, the Confederate polis. The city's morale had risen and fallen along with the national fortunes; as one resident noted, "Richmond was indeed the Confederate barometer, as well as the heart and brain of our . . . nation."[56] The city had prayed with Jackson, danced with Stuart, and sought to emulate the nobility of Lee. Spiritually, most of all, Richmond and the Confederacy were one. Even the enemy knew this, for when the time came they sang:

> Now Richmond has fallen, rebellion is done,
> Let all men rejoice for the victory is won!
> The city where slavery once dwelt in her pride
> Is now in our hands and the rebellion has died,
> Now Richmond is taken, they'll harm us no more,
> For treason is crushed and rebellion is o'er.
> Our armies have triumphed, the traitors have fled
> We've captured their city, secession is dead.[57]

Nation and capital had had an extraordinary impact upon each other. Now like spent swimmers they clung to each other and went under as one.

[56] Sallie Brock Putnam, *Richmond during the War: Four Years of Personal Observation*, p. 187.

[57] From *The Singing Sixties: The Spirit of the Civil War Days Drawn from the Music of the Times*, by Willard A. and Porter W. Heaps, pp. 353–354. Copyright 1960 by the University of Oklahoma Press.

12

Sans Everything

N April 1, 1865, the *Sentinel* proclaimed: "We are very hopeful of the campaign which is opening, and trust that we are
to reap a large advantage from the operations evidently near at
hand. But our people should clearly comprehend, that whatever
the temporary result, and though misfortune beyond what seems
in the bounds of possibility should befall us, our independence will
still be in our option, and our final success will *still* be beyond the
power of our enemies to prevent it."[1] However, Richard M. Smith,
the *Sentinel's* editor, was merely saying what was expected of him.
So were Foote, Benjamin, Anderson, the Congress, the council, and
almost everyone else. All but the blind zealots had known for
weeks, even months, that the city, state, army, everything, was
doomed.

When Admiral Raphael Semmes assumed command of the entire Confederate navy on February 18, his fleet numbered eight vessels.[2] At the last Lee had roughly 54,000 troops to fight off Grant's

[1] *Richmond Sentinel*, April 1, 1865.
[2] Raphael Semmes, *Memoirs of Service Afloat during the War between the
States*, pp. 799–808.

115,000.[3] Near the end of March, 1865, R. G. H. Kean recorded, "Through the effect of Sheridan's raid [in the Shenandoah Valley] Richmond is rapidly approaching a state of famine. Bacon is $20 a pound, flour $1,200 a barrel, butter $25 a pound, beef—and that the worst—$10 to $12, wood $200 a cord, etc., and the supply exceedingly meager."[4] The Confederate state of Richmond was near expiration.

Perhaps Josiah Gorgas best described the capital's misgivings. On March 6 he wrote: "The crisis of our fate is rapidly approaching, and men's minds are harassed with doubts, fears and perplexity. The weak are for submission and those who have more fortitude are affected by the fears of the timid. A few men remain strong and if they have them conceal their fears. Wherever three or four are gathered together there are ominous whispers and dubious shakings of the head. Even those whose faiths remain unshaken find it difficut to give a reason for their faith."[5] By all rational criteria the Cause was already lost. Even President Davis saw the end. He wrote to his wife, "If I live you can come to me when the struggle is ended, but I do not expect to survive the destruction of constitutional liberty."[6] Richmond lay in suspended animation. She felt her doom approaching, but she would not act upon the knowledge.

Grant kept extending his lines westward. Finally, Lee's force would stretch no farther. Very early on April 2 a general Federal advance broke through the gray curtain of earth and men. Lee had to act quickly to avoid a rout. Hoping desperately to unite with Joe Johnston's remnant army, the general in chief decided to retreat into North Carolina.[7] He telegraphed the war office, "I see no prospect of doing more than holding our position here till night. I am

[3] Richard B. Morris, ed., *Encyclopedia of American History*, p. 245.

[4] Edward Younger, ed., *Inside the Confederate Government: The Diary of Robert Garlick Hill Kean, Head of the Bureau of War*, p. 204.

[5] Frank E. Vandiver, ed., *The Civil War Diary of General Josiah Gorgas*, p. 174.

[6] Varina Howell Davis, *Jefferson Davis, Ex-President of the Confederate States of America: A Memoir by His Wife*, II, 575.

[7] Douglas S. Freeman, *Lee's Lieutenants: A Study in Command*, III, 675–680.

not certain I can do that." And he counseled the immediate evacuation of Richmond.[8]

Lee's dreadful message reached the war office at 10:40 on that balmy Sunday morning.[9] A courier bore the telegram one block up Ninth Street to St. Paul's Church where Jefferson Davis was on his knees, engrossed in the ante-communion service Dr. Minnegerode was reading. The President took the telegram, read it, then quietly put on his overcoat and left. His departure created no disturbance; affairs of state had interrupted Davis's worship before. Soon, however, the sexton was calling away everyone connected with the government or military. By the time the city's churches had concluded their services, Richmonders knew, or sensed, the worst.

President Davis assembled the heads of departments and bureaus in his office and told them of the impending flight. There was much to do before the evacuation that night, for Davis had never emphasized planning for defeat. Now within twelve hours the entire government must pack, load, and leave.[10]

Even Judah Benjamin allowed his composure to slip. At two o'clock in the afternoon he summoned French Consul Alfred Paul to his office. Paul recalled, "I found him extremely agitated, his hands shaking, wanting and trying to do and say everything at once; he was preparing to leave at five o'clock with the President and his other colleagues. . . . Mr. Benjamin said to me in a trembling voice, 'I have nothing in particular to say to you, but I wanted to be sure to shake your hand before my departure. . . . General Lee insists on the immediate evacuation of the city by the govern-

---

[8] Clifford Dowdey, *The Land They Fought For: The Story of the South as the Confederacy, 1832–1865*, p. 400.

[9] *Ibid.*

[10] Jefferson Davis, *The Rise and Fall of the Confederate Government*, II, 566–567; Emmie Crump Lightfoot Papers; Dr. Minnegerode's description of the President receiving the evacuation message is in Elizabeth Wright Weddell, *St. Paul's Church, Its Historic Years and Memorials*, I, 243–244, cited in William J. Kimball, ed., *Richmond in Time of War*, pp. 141–142. Josiah Gorgas did not learn of the evacuation until 1:00 P.M. (Vandiver, ed., *Diary of . . . Gorgas*, p. 179). Most observers, however, date their knowledge of the impending fall earlier. Dr. Minnegerode received the news before he served communion after the President's departure. For a good study of the evacuation and occupation see Rembert Patrick, *The Fall of Richmond*.

ment, it is simply a measure of prudence. I hope that we will return in a few weeks.' "[11] Benjamin's explanations were illusory. He knew that the evacuation was final. Perhaps, as Secretary of State, he sought to present a bold front to Paul as a representative of France. More likely Judah Benjamin was presenting a bold front to himself.

At four o'clock the city council met to discuss the fate of those remaining in the doomed city. Mayor Mayo officially announced the Confederacy's decision to abandon the capital. The city fathers requested that Governor Smith leave two companies of militia to keep order in the city. Smith concurred and appeared in person to report what he knew of the government's plans. As further insurance against possible disorder, the council appointed twenty-five citizens in each ward to dispose of all liquor supplies in the city. Finally, the council resolved: "That in the event of the evacuation of the city, the Council and a committee of citizens to be appointed by the President, together with a Mayor, shall be authorized to meet the Federal authorities to make such arrangements for the surrender of the city as may best protect the interests of the citizens."[12] The city council then adjourned until nine o'clock the next morning.[13]

Outside the council chamber, Richmond's streets flowed with people and property. "The office-holders were now making arrangements to get off. Every car was ordered to be ready to take them South. . . . The people were rushing up and down the streets, vehicles of all kinds were flying about, bearing goods of all sorts and people of all ages and classes who could go beyond the corporation lines."[14] The work of evacuation continued through the

[11] Alfred Paul to Drouyn de Llys, April 11, 1865, New York, Archives de Ministre des Affaires étrangères, Etats-Unis, Correspondence politique des consuls, Richmond 23, pp. 146–252, cited in Warren F. Spencer, "A French View of the Fall of Richmond: Alfred Paul's Report to Drouyn de Llys, April 11, 1865," *Virginia Magazine of History and Biography* 73 (April, 1965): 181.
[12] Richmond City Council, Minutes, April 2, 1865.
[13] *Ibid.* The entry in the council minutes for April 3, 1865, reads, "The city was, on this day, occupied by the United States forces, and the Council did not, therefore, meet."
[14] Judith W. McGuire, *Diary of a Southern Refugee during the War*, p. 344.

night. By the early hours of Monday, April 3, the government had packed and loaded all that the available wagons and railroad cars could carry. Only a token military force was to be left behind to fire Mayo's Bridge when the last of Lee's army had crossed. The trains pulled away; the wagons rattled off into the night.[15]

No one was quite sure how the fire started. Josiah Gorgas attributed the blaze to the firing of the railroad bridges across the James.[16] War Clerk J. B. Jones felt that explosions set off at the powder magazine and arsenal started it.[17] Major General Godfrey Weitzel, commander of the Federal troops who would shortly occupy Richmond, "understood from leading citizens of Richmond the fires had been started in the large tobacco warehouses which had been fired by the order of General Ewell in order that their contents might not fall into our hands."[18] Weitzel's intelligence agrees with the account of Emmie Sublett, a thirteen-year-old girl who lived close enough to the area of the fire to know of its origin. She wrote to a friend that the fire began "about three or a little earlier, and raged furiously; you know the warehouses and some of the public buildings were set on fire, from which the others caught."[19]

Whatever its origin, the fire engulfed a large portion of the city from the river up to Capitol Square. Very few Richmonders had gone to bed on Sunday night, and those who had were awakened early by the explosions as the fire engulfed the powder magazine and arsenal. And in the intervals between the explosions, at least one resident "shuddered at the dreadful silence. Richmond burning and no alarm. It was terrible."[20]

Captain Clement Sulivane, commanding the last Confederate

[15] See Vandiver, ed., *Diary of . . . Gorgas*, pp. 179–180; McGuire, *Diary of a Southern Refugee*, pp. 343–347; J. B. Jones, *A Rebel War Clerk's Diary at the Confederate States Capital*, ed. Howard Swiggett, II, 465.

[16] Vandiver, ed., *Diary of . . . Gorgas*, p. 180.

[17] Jones, *Rebel War Clerk's Diary*, II, 467–468.

[18] Major General Godfrey Weitzel, Letter Press Books.

[19] Emmie Sublett to Emmie Anderson, April 29, 1865, cited in *Confederate Museum Newsletter* 5 (April, 1968): 3–5.

[20] Mrs. Mary A. Fontaine to Mrs. Marie Burrows Sayre, April 30, 1865, Fontaine Letter.

force in the city, was powerless to combat the leaping flames. His orders were to hold Mayo's Bridge until Lee's rear guard crossed, then to destroy this last span across the James. Sulivane watched as the flames illuminated the city. A mob gathered and began wildly looting and stealing. Several thousand descended upon the commissary depot at Fourteenth and Cary streets. The Confederacy had been unable to transport the stores of food, and the mob was hungry. The city council's committees had faithfully poured barrel after barrel of whiskey into the streets. Now the rioters scooped and drank from the gutters. The frenzy mounted as the fire spread and at last consumed the commissariat.

Sulivane was anxious. Dawn approached and still Lee's rear guard had not come. The tar, pine knots, and kerosene were in place on the bridge. It could not be long until the enemy's arrival. At last General Gary's hard-pressed troops appeared. Ambulances, then cavalry, dashed across the bridge. "All over, goodbye; blow her to hell." Sulivane crossed ahead of the flames, sent his command on its way, and turned to watch.[21]

The last Rebel had departed. Richmond's Confederate epic was over. Pain and hardship and anxiety and strain were no more, but no more either were the challenge, the excitement, the life of this great drama. Dawn had come and elsewhere the sun shone brightly. Over the burning Confederate Capital the sun was a "great red ball veiled in mist."[22] The smoke from Richmond's funeral pyre defied the light and "made the sun shed a *dark red light over the whole.*"[23] Within the city respectable folk remained behind bolted doors and peered out of drawn shutters. The mob of hungry pillagers had been swelled by those made homeless by the fire.

Around eight o'clock in the morning General Weitzel's bluecoated columns entered the city. Weitzel later recalled: "We found

[21] Captain Clement Sulivane, "The Fall of Richmond, I. The Evacuation," in Robert Underwood Johnson and Clarence Clough Buel, eds., *Battles and Leaders of the Civil War*, IV, 725–726.

[22] Mrs. Mary A. Fontaine to Mrs. Marie Burrows Sayre, April 30, 1865, Fontaine Letter.

[23] Emmie Sublett to Emmie Anderson, April 29, 1865, cited in *Confederate Museum Newsletter* 5 (April, 1968): 3–5.

ourselves in perfect pandemonium. Fires and explosions in all directions; whites and blacks either drunk or in the highest state of excitement running to and fro on the streets apparently engaged in pillage or in saving some of their scanty effects from the fire; it was a yelling howling mob."[24]

Sulivane watched Union cavalry pass up Main Street; then the endless blue column of infantry started its march through the city. He heard the "very welkin ring with cheers" as the Federals reached Capitol Square. "And then we turned and slowly rode on our way."[25]

[24] Weitzel, Letter Press Books.
[25] Sulivane, "The Fall of Richmond," in Johnson and Buel, eds., *Battles and Leaders*, IV, 726.

BIBLIOGRAPHY

The sources of Richmond's wartime history are numerous. Reiteration and significant omissions occasionally mar the voluminous record. In general, however, the researcher's most important function is that of interpreting and compressing his abundantly available materials.

Most important of the manuscript sources are the minute books of Richmond's city council. The minutes offer insight into the workings of Richmond's municipal government, as well as into the minds of the councilmen. As far as I can discover, the council's minutes have never been used extensively. Since my research, the minute books have found publication as *Richmond at War: The Minutes of the City Council 1861–1865*, edited by Louis Manarin. The Personal Property Tax Books and the Real Estate Tax Books offer valuable information on such topics as land value, personal wealth, male population, slave population, and the like. Unfortunately the Real Estate Tax Books after 1863, and Personal Property Tax Books after 1862 are unavailable. The minute books of Richmond's Hustings Court provide some indication of the crime rate and the nature of crimes committed in the wartime capital.

The War Department Collection of Confederate Records, in the National Archives, contains much material on the functions of the Confederacy in Richmond, some of which is pertinent in a study of the city. Among the Records of the Medical Director at Richmond a "letters sent" file contains a number of detailed reports on Richmond hospitals. A collection of hospital reports presents statistics, month by month from the fall of 1862, on the population, deaths, discharges, and admittances in each of Richmond's hospitals.

The Social Statistics compiled from the Eighth Census give a good view of Richmond in 1860. Such items as the numbers and kinds of schools, periodicals, and churches make this source an important one. Although the relevance to Confederate Richmond is limited, the minutes of the Virginia Branch of the American Colonization Society from November 4, 1823, to February 5, 1859, chronicle the activities and influence of this highly significant organization.

The Louis T. Wigfall papers at The University of Texas at Austin are a valuable record of the infighting within official circles in Richmond. The Kate Mason Rowland Papers and a few of the other smaller collections at the Confederate Museum are useful. On the whole, however, the manuscript sources of Richmond's Confederate years are disappointing.

One very good reason for the paucity of manuscript materials is that many diaries, memoirs, reminiscences and collected letters have found publication. Two valuable collections of primary sources are William J. Kimball's *Richmond in Time of War*, and Katherine M. Jones's *Ladies of Richmond: Confederate Capital.* Kimball's volume is a "canned source" designed primarily to be used in teaching research-paper techniques. It contains, however, several little-known and enlightening entries. The Jones work arranges quotations from Richmond ladies chronologically and in this way presents a version of Richmond's wartime history.

First among the ladies whose published diaries and memoirs are especially important is Mary Boykin Chesnut. Her *Diary from Dixie* presents a vivid portrait of social life in the capital. Mrs. Chesnut's close friend Varina Howell Davis, in her *Jefferson Davis, Ex-President of the Confederate States of America: A Memoir by His Wife*, offers insight into her own experience as guest and matriarch in Richmond. Invaluable as a guide to hardship and refugee life in the capital is Judith W. McGuire's *Diary of a Southern Refugee during the War.* Sallie Brock Putnam's *Richmond during the War: Four Years of Personal Observation* is an interesting, although sometimes factually inaccurate record of the attitudes of a native Richmonder. Bell Wiley's edition of Phoebe Yates Pember's *A Southern Woman's Story* provides a graphic picture of a hospital matron and the lively writing style makes this little volume one of the most interesting and important accounts of Richmond life.

The *Memoirs of Governor William Smith* (edited by John W. Bell) presents a good account of Smith's attempts to feed his constituents. Letters, speeches, and the like are appended.

The diaries and memoirs of governmental officials in Richmond are quite important. *The Letters of Warren Akin, Confederate Congressman* (edited by Bell Wiley) gives an illuminating look at the daily life of a Georgian alone in Richmond during 1864–1865. The difficulties of life and the almost constant political activity in the capital are covered in Franklin B. Sexton's diary (edited by Mary S. Estill) "The Diary of a Confederate Congressman, 1862–63," *Southwestern Historical Quarterly* 38 (April, 1935): 270–301; 39 (July, 1935), 33–65.

Best known, and perhaps deservedly so, among Richmond diaries is J. B. Jones's *Rebel War Clerk's Diary at the Confederate States Capital*. Jones tampered with the original diary before he published it, and therefore much of the remarkable insight and many sage observations stem from hindsight. Still, as a day-by-day account of what one Richmonder close to important people and events thought and did, the work is unequaled. Another war office diary is that of the Head of Bureau of War, Robert G. H. Kean (*Inside the Confederate Government; the Diary of Robert Garlick Hill Kean*, edited by Edward Younger). Kean held a key position, and therefore his observations are more informed than those of Jones although his diary does not contain the color and volume of Jones's work. *The Civil War Diary of General Gorgas* (edited by Frank E. Vandiver) contains the opinions and attitudes of the talented chief of ordnance. Gorgas's diary presents a contrast to Jones's and Kean's in terms of political opinion. Jones was a great hater. He grew to despise Jefferson Davis, Judah Benjamin, John H. Winder, and others. Kean also held strong opinions about the Confederate leadership. He was the protégé of George W. Randolph and grew to dislike Davis for displacing Randolph, and James A. Seddon for being Randolph's successor. Gorgas was more moderate. He liked Davis, tolerated Congress, and displayed no lasting hates.

In a class by themselves are two works of T. C. DeLeon, *Four Years in Rebel Capitals* and *Belles, Beaux, and Brains of the 60's*. The gregarious DeLeon was a keen observer, and he recorded his views in skillful prose. His descriptions of society at the capital are unmatched.

Among the myriad of prisoners' accounts, Alfred Ely's *Journal* is probably the least biased. Most of the literature on Richmond's prisons is highly questionable. Prisoners tell tales of harsh treatment while prison officers go to the other extreme in describing the justness of their regimes. Captain I. N. Johnston's *Four Months in Libby and the Campaign against Atlanta* tells (as only a participant could) the exciting story of the 1864 tunnel escape.

Hospital experiences, too, are rather well documented. The best accounts come from Phoebe Yates Pember (*A Southern Woman's Story*), Mrs. Fannie A. Beers (*Memories*), and the *Mason Smith Family Letters 1860–1868* (edited by Daniel E. Huger Smith, Alice R. Huger Smith, and Arney R. Childs).

Soldiers continually passed through Richmond and enjoyed the pleasures of the city. Among the many materials some of these warriors left behind are the *Wartime Papers of R. E. Lee* (edited by Clifford Dowdey) and Benjamin Washington Jones's *Under the Stars and Bars*. Lee's letters to his wife, as well as his official correspondence, reflect conditions in Richmond and military conditions in front of the capital. Jones spent much of the war in garrison camps about the city, and his book, composed of letters to a friend, gives a good picture of the city through a soldier's eyes.

The list of sources which follows is largely restricted to material cited in the footnotes with a few significant additions.

I
MANUSCRIPT MATERIALS

American Colonization Society, Virginia Branch. Minutes, November 4, 1823–February 5, 1859. Virginia Historical Society Library. Richmond, Virginia.

Bagby, George W. Diary, 1860–1862. George William Bagby Papers. Virginia Historical Society Library. Richmond, Virginia.

Bureau of the Census. Eighth Census, Social Statistics. Microfilm of MS returns in Virgina State Library, Richmond, Virginia.

Cedar Creek Friends. Minutes. Virginia State Library. Richmond, Virginia.

City of Richmond. City Council Minutes, 1860–1865. Virginia State Library. Richmond, Virginia.

City of Richmond. Hustings Court Minutes, 1860–1865. Virginia State Library. Richmond, Virginia.

City of Richmond. Personal Property Tax Books, 1860–1865. Virginia State Library. Richmond, Virginia.

City of Richmond. Real Estate Tax Books, 1859–1863. Virgina State Library. Richmond, Virginia.

Claiborne Family. Papers. Virginia Historical Society Library. Richmond, Virginia.

Fontaine, Mrs. Mary A. Letter. Confederate Museum. Richmond, Virginia.

Harrison, Dr. Jacob Prosser. Correspondence. Harrison Family Papers. Virginia Historical Society Library. Richmond, Virginia.

Haxall and Crenshaw. Papers. Confederate Museum. Richmond, Virginia.

Holloway, Dr. J. M. Papers. Virginia Historical Society Library. Richmond, Virginia.

Lightfoot, Emmie Crump. Papers Relating to Personal Experience in and around Richmond during the Confederacy. Confederate Museum. Richmond, Virginia.

Lynn, Clara Minor. Papers. Confederate Museum. Richmond, Virginia.

Randolph, Tucker. Journal. Confederate Museum. Richmond, Virginia.

Richmond Soup Association. Journal. Confederate Museum. Richmond, Virginia.

Rives, William Cabell. Papers. Manuscript Division, Alderman Library, University of Virginia. Charlottesville, Virginia.

Rowland, Kate Mason. Papers. Confederate Museum. Richmond, Virginia.

Taliaferro, Jacqueline. Diary. In possession of Harry T. Taliaferro, Jr. Richmond, Virginia.

Virginia Capital Bicentennial Commission, comp. Sketches of Societies and Institutions, Together with Descriptions of Phases of Social, Political and Economic Development in Richmond, Virginia. Richmond, 1937. Typed papers in the Virginia State Library, Richmond.

Virginia Executive Council. Minutes, 1861. Virginia State Library. Richmond, Virginia.

War Department Collection of Confederate Records. Hospital reports of the Medical Director at Richmond. Record Group 109. National Archives. Washington, D.C.

War Department Collection of Confederate Records. Letters sent file of the Medical Director at Richmond. Record Group 109. National Archives. Washington, D.C.

Weitzel, Major General Godfrey. Letter Press Books. T. S. Cincinnati Historical Society. Cincinnati, Ohio.

Wigfall, Louis T. Papers. The University of Texas Archives. Austin, Texas.

II

BOOKS, ARTICLES, DISSERTATIONS

Ambler, Charles Henry, ed. *Correspondence of Robert M. T. Hunter, 1826–1876. American Historical Association Annual Report, 1916.* Vol. II. Washington, D.C., 1918.

Anderson, Joseph R. "Anderson's Brigade in the Battles around Richmond." *Confederate Veteran* 31 (December, 1923): 448–451.

Avary, M. L. *A Virginia Girl in the Civil War, 1861–1865.* New York: D. Appleton and Co., 1903.

Bailey, James H. *Henrico Home Front 1861–1865 A Picture of Life in Henrico County, Virginia: Based upon Selections from the Minute Books of the Henrico County Court.* Richmond: Henrico County Civil War Centennial Commission, 1963.

Beers, Mrs. Fannie A. *Memories: A Record of Personal Experience and*

Adventure during Four Years of War. Philadelphia: J. B. Lippincott Co., 1888.

Bell, John W., ed. *Memoirs of Governor William Smith of Virginia, His Political, Military, and Personal History.* New York: The Moss Engraving Co., 1891.

Bill, Alfred Hoyt. *The Beleaguered City.* New York: Alfred A. Knopf, 1946.

Bondurant, Agnes Meredith. *Poe's Richmond.* Richmond: Garrett and Massie, 1942.

Boney, F. N. *John Letcher of Virginia: The Story of Virginia's Civil War Governor.* Southern Historical Publications No. 11. University: University of Alabama Press, 1966.

Borcke, Heros von. *Memoirs of the Confederate War for Independence.* 2 vols. London: William Blackwood and Sons, 1866.

Brenaman, J. N. *A History of Virginia Conventions.* Richmond: J. L. Hill Printing Co., 1902.

Bruce, Kathleen. *Virginia Iron Manufacture in the Slave Era.* New York: Century Co., 1930.

Burrows, J. L. "Recollections of Libby Prison." *Southern Historical Society Papers* 11 (February, March 1883): 83–92.

Capers, Henry D. *Life and Times of Christopher G. Memminger.* Richmond: Everett Waddey Co., 1893.

Cappelmann, Mary Dudley. *A Brief History of the Fire Department and Police Department of Richmond Virginia.* Richmond, 1931.

Chesnut, Mary Boykin. *A Diary from Dixie.* Edited by Ben Ames Williams. Boston: Houghton Mifflin Co., 1961.

Christian, W. Ashbury. *Richmond, Her Past and Present.* Richmond: L. H. Jenkins, 1912.

Claiborne, John Herbert. *Seventy-five Years in Old Virginia, With Some Account of the Life of the Author and Some History of the People amongst Whom His Lot Was Cast,—Their Character, Their Condition, and Their Conduct before the War, during the War, and after the War.* New York: Neale Publishing Co., 1904.

Clark, Sam L., ed. "A Confederate Officer Visits Richmond." *Tennessee Historical Quarterly* 11 (March, 1952): 86–91.

Clay, Mrs. Clement C. *A Belle of the Fifties: Memoirs of Mrs. Clay, of Alabama, Covering Social and Political Life in Washington and the South, 1853–66.* Edited by Ada Sterling. New York: Doubleday, Page and Co., 1905.

Cleveland, Henry. *Alexander H. Stephens, in Public and Private: with Letters and Speeches, before, during, and since the War.* Philadelphia: National Publishing Co., 1866.

Confederate Memorial Literary Society. *Illustrated Guide to Richmond, the Confederate Capital: With a Facsimile Reprint of the City Intelligencer of 1862.* Richmond, 1960.

Confederate States of America, Congress, House, Committee to Enquire into Treatment of Prisoners at Castle Thunder. *Evidence Taken before the Committee of the House of Representatives, Appointed to Enquire into the Treatment of Prisoners at Castle Thunder.* Richmond, 1863.

————, Congress, House, Hospital Committee. *Report of the Hospital Committee.* Richmond, 1862.

Coulter, E. Merton. *The Confederate States of America, 1861–1865.* A History of the South Series, edited by Wendell Holmes Stephenson and E. Merton Coulter, vol. 7. Baton Rouge: Louisiana State University Press, 1950.

Crandall, Marjorie Lyle. *Confederate Imprints: A Check List Based Principally on the Collection of the Boston Athenaeum.* 2 vols. Boston: Boston Athenaeum, 1955.

Cunningham, Horace Herndon. *Doctors in Grey: The Confederate Medical Service.* Baton Rouge: Louisiana State University Press, 1958.

Daniel, Frederick S., ed. *The Richmond Examiner during the War; or the Writings of John M. Daniel with a Memoir of His Life.* New York: Frederick S. Daniel, 1868.

Davis, Jefferson. *The Rise and Fall of the Confederate Government.* 2 vols. New York: D. Appleton and Co., 1881.

Davis, Rev. Nichols A. *The Campaign from Texas to Maryland, with the Battle of Fredericksburg.* Richmond: Presbyterian Committee of Publication of the Confederate States, 1863.

Davis, Varina Howell. *Jefferson Davis, Ex-President of the Confederate States of America: A Memoir by His Wife.* 2 vols. New York: Belford Co., 1890.

DeLeon, T. C. *Belles, Beaux, and Brains of the 60's.* New York: G. W. Dillingham Co., 1907.

————. *Four Years in Rebel Capitals: An Inside View of Life in the Southern Confederacy from Birth to Death.* Mobile, Ala.: The Gossip Printing Co., 1890.

Dew, Charles B. *Ironmaker to the Confederacy: Joseph R. Anderson and the Tredegar Iron Works.* New Haven: Yale University Press, 1966.

Dodd, William E. *Jefferson Davis.* Philadelphia: G. W. Jacks and Co., 1907.

Doggett, Davis Seth. *The War and Its Close: A Sermon Delivered in Centenary Church, Richmond, April 8, 1864.* Richmond, 1864.

Dover Baptist Association. *Minutes of the Dover Baptist Association.* Richmond, 1860–1864.

Dowdey, Clifford. *Experiment in Rebellion.* New York: Doubleday & Co., 1946.

————. *The Land They Fought For: The Story of the South as the Confederacy, 1832–1865.* New York: Doubleday & Co., 1955.

————, ed. *The Wartime Papers of R. E. Lee.* Boston: Bramhall House, 1961.

Eaton, Clement. *A History of the Southern Confederacy.* New York: Macmillan Co., 1954.

Eckenrode, Hamilton J. *Jefferson Davis, President of the South.* New York: Macmillan Co., 1923.

Eggleston, George Cary. *A Rebel's Recollections.* New York: G. P. Putnam's Sons, 1905.

Ely, Alfred. *Journal of Alfred Ely, a Prisoner of War in Richmond.* Edited by Charles Lanman. New York: D. Appleton and Co., 1862.

Estill, Mary S., ed. "The Diary of a Confederate Congressman, 1862–63." *Southwestern Historical Quarterly* 38 (April, 1935): 270–301; 39 (July, 1935): 33–65.

Evans, Marvin Davis, "The Richmond Press on the Eve of the Civil War." *The John P. Branch Historical Papers on Randolph-Macon College,* New Series, 1 (January, 1951).

Ezekiel, Herbert Tobias, and Gaston Lichtenstein. *The History of the Jews of Richmond from 1769 to 1917.* Richmond, 1917.

Fahrner, Alvin Arthur. "The Public Career of William 'Extra Billy' Smith." Doctoral dissertation, University of North Carolina, 1953.

Fifty Years a Pastor: An Account of the Observance of the Semi-Centennial Anniversary of the Installation of Rev. Moses Drury Hoge, D.D., L.L.D., in the Pastorate of the Second Presbyterian Church, Richmond, Virginia. Richmond, 1895.

Fleet, Betsy; John D. P. Fuller; and W. Clement Eaton, eds. *Green Mount: A Virginia Plantation Family during the Civil War: Being the Journal of Benjamin Robert Fleet and Letters of His Family.* Lexington: University of Kentucky Press, 1962.

Flournoy, H. W., ed. *Calendar of Virginia State Papers and Other Manuscripts from January 1, 1836, to April 15, 1869, Preserved in the Capital at Richmond.* 2 vols. Richmond, 1893.

Freeman, Douglas Southall. *The Last Parade.* Richmond, 1932.

————. *Lee's Lieutenants: A Study in Command.* 3 vols. New York: Charles Scribner's Sons, 1942–1944.

————. *The South to Posterity: An Introduction to the Writings of Confederate History.* New York: Charles Scribner's Sons, 1939.

Fremantle, Arthur James Lyon. *The Fremantle Diary, Being the Journal of Lieutenant Colonel Arthur James Lyon Fremantle, Coldstream Guards, on His Three Months in the Southern States.* Edited by Walter Lord. Boston: Little, Brown & Co., 1954.

Girard, Charles. *A Visit to the Confederate States of America in 1863: Memoir Addressed to His Majesty Napoleon III.* Tuscaloosa: University of Alabama Press, 1962.

Glass, Robert C., and Carter Glass, Jr. *Virginia Democracy: A History of the Achievements of the Party and Its Leaders in the Mother of Commonwealths, the Old Dominion.* Springfield, Ill.: Democratic Historical Association, 1937.

Greenberg, Mrs. Davis J. *Through the Years: A Study of the Richmond Jewish Community.* Richmond: Richmond Jewish Community Council, 1955.

Harris, Lt. William Charles. *Prison-Life in the Tobacco Warehouse at Richmond. By a Balls Bluff Prisoner.* Philadelphia: George W. Childs, 1862.

Harrison, Constance Cary. *Recollections Grave and Gay.* New York: Charles Scribner's Sons, 1911.

Harrold, John. *Libby, Andersonville, Florence, The Capture, Imprisonment, Escape and Rescue of John Harrold, A Union Soldier in the War of the Rebellion, with a Description of Prison Life among the Rebels—The Treatment of Union Prisoners—Their Privations and Sufferings.* Philadelphia: W. B. Selheimer, 1870.

Harvie, Mrs. John B., ed. *Beacon on a Hill: A Brief History of 100 Years of Christian Service, 1855–1955.* Richmond: Pine Street Baptist Church, 1955.

Harwell, Richard. *More Confederate Imprints.* 2 vols. Richmond: Virginia State Library, 1957.

Heaps, Willard A., and Porter W. Heaps. *The Singing Sixties: The Spirit of the Civil War Days Drawn from the Music of the Times.* Norman: University of Oklahoma Press, 1960.

Heartsill, William Williston. *Fourteen Hundred and 91 days in the Confederate Army: A Journal Kept by W. W. Heartsill, for Four Years, One Month, and One Day or Camp Life; Day-by-Day of the W. P. Lane Rangers, from April 19, 1861 to May 20, 1865.* 1876. 2d edition. Edited by Bell I. Wiley. Jackson, Tenn.: McCowat-Mercer Press, 1953.

Hill, Louise B. *State Socialism in the Confederate States of America.*

Southern Sketches, no. 9. Edited by J. D. Eggleston. Charlottesville, Va.: Historical Publishing Co., 1936.

Hoole, William Stanley. *Alias Simon Suggs: The Life and Times of Johnson Jones Hooper.* University: University of Alabama Press, 1952.

Hopley, Catherine Cooper. *Life in the South: From the Commencement of the War by a Blockaded British Subject. Being a Social History of Those Who Took Part in the Battles, from a Personal Acquaintance with Them in Their Homes. From the Spring of 1860 to August, 1862.* 2 vols. London: Chapman and Hall, 1863.

Hudson, Arthur Palmer. *Folklore Keeps the Past Alive.* Athens: University of Georgia Press, 1962.

Hume, Major Edgar Erskine. "The Days Gone By: Chimborazo Hospital Confederate States Army—America's Largest Military Hospital." *The Military Surgeon: Journal of the Association of Military Surgeons of the United States* 75 (September, 1934): 156–166.

James, W. C. *Leigh Street Baptist Church, 1854–1954: A Brief History of its First One Hundred Years in the Service of Christ.* Richmond: Whittet and Shepperson, 1954.

Jeffery, William H. *Richmond Prisons, 1861–1862: Compiled from the Original Records Kept by the Confederate Government, Kept by Union Prisoners of War, Together with the Name, Rank, Company, Regiment and State of the Four Thousand Who Were Confined There.* St. Johnsbury, Vt.: Republican Press, 1893.

Johnson, Ludwell H. "Commerce between Northeastern Ports and the Confederacy, 1861–1865." *Journal of American History* 54 (June, 1967): 30–42.

Johnson, Robert Underwood, and Clarence Clough Buel, eds. *Battles and Leaders of the Civil War.* 4 vols. New York: Century Co., 1887.

Johnston, Angus J., II. "Virginia Railroads in April, 1861." *Journal of Southern History* 22 (August, 1957): 307–330.

Johnston, Captain I. N. *Four Months in Libby and the Campaign against Atlanta.* Cincinnati: Methodist Book Concern, 1864.

Johnston, Joseph E. *Narrative of Military Operations Directed during the Late War between the States.* New York: D. Appleton and Co., 1874.

Jones, Benjamin Washington. *Under the Stars and Bars: A History of the Surry Light Artillery: Recollections of a Private Soldier in the War between the States.* Richmond: Everett Waddley Co., 1909.

Jones, J. B. *A Rebel War Clerk's Diary at the Confederate States Capital.* Edited by Howard Swiggett. 2 vols. New York: Old Hickory Bookshop, 1935.

Jones, J. William, comp. "The Kilpatrick-Dahlgren Raid against Richmond." *Southern Historical Society Papers* 13 (January–December, 1855): 546–560.

Jones, Katherine M., ed. *Ladies of Richmond: Confederate Capital.* New York: Bobbs-Merrill Co., 1962.

Jones, Virgil Carrington. *Eight Hours before Richmond.* New York: Henry Holt & Co., 1957.

Kent, Mrs. E. C. *Four Years in Secessia: A Narrative of a Residence at the South previous to and during the Southern Rebellion up to November, 1863, When the Writer Escaped from Richmond.* Buffalo: Franklin Printing House, 1865.

Kimball, William J., ed. *Richmond in Time of War.* Boston: Houghton Mifflin Co., 1960.

Little, John P. *History of Richmond.* Richmond: Dietz Press, 1933.

Manarin, Louis H., ed. *Richmond at War: The Minutes of the City Council, 1861–1865.* Richmond Civil War Centennial Committee Publications, No. 17. Chapel Hill: University of North Carolina Press, 1966.

Manchester Baptist Church. *A Century of Service: A History of Bainbridge Street Baptist Church 1857–1957.* Richmond: Whittet and Shepperson, 1957.

M'Anery, John. "Dahlgren's Raid on Richmond." *Confederate Veteran* 29 (January, 1921): 20–21.

Matthews, James M., ed. *Statutes at Large of the Confederate States of America, Commencing with the First Session of the First Congress.* Richmond: 1862–1864.

————, ed. *Statutes at Large of the Provisional Congress of the Confederate States of America.* Richmond: 1864.

Maury, Col. Richard L. "The First Marine Torpedoes Were Made in Richmond, Va., and Used in James River." *Southern Historical Society Papers* 31 (1903): 326–333.

McGuire, Judith W. *Diary of a Southern Refugee during the War.* New York: E. J. Hale and Son, 1867.

Meade, Robert D. *Judah P. Benjamin: Confederate Statesman.* New York: Oxford University Press, 1943.

————. "The Relations between Judah P. Benjamin and Jefferson Davis: Some New Light on the Working of the Confederate Machine." *Journal of Southern History* 5 (November, 1939): 468–478.

Merrell, William Howard. *Five Months in Rebeldom; or, Notes from the Diary of a Bull Run Prisoner at Richmond.* Rochester: Adams and Dabney, 1862.

Mordecai, Samuel. *Richmond in By-Gone Days.* Reprinted from 2nd ed. 1860, Richmond: Garrett and Massey, 1946.

Morris, Richard B., ed. *Encyclopedia of American History.* Revised edition. New York: Harper and Row, 1961.

Nichols, G. W. *A Soldier's Story of His Regiment (61st Ga.) and Incidentally of the Lawton-Gordon-Evans Brigade, Army Northern Virginia.* Kennesaw, Ga.: G. W. Nichols, 1898.

Norwood, William. *God and Our Country—A Sermon.* Richmond: 1863.

Owen, William Miller. *In Camp and Battle with the Washington Artillery of New Orleans: A Narrative of Events during the Late Civil War from Bull Run to Appomatox and Spanish Fort.* Boston: Ticknor and Co., 1885.

Park, Robert Emory. "War Diary of Captain Robert Emory Park." *Southern Historical Society Papers* 26 (1898): 1–31.

Patrick, Rembert W. *The Fall of Richmond.* Baton Rouge: Louisiana State University Press, 1960.

———. *Jefferson Davis and His Cabinet.* Baton Rouge: Louisiana State University Press, 1944.

———, ed. *The Opinions of the Confederate Attorneys General, 1861–1865.* Buffalo: Dennis and Co., 1950.

Pollard, Edward A. *The First Year of the War.* Richmond: West and Johnston, 1862.

Pollard, Julia Cuthbert. *Richmond's Story.* Richmond: Richmond Public Schools, 1954.

"Proceedings of the Confederate Congress." *Southern Historical Society Papers* 44–52 (1923–1959).

Pryor, Mrs. Roger A. *Reminiscences of Peace and War.* New York: Macmillan Co., 1904.

Putnam, George Haven. *A Prisoner of War in Virginia 1864–5; Reprinted, with Additions, from the Report of an Address Delivered before the N.Y. Commandery of the U.S. Loyal Legion, December 7, 1910. Third Edition* [1914], *with a List of Commissioned Officers Confined in Danville, Virginia, 1864–5, and an Appendix Presenting Statistics of Northern Prisons from the Report of Thomas Sturgis, 1st Lieut. 57th Mass. Vol.* New York: G. P. Putnam's Sons, 1917.

Putnam, Sallie Brock. *Richmond during the War: Four Years of Personal Observation.* New York: G. W. Carleton and Co., 1867.

Rabun, James Z. "Alexander H. Stephens and Jefferson Davis." *American Historical Review* 58 (January, 1953): 290–321.

Ramsdell, Charles W. *Behind the Lines in the Southern Confederacy.* Baton Rouge: Louisiana State University Press, 1944.

————. "The Control of Manufacturing by the Confederate Government." *Mississippi Valley Historical Review* 8 (December, 1921): 231–249.

————, ed. *Laws and Joint Resolutions of the Last Session of the Confederate Congress (November 7, 1864–March 18, 1865) Together with the Secret Acts of Previous Congresses.* Durham, N.C.: Duke University Press, 1941.

Randall, James G., and David Donald. *Civil War and Reconstruction.* 2nd ed. Boston: D. C. Heath and Co., 1961.

Reynolds, Daniel N. "Memoirs of Libby Prison." Edited by Paul H. Giddens. *Michigan History Magazine* 23 (Autumn, 1939): 391–398.

Richardson, James D., ed. *A Compilation of the Messages and Papers of the Confederacy including the Diplomatic Correspondence, 1861–1865.* 2 vols. Nashville: United States Printing Co., 1905.

"The Richmond Ambulance Corps." Richmond *Dispatch,* December 12, 1897. Reprinted in *Southern Historical Society Papers* 25 (1897): 113–115.

Richmond, Approaches to Its History by Various Hands. Richmond: Whittet and Shepperson, 1936.

Richmond Police and Fire Department Directory. Richmond, 1896.

Robinson, William M. *Justice in Grey: A History of the Judicial System of the Confederate States of America.* Cambridge: Harvard University Press, 1941.

Ross, Fitzgerald. *Cities and Camps of the Confederate States.* Edited by Richard B. Harwell. Urbana: University of Illinois Press, 1958.

Rowland, Dunbar, ed. *Jefferson Davis, Constitutionalist: His Letters, Papers, and Speeches.* 10 vols. Jackson, Miss: Mississippi Department of Archives and History, 1923.

Scheibert, Captain Justus. *Seven Months in the Rebel States during the North American War, 1863.* Translated by Joseph C. Hayes. Edited by William Stanley Hoole. Tuscaloosa: University of Alabama Press, 1958.

Schwab, John C. "Prices in the Confederate States, 1861–65." *Political Science Quarterly* 14 (June, 1899): 281–304.

Scott, Mary Wingfield. *Houses of Old Richmond.* Richmond: The Valentine Museum, 1941.

————. *Old Richmond Neighborhoods.* Richmond: Whittet and Shepperson, 1950.

Semmes, Raphael. *Memoirs of Service Afloat during the War between the States.* Baltimore: Kelly, Piet and Co., 1869.

Shanks, Henry T. *The Secession Movement in Virginia, 1847–1861.* Richmond: Garrett and Massie, 1934.

Shepard, John, Jr. "Religion in the Army of Northern Virginia." *North Carolina Historical Review* 25 (July, 1948): 341–376.

Shields, John C. "Old Camp Lee." *Southern Historical Society Papers* 26 (1898): 241–246.

Silber, Irwin, comp. and ed. *Songs of the Civil War.* New York: Columbia University Press, 1960.

Small, Abner R. *The Road to Richmond: The Civil War Memoirs of Major Abner R. Small of the Sixteenth Maine Volunteers. Together with the Diary Which He Kept When He Was a Prisoner of War.* Edited by Harold Adams Small. Berkeley: University of California Press, 1870.

Smith, Daniel E. Huger; Alice R. Huger Smith; Arney R. Childs, eds. *Mason Smith Family Letters 1860–1868.* Columbia: University of South Carolina Press, 1950.

Spencer, Warren F. "A French View of the Fall of Richmond: Alfred Paul's Report to Drouyn de Llys, April 11, 1865." *Virginia Magazine of History and Biography* 73 (April, 1965): 178–188.

Stanard, Mary Newton. *Richmond, Its People and Its Story.* Philadelphia: J. B. Lippincott Co., 1923.

Stephenson, Nathaniel W. *The Day of the Confederacy: A Chronicle of the Embattled South.* New Haven: Yale University Press, 1919.

Strangers Guide and Official Directory for the City of Richmond: Showing the Location of Public Buildings and Offices of the Confederate, State, and City Governments, Residences of the Principal Officers, etc. Richmond, 1863.

Strode, Hudson. *Jefferson Davis.* 3 vols. New York: Harcourt, Brace and World, 1955–1964.

Sublett, Emmie. Letter. In *Confederate Museum Newsletter* 5 (April, 1968): 3–5.

Timberlake, W. L. "The Last Days in Front of Richmond." *Confederate Veteran* 22 (July, 1914): 303.

———. "In the Siege of Richmond and After." *Confederate Veteran* 29 (November, 1921): 412–414.

Todd, Richard C. *Confederate Finance.* Athens: University of Georgia Press, 1954.

"The Treatment of Prisoners during the War between the States." *Southern Historical Society Papers* 1 (March, 1876).

Trexler, Harrison A. *The Confederate Ironclad "Virginia" ("Merrimac").* Chicago: University of Chicago Press, 1938.

———. "The Davis Administration and the Richmond Press, 1861–1865." *Journal of Southern History* 16 (May, 1950): 176–195.

Tyler, Lyon Gardiner, ed. *Encyclopedia of Virginia Biography*. 6 vols. New York: Lewis Historical Publishing Co., 1915.

United States, Bureau of the Census. Eighth Census, 1860. *Manufactures of the United States in 1860; Compiled from the Original Returns under the Direction of the Secretary of the Interior*. Washington, D.C.: Government Printing Office, 1865.

————, Bureau of the Census. Eighth Census, 1860. *Statistics of the United States, (including mortality, property, etc.) in 1860; Compiled from the Original Returns and Being the Final Exhibit of the Eighth Census, under the Direction of the Secretary of the Interior*. Washington, D.C.: Government Printing Office, 1866.

————, Congress, House. *War of the Rebellion: A Compilation of the Official Records of the Union and Confederate Armies*. Compiled under the direction of the Secretary of War. 4 series in 70 vols. (127 books, and index). Washington, D.C.: Government Printing Office, 1880–1901.

————, Congress, Senate. *Journal of the Congresses of the Confederate States of America 1861–1865*. 7 vols. Washington, D.C.: Government Printing Office, 1904–1905.

Vandiver, Frank E. *Basic History of the Confederacy*. Princeton: D. Van Nostrand Co., 1962.

————. *Jefferson Davis and the Confederate State*. Oxford: Clarendon Press, 1964.

————. "Jefferson Davis and Confederate Strategy." In *The American Tragedy: The Civil War in Retrospect*, edited by Bernard Mayo. Hampden-Sydney, Va.: Hampden-Sydney College, 1959.

————. *Jubal's Raid: General Early's Famous Attack on Washington in 1864*. New York: McGraw-Hill, 1960.

————. *Mighty Stonewall*. New York: McGraw-Hill, 1957.

————. *Ploughshares into Swords: Josiah Gorgas and Confederate Ordnance*. Austin: University of Texas Press, 1952.

————, ed. *The Civil War Diary of General Josiah Gorgas*. University: University of Alabama Press, 1947.

Vanfelson, Charles A. *The Little Red Book or Departmental Directory for the Use of the Public in the Confederate States of America*. Richmond, 1861.

Van Riper, Paul P., and Harry N. Schreiber. "The Confederate Civil Service." *Journal of Southern History* 25 (November, 1959): 448–470.

Virginia Convention. *Ordinances Adopted by the Convention of Virginia, in Secret and Adjourned Sessions in April, May, June and July 1861*. Richmond, 1861.

Virginia General Assembly. *Acts of the General Assembly of the State of Virginia, Passed in 1861 in the Eighty-fifth Year of the Commonwealth.* Richmond, 1861.

———. *Acts of the General Assembly of the State of Virginia, Passed in 1861–2, in the Eighty-sixth Year of the Commonwealth.* Richmond, 1862.

———. *Acts of the General Assembly of the State of Virginia, Passed at the Extra Session, 1862, in the Eighty-sixth Year of the Commonwealth.* Richmond, 1862.

———. *Acts of the General Assembly of the State of Virginia, Passed at the Called Session, 1862, in the Eighty-seventh Year of the Commonwealth.* Richmond, 1862.

———. *Acts of the General Assembly of the State of Virginia, Passed at the Adjourned Session, 1863, in the Eighty-seventh Year of the Commonwealth.* Richmond, 1863.

———. *Acts of the General Assembly of the State of Virginia, Passed at the called Session, 1863, in the Eighty-seventh Year of the Commonwealth.* Richmond, 1863.

———. *Acts of the General Assembly of the State of Virginia, Passed at the Session of 1863–4, in the Eighty-eighth Year of the Commonwealth.* Richmond, 1864.

———. *Documents of the Session of 1861.* Richmond, 1861.

Wade, Richard C. *Slavery in the Cities: The South, 1820–1860.* New York: Oxford University Press, 1964.

Waitt, Robert W., Jr. *Confederate Military Hospitals in Richmond.* Richmond: Richmond Civil War Centennial Committee, 1964.

Weeks, Nan F. *Grace Baptist Church Richmond, 1833–1958.* Richmond, Va.: Garrett and Massie, 1958.

White, Blanche Sydnor. *First Baptist Church, Richmond, 1780–1955, One Hundred and Seventy-five Years of Service to God and Man.* Richmond, Va.: Whittet and Shepperson, 1955.

Wiley, Bell I. *The Life of Johnny Reb: The Common Soldier of the Confederacy.* New York: The Bobbs-Merrill Co., 1943.

———. *Southern Negroes, 1861–1865,* Yale Historical Publications 31. New Haven: Yale University Press, 1938.

———, ed. *The Letters of Warren Akin, Confederate Congressman.* Athens: University of Georgia Press, 1959.

———, ed. *A Southern Woman's Story: Life in Confederate Richmond by Phoebe Yates Pember including Unpublished Letters Written from the Chimborazo Hospital.* Jackson, Tenn.: McCowat-Mercer Press, 1959.

Williams, Kenneth P. *Lincoln Finds a General*, 2 vols. New York: Macmillan Co., 1949.

William, T. Harry. *Lincoln and His Generals*. New York: Alfred Knopf, 1952.

Wise, John S. *The End of an Era*. Boston: Houghton Mifflin Co., 1902.

Worsham, John H. *One of Jackson's Foot Cavalry, His Experience and What He Saw during the War 1861–1865, including a History of "F Company," Richmond, Va., 21st Regiment Virginia Infantry, Second Brigade, Jackson's Division, Second Corps, A. N. Va.* New York: Neale Publishing Co., 1912.

Wright, Mrs. D. Giraud. *A Southern Girl in '61: The War-Time Memories of a Confederate Senator's Daughter*. New York: Doubleday, Page and Co., 1905.

Wright, Gordon. "Economic Conditions in the Confederacy as Seen by the French Consuls." *Journal of Southern History* 7 (May, 1941): 195–214.

Yearns, Wilfred B. *The Confederate Congress*. Athens: University of Georgia Press, 1960.

Younger, Edward, ed. *Inside the Confederate Government: The Diary of Robert Garlick Hill Kean, Head of the Bureau of War*. New York: Oxford University Press, 1957.

Zornow, William Frank. "Aid for the Indigent Families of Soldiers in Virginia, 1861–1865." *Virginia Magazine of History and Biography* 66 (October, 1958): 454–458.

III
Periodicals

Age: A Southern Eclectic Magazine (Richmond)
Bohemian (Richmond)
Daily Richmond Enquirer
Magnolia: A Southern Home Journal (Richmond)
Record of News, History and Literature (Richmond)
Religious Herald (Baptist, Richmond)
Richmond Daily Dispatch
Richmond Daily Examiner
Richmond Daily Whig
Richmond Sentinel
Smith and Barrow's Monthly (Richmond)
Southern Illustrated News (Richmond)
Southern Literary Messenger (Richmond)
Southern Punch (Richmond)

INDEX

220

Index